PENGUIN CANADA

ALL YOU CAN EAT

As a reporter and columnist for *The Globe
and Mail*, *Maclean's* and the *National Post*,
Linda McQuaig has written extensively on
politics, economics and social values, and
has developed a reputation for challenging
Canada's Establishment.

McQuaig's previous five books, which
include *Shooting the Hippo*, *The Cult of
Impotence* and *The Wealthy Banker's Wife*, have
all been controversial national bestsellers.

# ALL YOU CAN EAT

## GREED, LUST
### AND THE NEW CAPITALISM

## LINDA McQUAIG

PENGUIN
CANADA

PENGUIN CANADA

Published by the Penguin Group

Penguin Books, a division of Pearson Canada, 10 Alcorn Avenue, Toronto, Ontario, Canada
    M4V 3B2

Penguin Books Ltd, 80 Strand, London WC2R 0RL, England

Penguin Putnam Inc., 375 Hudson Street, New York, New York 10014, U.S.A.

Penguin Books Australia Ltd, 250 Camberwell Road, Camberwell, Victoria 3124, Australia

Penguin Books India (P) Ltd, 11, Community Centre, Panchsheel Park,
    New Delhi – 110 017, India

Penguin Books (NZ) Ltd, cnr Rosedale and Airborne Roads, Albany, Auckland 1310,
    New Zealand

Penguin Books (South Africa) (Pty) Ltd, 24 Sturdee Avenue, Rosebank 2196, South Africa

Penguin Books Ltd, Registered Offices: 80 Strand, London WC2R 0RL, England

First published in Viking by Penguin Books Canada Limited, 2001
Published in Penguin Canada by Penguin Books, a division of Pearson Canada, 2002

10 9 8 7 6 5 4 3 2 1

Author representation: Westwood Creative Artists, 94 Harbord Street,
Toronto, Ontario M5S 1G6

Manufactured in Canada.

NATIONAL LIBRARY OF CANADA CATALOGUING IN PUBLICATION DATA

McQuaig, Linda, 1951–
    All you can eat : greed, lust, and the new capitalism / Linda McQuaig.

Includes bibliographical references and index.

ISBN 0-14-026222-9

1. Capitalism. 2. Capitalism—History. 3. Economic history—1990–
I. Title.

HB501.M28  2002      330.12'2     C2002-902389-0

Visit Penguin Books' website at **www.penguin.ca**

To Amy, with all the love in
the world!

"Property is but the creation of the law. Whoever makes the law has the power of appropriating the national wealth. If they did not make the law, they would not have the property."

—*POOR MAN'S GUARDIAN,* 1835

"While laissez-faire economy was the product of deliberate state action, subsequent restrictions on laissez-faire started in a spontaneous way. Laissez-faire was planned; planning was not."

—KARL POLANYI

"[T]hey call it freedom when themselves are free."

—OLIVER GOLDSMITH

"Our animal dependence on food has been bared and naked fear of starvation permitted to run loose. Our humiliating enslavement to the 'material,' which all human culture is designed to mitigate, [has been] deliberately made more rigorous. This is the root of the 'sickness of an acquisitive society.'"

—KARL POLANYI

"Shut up and shop! Shut up and shop! Shut up and shop!"

—JELLO BIAFRA

# Contents

# Preface to the Paperback Edition

IT WAS PROBABLY THE TOUGHEST THING George W. Bush ever had to do.

After all the titans of corporate America had done for him, it had to be hard for Bush to turn on them like that. But as each day seemed to bring fresh media revelations of corporate fraud and corruption, with investors losing their life savings and employees losing their jobs, the U.S. President felt compelled in July 2002 to lecture Wall Street about the need to behave responsibly. The audience wasn't just the roomful of corporate executives on hand, but also the broader public watching the President deliver his stern message on TV, against a backdrop on which the slogan "Corporate Responsibility" was printed dozens of times, as if the sheer repetition would make the President look serious about the issue. As a slogan coming from the Bush administration, however, "Corporate Responsibility" seemed only slightly more plausible than, perhaps, "Make the Rich Pay."

Of course, Bush's discomfort with getting tough on corporate friends had a lot to do with his own background in the corporate world. The scandals were clearly getting close to home. There was the embarrassment of explaining his own behaviour as a corporate director, when he sold his shares in Harken Energy in 1990 just before ordinary shareholders, who didn't have access to inside information, discovered they faced massive losses. Clearly, the President's speechwriter had to choose words with particular care for the Wall Street address. "Corporate leaders who violate the public trust should never be given that trust again," Bush said, without mentioning whether or not there was anything wrong with such people going on to be President.

Where would it all lead? The public was becoming cynical about the loose boardroom morals that seemed rampant on Wall Street and fairly common among those occupying senior positions at the White House. But what if the skepticism went even farther? What if the public began to question the very nature of the unbridled capitalism under which members of the financial elite had managed—legally and illegally, it turns out—to change, bend, twist and contort the rules in every possible way in order to further enrich themselves over the past two decades?

Take Bush's tax cut, for instance. Over the next decade, it will transfer massive wealth to a financial elite that has already benefited enormously from the tax changes of the past decade. The Washington-based Citizens for Tax Justice notes that more than half of all the tax savings in the Bush plan will go to the richest one per cent of Americans. These people—whose annual incomes will average $1.5 million by the time the cuts are phased in—can count on a ten-year tax saving of $342,000—*each*. This ongoing transfer of wealth to the richest Americans has had a significant impact in Canada, with the elite here using it as a lever to effectively push for tax cuts for themselves. In 2000, the Chrétien government announced more than $100 billion in tax cuts, with savings skewed to the upper end—including generous new tax treatment of capital gains and corporate stock options beneficial almost exclusively to the wealthy—despite polls showing that most Canadians preferred to see the federal surpluses spent on social re-investment.

When rapacious behaviour on the part of the elite becomes the basis of public policy, it surely sends a message that any manoeuvring in the quest for personal enrichment is acceptable . . . at least for those with access to a good accounting firm.

It's interesting to note how far things have moved from the early postwar years, when governments were expected to protect something called the "public good." It was understood back then that, while the marketplace could generate great material wealth, it was also capable of generating extreme inequality and leaving large segments of society highly vulnerable. There was widespread agreement that the market, and the powerful corporations that dominate it, should be subject to the broader control of society.

In the last two decades, however, this crucially democratic notion has been largely discarded. Under the New Capitalism—with its deregulation, privatization and the reduction in government redistribution—the market has been given virtual pre-eminence. All this has been aggressively encouraged by a network of business-funded think-tanks arguing that such policies are inevitable, given human nature, even though they are almost unique in human history.

But the scandals being unveiled in the corporate world are more than just an indication of how much—and how dangerously—the New Capitalism has nurtured a reckless culture of greed and acquisitiveness. The extent of the greed has long been known. Advocates of the New Capitalism have insisted, however, that the unleashing of greed from social constraints is nothing to be alarmed at. Rather, they've argued, it is something to be celebrated, since it produces a raw energy and exuberance that promises to lift the world to undreamed-of levels of prosperity. "The economic problem has been solved," gushed Dinesh D'Souza, one of the enthusiasts of the New Capitalism in his book *The Culture of Prosperity,* "We know how to create wealth. . . . But there is only one way to do it, and that is the American way of technological capitalism."

In fact, it turns out that much of the success so giddily proclaimed by D'Souza and other prophets of the New Capitalism has been an illusion. We now discover that some of the biggest success stories of the new era—Enron, WorldCom, Global Crossing, Adelphia—aren't actually harbingers of a new age of material bounty for the world. In fact, it turns out these companies aren't actually successful—aren't even solvent—once the accounting is done honestly. The huge telecommunications industry that lies at the centre of the New Economy and the skyrocketing stock market of recent years has been revealed to be about as sturdy as a house built of toothpicks.

D'Souza's cocky claims about the wonders of the New Capitalism now seem not only bombastic, but also hopelessly misleading. Let's play that again: "We know how to create wealth. . . . But there is only one way to do it." What way would that be? Lying, cheating, cooking the books? Have we really unlocked the mysteries of ever-increasing wealth or have we just been fooled into celebrating a gigantic accounting scam? The New Capitalism turns out to be based not just on greed and self-interest, as we've long known, but also on claims that are fraudulent and flaky.

Certainly, the scandals should help us finally see through one of the myths central to the New Capitalism—that freeing up the market will bring us untold efficiency. The market has been portrayed as an arena of efficiency, where decisions are based on scientific laws like supply and demand, and where one succeeds on merit, not on the kind of crony connections that ruled the old-style tribal economies of pre-market days.

But today's brand of capitalism bears little resemblance to this rational, scientific model. The model may work like that at lower levels, where workers are effectively disciplined by market forces. At the top, however, the old-boy crony network continues to thrive. Corporate CEOs, even those running badly failing enterprises, routinely win multi-million dollar stock option packages from corporate boards filled with friends and colleagues who apparently sense that a rising tide of corporate compensations lifts all boats—and that their turn will come up soon. The collegial atmosphere of all this would make even the most primitive tribal chief feel right at home. But it's hard to see anything particularly efficient about it.

It's also hard to imagine how Adam Smith's vision of everyone rationally pursuing their own self-interest can even happen when widespread accounting trickery prevents the players from seeing the true value of companies they're investing in or working for, and therefore seeing where their self-interest actually lies.

As markets continued to plunge and ordinary citizens began questioning the prevailing economic wisdom with new-found cynicism, Bush struggled to imbue today's capitalism with some moral substance. "In the long run" he told the TV audience, "there is no capitalism without conscience, there is no wealth without character."

Really? As a philosophical observation, this is about on a par with "Shopping is good." One can only speculate what Bush meant by such a loopy pronouncement. Was he suggesting that having money builds character or that having character builds money? Either way, those guys driving around in Jaguars must be saints.

One suspects that, above all, Bush was praying for a return to simpler times, when he was able to cast as the enemy a band of foreign terrorists or even the Kyoto accords or big government—anything but what lay at the very heart of global capitalism. In fact, the most immediate threat to the well-being of ordinary people seemed suddenly to be coming, not from shadowy figures in faraway caves, but from guys in business suits in nearby corporate boardrooms.

Linda McQuaig
July, 2002

# CHAPTER ONE

# Nudists and Capitalists

*London, 1321*

LIKE ANY CRIME, THIS one had seemed full of promise in the planning stage. All he had to do was put just a little less dough into each baking pan, and the bread would come out a little lighter than usual. He could then sell a bunch of these underweight loaves to the first suckers who wandered into his shop—and pocket a little extra profit in the process. It seemed foolproof at the time.

It seemed less so now. Standing in the prisoner's dock in the formidable, high-ceilinged London courtroom, the accused baker, William le Bole of Bread Street, felt the deep remorse of a man who now sees clearly that the chances of getting caught were too high to have justified the risk. What kind of recklessness had led him to think he could get away with such a clear-cut breach of the law?

The smugness of the look on the prosecutor's face said it all—the case against le Bole was airtight. The evidence of the two grain dealers had been compelling: they had sold le Bole a quarter of good wheat for eight shillings. Once his overhead was added—three halfpence for three journeymen, a halfpenny for two apprentices, a halfpenny for salt, twopence for wood, three halfpence for the sieve, a farthing for the candle, plus the cost of rent on the oven—it was pretty clear to everyone what a halfpenny loaf of light bread for sale the next day should have weighed. Caught red-handed with the underweight loaves on his shelves, le Bole had panicked and declared the bread not of his baking. Wrong line.

If only he could retract that line now, confess fully his intention to make an extra profit at the expense of others and fall prostrate on the ground before the court.

That strategy had worked, after all, for Thomas Lespicer, the Portsmouth fishmonger whose transgression was every bit as serious. Lespicer had come to London in the spring of 1311 with six pots of lampreys (a fish with a long ulcer-like pipe on the top of its head). But instead of selling his lampreys for four days in his specified spot under the wall of St. Margaret's Church, Lespicer had taken all six pots to the house of another fishmonger. The two men had stowed the fish there for a couple of days, with the full intention of selling the lampreys at an elevated price once local supplies ran low. They might well have got away with their clever scheme, except that the fish had begun to give off the tangy aroma that lampreys do after a while out of water, and the men were caught trying to discreetly move six pots of them to market. Luckily, they had the presence of mind to plead guilty and confess fully their intention to make an unduly large profit at the expense of others. As a result, they got off scot-free; they only had to swear they would never conspire to push up the price of lampreys again.

Of course, there were others with an eye for turning a quick profit who had been dealt with much more harshly. Usurers seemed to fare particularly badly; lending money for profit—anything beyond covering one's immediate costs—was considered a serious assault on the well-being of the community. "Lend freely, expecting nothing in return," was the dictate of the medieval Christian church. Those found doing otherwise were commonly denied Christian burial—a huge deal in an age when people spent much of their lives preparing for the moment when it was determined whether they were on their way to heaven or hell. In cases where usury was discovered after death, the corpse of the usurer was excavated from the church burial ground and transferred to a local dunghill—not considered a good omen of the direction one was headed.

All these grim thoughts were rattling around in le Bole's mind, leaving him feeling incredibly small and powerless under the vaulted ceiling of the courtroom, when the twelve men of the jury returned. It would have been hard to read their expressions as anything other than sour and mean-spirited—perhaps taciturn at best. Things, he felt sure, were not about to go his way. And he was right. The jury found le Bole in clear breach of the law, guilty of indulging his desire for excessive private gain to the detriment of the well-being of the community. That meant the maximum penalty of three hours in the pillory—that is, standing in the town square with head and hands held in place by a wooden frame, for the purpose of being subjected to public ridicule. For the added offence of lying to the court, le Bole had his sentence bumped up to being drawn through the city on a hurdle—a kind of pillory on wheels.

It would be a while before le Bole would consider trying to make an extra profit again.

∾

*Washington, D.C., 1999*

IF THERE WAS ONE thing the executives of Metalclad Corp. had no trouble admitting, it was their deep and abiding interest in making profits—the more the better. That was what had attracted them to Guadalcazar in the first place. The central Mexican town wouldn't normally have even shown up on the radar screen at the corporate headquarters of a big company like Delaware-based Metalclad. But the firm had determined that Guadalcazar was the perfect spot to build a landfill site for toxic waste. Everything was ready to go. But executives back at Metalclad's head office were taken off guard by the news that the town of Guadalcazar had refused to grant them a building permit.

There was a time, not that long ago, when a decision like this would have prompted the company to fold its tent, pack up its toxic substances and move on. But Metalclad knew that it was not without recourse these days; it knew that some two-bit Mexican town couldn't just kick sand in the face of a big corporation and get away with it. Not any more. Not in the age of NAFTA.

And so it was that Guadalcazar's decision not to grant a building permit came under fierce attack from a high-powered gang of corporate lawyers at a NAFTA tribunal hearing in downtown Washington in the summer of 1999.

Now, to those not familiar with the workings of NAFTA—the North American Free Trade Agreement—this whole scene might seem confusing. First of all, one might ask, isn't NAFTA a *trade* deal? So why would a NAFTA tribunal be interested in the decision of the town of Guadalcazar to withhold a building permit from Metalclad— a matter that seems to have little to do with trade? The simple answer is that NAFTA is far more than a trade deal. Indeed, a central focus of NAFTA is the establishment of a set of legal rights for corporations and corporate investors. Among other things, those legal rights entitle corporations to compensation if the actions of a foreign government interfere with their ability to earn profits. That is exactly what Metalclad accused the town of Guadalcazar of doing, and that's why it brought its case to a NAFTA tribunal.

But let's not forget what the alleged offence is here—the people of Guadalcazar denied Metalclad permission to build a toxic-waste landfill in their town because they feared it would pollute their drinking water. In fact, the townspeople had had a previous bad experience. Another company had operated a toxic-waste facility on this very site, and there had been concerns about polluted water. When Metalclad tried to reopen the landfill site, the local population turned out in force to protest. Responding to popular sentiment, the town council refused to issue Metalclad a building permit. Wrong decision.

As the NAFTA tribunal hearing progressed in a conference room inside the headquarters of the World Bank, the lawyers representing Mexico could tell that things weren't going well. They probably experienced that same sinking feeling that William le Bole had experienced back in 1321. And with reason—like le Bole, they lost the case. The NAFTA tribunal found, among other things, that the necessary federal permits had been obtained and it wasn't up to the town to judge the environmental risks involved in the case. The three judges on the NAFTA tribunal panel were apparently satisfied that Metalclad would not pollute the local water (easy for them to say!).

The good news was that no Mexicans were to be dragged through downtown Washington on a mobile pillory. The bad news was that the panel ordered Mexico to pay Metalclad damages of $16.7 million (U.S.).

It will probably be a while before the people of Guadalcazar put their collective interests before private profit-making again.

❧

THE LEGAL SYSTEM THAT le Bole faced in 1321 and the one that the Mexicans faced in 1999 are in some ways similar. They both have wide-ranging powers intended to enforce economic goals. But the economic goals they seek to enforce could hardly be more different. Indeed, they are almost diametrically opposed—one system seeks to control greed and material acquisitiveness; the other seeks to make these the central organizing principles of society.

Certainly, the medieval legal code that le Bole suffered under was a clumsy and heavy-handed system aimed at achieving what most of us today would regard as an impossible task—curbing human greed (that is, restricting the impulse for personal gain, material acquisitiveness, profit-making, etc.). The architects of these medieval laws weren't naive. They didn't believe they could stamp out human greed. But they did believe the full force of the law should be applied to try to rein in this aspect of human behaviour as much as possible. Hence the need for a coercive legal system with some tough sanctions. Being pulled through town on a wooden frame, as neighbours and strangers shout words of derision, might not be enough to drive the demon greed out of a man's soul forever, but it would likely make him pause before he decided to shortchange his baking pans the next time the thought popped into his head.

Fast-forward to the present, and we see a very different system in play. Gone are the negative feelings about greed; greed and material acquisitiveness are now unabashedly praised as the engine of growth. Gone is the notion that one should try to control one's appetite for material gain; there's now virtually no limit to the number of expensive consumer items one is expected to acquire as part of a normal lifestyle. Gone is any insistence that one should lend freely—or do anything else, for that matter—expecting nothing in return. Gone also is the concept that the individual's pursuit of gain should be subordinated to the well-being of the whole community. A closer description of today's sentiment is expressed breezily in a Mitsubishi magazine advertisement for Internet-connected cellphones, which says: "The world doesn't revolve around you . . . But we're working on it."

Interestingly, the enemy today is no longer believed to be individual greed but rather any collective action aimed at curbing that greed, restraining it in the name of the broader collective interest. Our laws today seek to hold that collective interest in check and enforce the supremacy of individual profit-making. That's how the town of Guadalcazar got into trouble. It tried to defend the collective interest of the local people, who decided they didn't want a private company storing toxic wastes near their drinking water. But NAFTA gives precedence to the rights of individual investors and corporations, who want to turn a profit. This subordination of the collective interest to the private pursuit of profit is basic, in fact, to the goals of NAFTA, as well as to the goals of the other major institutions that set the rules for today's global economy—the WTO (World Trade Organization), the IMF (International Monetary Fund) and the World Bank.

So while we have rejected the repressiveness of the medieval world's restrictions on individual gain, it's interesting to note that today we are repressive in the opposite direction—in our restrictions on attempts to defend the collective interests of the broader community. Despite the popular hype that today's economic order represents the liberation of mankind, it is perhaps more accurate to see it as merely a different kind of repressive system—one that represses collective interests to free up individual material acquisitiveness.

When you think about it, our approach is surely just as odd.

THIS BOOK IS ABOUT GREED—not about how bad it is or how guilty we should feel about giving in to it and indulging ourselves. Rather, this book is about the curious way our society has made greed and material acquisitiveness its central organizing principles. I describe this as "curious" because there is nothing natural or inevitable about our approach. Indeed, our approach is something of an aberration. The pursuit of private profit and the impulse to accumulate material possessions have always been present, in some form, in human societies. But through most of history and in just about every corner of the globe, the pursuit of material gain was not the central activity of society, as it is today. Rather it was relegated to a lower position, considered less important than other aspects of life—like religion, family, clan, community and kingdom. The attainment of material possessions was considered a less important mark of distinction and status than the display of other forms of human behaviour—like bravery, loyalty, devotion, service, honour and dedication to duty.

The late economic historian and anthropologist Karl Polanyi—whose ideas are central to this book—made the provocative point that it is only in the last few centuries, and only in parts of the Western world, that greed and the endless pursuit of material gain have been given almost free rein, that they have been massaged, encouraged and even considered the very essence of the human personality. This amounts to a massive transformation of society, and this book will explore aspects of this transformation and their impact on the world. Polanyi went on to argue that this transformation was not part of some natural evolution, based on the reality of human nature, but rather was a deliberately imposed redesign of society, carried out by a small but powerful elite in order to enhance its own interests. It could be added that it is only in the last decade or so that things have been pushed an amazing step further—to the point where elaborate international legal systems have been put in place to ensure not only that greed and the pursuit of material gain are given legal protection, but that they are given *supremacy*.

❧

IN HER TINY JAIL CELL in Lima, Peru, Maria Sybila Arredondo savoured a huge victory. The most prestigious human rights body in the world—the United Nations Human Rights Committee—had reviewed her case in detail, concluded that she had been unjustly imprisoned for ten years and called on Peruvian authorities to release her immediately and compensate her for her suffering.

In 1990, Arredondo had been working as a human rights advocate, specializing in helping indigenous people, when she was arrested in Lima. She was charged with belonging to a terrorist organization, apparently because she was in the company of several people considered to be connected to a terrorist organization. She was tried by a "faceless" military court and convicted. While the case has been under appeal for a decade, she has remained in the High Security Prison for Women in Lima. There she is confined to a cell that measures three metres by three metres, and is allowed out into the general prison population for only half an hour a day. She is not permitted any writing materials, newspapers, magazines, radio or television, and is permitted to see her daughter only once a month, for thirty minutes, and her five-year-old grandson once every three months.

Arredondo's daughter, Carolina Teillier Arredondo, was able to get her mother's case to the UN Human Rights Committee in Geneva. Normally, the committee won't hear such cases until all domestic legal avenues have been exhausted. But although Arredondo's appeal in the Peruvian courts was still outstanding, the UN committee decided the delay had been unreasonable. So in July 2000, a sixteen-member panel examined the evidence, including submissions from Carolina Teillier Arredondo, on behalf of her mother, and from the Peruvian government. The following month, the committee concluded that Peru had violated several articles of the International Covenant on Civil and Political Rights. The committee called for Arredondo's immediate release and compensation, and notified Peru that it is under an obligation to ensure similar violations do not occur in the future.

It all sounds very reassuring—an abusive government is held accountable by an international body, which orders the release of an innocent citizen held in a faraway prison. While we may never be able to stamp out these kinds of horrible abuses, it is encouraging to see that the international community has taken steps to ensure there are ways to override the authority of abusive governments, that there is a system in place to protect the most basic rights of all individuals. It suggests that we are living in a civilized world. There is only one problem with this reassuring scenario—in reality, the UN Human Rights Committee has no power. It can call for whatever it wants and tell countries as much as it likes about their obligations, but it has no enforcement mechanism. The UN committee sent a letter notifying Peruvian authorities of its decision that Arredondo should be immediately released. But the Peruvian authorities didn't bother to respond to the letter. More than a year later, Arredondo is still in jail.

Corporate investors who believe their rights have been violated can count on swifter remedies. When Metalclad considered that its profit-making rights had been violated by the actions of Mexico and the town of Guadalcazar, it didn't have to drag its case for years through the domestic court system of Mexico. Instead, it was able to take its grievance directly to a NAFTA tribunal. And the tribunal, after listening to both sides, concluded that Metalclad's rights had been violated, and ordered multimillion-dollar damages, which Mexico was obliged to pay.

So Maria Sybila Arredondo sits in her tiny Peruvian cell, the victim for more than a decade of what international authorities concluded were serious and unacceptable violations of her human rights, and her tormenter, the government of Peru, has received nothing more than a slap on the wrist. Meanwhile, a corporation that feels its profit-making rights were violated—by what many people would regard as legitimate action on the part of a municipal government in Mexico to protect its citizens—is given quick justice, and Mexico is forced to pay many millions of dollars to its corporate "victim." This situation amounts to what the Ottawa trade lawyer Steven Shrybman calls "a revolutionary development in international law."

Shrybman's point is that NAFTA, which came into effect in the early 1990s, is a departure from previous international law in that it provides more protection for corporate rights than any other kind of rights. International law is always a difficult area, since it supersedes the jurisdictions of individual nations. But the world community has nevertheless attempted to come together and work out international laws aimed at protecting human and labour rights and the environment. But in these areas, there is rarely any action taken against abuses. The International Labour Organization (ILO), for instance, monitors abuses of the rights of workers worldwide, but it generally does nothing to punish countries that violate its internationally set labour standards. Indeed, the weakness of the international legal protections for labour and environmental rights is illustrated by the fact that the U.S., the world's most powerful nation, hasn't even signed the ILO conventions on fundamental labour rights, and has recently announced its withdrawal from the Kyoto environmental accords. And we've already seen how weak the enforcement mechanism is for the most basic human rights. When Peru failed to release Maria Sybila Arredondo, it didn't face a penny in fines or any other type of international punishment or retaliation. When international watchdogs lack or fail to use a punishment mechanism, human rights, as well as environmental and labour rights, remain largely symbolic. It would be nice if countries obeyed laws protecting these rights, but they are completely free to ignore them if they wish.

That is not the case when it comes to violations of the profit-making rights of corporate investors. International corporate investors alone are in the enviable position of having a tribunal that watches over their rights and has real teeth to enforce those rights. The tribunal has the power to force sovereign governments to pay corporate investors unlimited amounts of money in damages if the tribunal concludes their rights have been violated. And these damage awards are enforceable through domestic courts. Strangely, then, of all the rights we've chosen to protect in international law, those of corporate investors get the strongest protections. Comments Shrybman, "If anyone doesn't need to be protected, it's these guys."

And let's not forget what we're protecting "these guys" from. It's not that they are facing imprisonment or physical abuse. This vast new apparatus of NAFTA is designed to protect the right of corporate investors to earn profits, and to be compensated fully for unrealized profits whenever government action or legislation—even when it is designed to protect its own citizens—interferes with this "right." Incredibly, then, we've actually created stronger international rights for corporations to be free from constaints on their profit-making than we have for humans to be from from beatings, torture and imprisonment.

We will discuss in chapter two the far-reaching transfer of power to corporations that is taking place under the auspices of NAFTA and other trade deals, as well as through institutions like the World Bank and the IMF. The point here is simply to note how these recent changes in international law have left our priorities badly skewed, and how this reflects the deep homage we now pay to individual greed.

NUDISTS MUST CERTAINLY RANK prominently among those who feel marginalized—or at least feel they've had little luck turning their cause into a broad-based movement. Everywhere around them, they see the fully clothed. Even in the hottest of weather, people obstinately wear clothing. To nudists, the behaviour and mindset of the fully clothed are nicely summed up in the expression "the textile world." This lovely, ironic phrase is the nudist's attempt to present the wearing of clothes as just one of the available options, rather than the universal norm. To the rest of us, however, wearing clothes is so automatic that we're not particularly conscious of having ever made a choice. Wearing clothes is just part of being normal.

It's a bit like that with capitalism these days. Capitalism is so pervasive that it simply seems like the universal norm. Even the premise of capitalism—that we will all be best off if we individually pursue our own self-interest—has taken on the aura of a law of nature, instead of being merely an intriguing and provocative but unproven thesis. And the values of capitalism—accumulating ever more, getting the largest share, beating out all competitors—just seem like normal human behaviour. The culture of capitalism so surrounds us that it has become invisible. The U.S. economist Robert Heilbroner once noted that the word "capitalism" almost never appears in the journal of the American Economics Association. It would be no more necessary to mention it, when it is the only economic system ever discussed in the journal, than it is necessary for the media to describe the millions of people walking around our cities as belonging to the textile world.

We take it as self-evident that the desire to endlessly accumulate material possessions is basic to the human condition. Some people consider it virtually the only thing basic to the human condition. In the study of economics, for instance, it occupies the very centre of the compass. The central character in economics is *Homo Economicus,* the human prototype, who is pretty much just a walking set of insatiable material desires. He uses his rational abilities to ensure the satisfaction of all his wants, which are the key to his motivation. And he isn't considered some weirdo; the whole point of him is that he represents traits basic to all of us—*Homo Economicus* 'R' Us, as it were. This constancy in basic human programming makes it possible, according to economists, to predict human behaviour. Offer enough material incentive, for instance, and we can push corporate executives into a frenzy of hard work; reduce support for welfare recipients, and they'll soon get their financial houses in order and hold down a job. Sure, human beings are intelligent and complex, but their basic motivation is quite simple, the theory goes, and it starts—and usually ends—with a voracious appetite for material gain.

One of the reasons for the success of this theory is that it is so obviously true—or at least partly true. The argument that humans are greedy and have large appetites for material possessions is hardly one that requires supporting evidence. Just state the argument and everyone will nod immediately in agreement—partly because they recognize that sort of inclination in themselves, partly because they've seen it constantly in others. It's pretty clear: *Homo Economicus* rules. After a while, any slight deviation from the *Homo Economicus* model starts to seem implausible or even suspect. Why would anybody do this or that without pay? Must be up to something.

But while the case for *Homo Economicus*—or the centrality of greed and insatiable acquisitiveness in the human personality—appears incontestable, it may hold true mostly for our own society. It may be, in other words, that such strongly acquisitive behaviour isn't really rooted in our nature, but rather is an acquired habit based on the institutions, attitudes and incentives that shape our society.

Polanyi noted that in primitive and traditional societies, the satisfaction of human material needs was an integral part of the overall life of the community. In other words, the quest for food and material goods was simply part of the overall process and organization of society. The function of meeting material needs was thus "embedded" in one's broader social relations, part of one's role as a member of family, clan and the larger community. Capitalism changed this, by redesigning society in a way that separated out human material desires, stimulated them and pushed them to the forefront, greatly expanding their importance. The quest for material goods became a world of its own—a world that was given precedence over all other aspects of society. Thus, under capitalism, the material motive was "dis-embedded" from society and from social control, with far-reaching implications for humans and their surroundings.

So the *Homo Economicus* model isn't really a model of human behaviour but rather a model of human behaviour as *capitalism has attempted to reshape it*. The intense focus on material acquisitiveness is something that capitalism has cultivated in us. The point is not to suggest that humans are nicer than the *Homo Economicus* model implies, simply different. By highlighting the individualistic, materialistic motive, capitalism has moved the focus away from what Polanyi insists is the most basic aspect of our nature—that we are social animals.

The essentially social nature of humans was identified centuries ago by Aristotle, and has been observed extensively in the social sciences—particularly psychology, sociology and anthropology—as well as being the subject of much theory in philosophy and religion. The point is that humans naturally seek to relate to and be accepted by other humans. They want to belong, to feel part of a larger human community. As part of that community—whether family, clan, club, gang, social network or society at large—they will generally participate and contribute willingly. In addition to a sense of belonging, they want position and status in the social order. They desire approval, recognition and respect from others; they want to be appreciated and considered worthy by their fellow humans. The more ambitious may dream of being honoured, treated like a "big man on campus" or fawned over by enthusiastic fans.

In emphasizing this social nature, Polanyi is not suggesting that humans are unselfish or uninterested in their own welfare. On the contrary, he is suggesting they are primarily concerned about their own welfare (although not always exclusively so). But this focus on their own welfare doesn't mean that their motivation is primarily materialistic in nature. In fact, their individual welfare hinges, to a large extent, on their social relationships and on the preservation and viability of their communities. To the extent that humans are focused on specifically material goals, their motivation may be largely based on their desire to achieve status and position in the social order. "[Man] does not aim at safeguarding his individual interest in the acquisition of material possessions, but rather at ensuring social good will, social status, social assets," argues Polanyi. "He values possessions primarily as a means to that end."

So while humans are focused on achieving status in the social order, every society has a different way of establishing how status will be determined, by what criteria the members of that society will be judged and ranked—who will enjoy respect and prestige and who won't. In our society, one's status is determined to a large extent by one's material success. A big income, an expensive car or an impressive home are indicators of personal success and achievement, of having "made it." Our media are full of stories of the rich; newspapers often run a "top ten" list of the richest individuals in the country or the world, reflecting the fact that the mere possession of such large quantities of money impresses us in some significant way—perhaps with envy, but at least with great interest and attention. Hollywood movies and hundreds of lifestyle magazines routinely depict a lavish lifestyle as synonymous with the good life, at least as a backdrop to any life we would want to lead. To be rich is an indicator of success in our society. The flip side—being poor—is considered, if not a disgrace, at least an indication of some kind of personal failure.

In other societies, one's status was determined by criteria other than material wealth and acquisitions. "In Iroquois society, it was the number of scalps you collected that mattered," explains economist and Polanyi scholar Abraham Rotstein. "Among Benedictine monks, it was your level of propriety or your skill in copying Biblical manuscripts. Among the Spartans, it was athletic prowess . . . Every society defines the standard by which people achieve prestige." Thus, humans are above all interested in establishing themselves and gaining acceptance and prestige among their fellow humans, and every society offers a different way of doing this. Defining rank and prestige by financial success and material accumulation is a feature distinctive to capitalist societies, not to human societies in general. "If so-called economic motives were natural to man, we would have to judge all early and primitive societies as thoroughly unnatural," Polanyi notes.

Robert Heilbroner makes a similar point, observing that the idea of material gain was largely foreign to most people in ancient Egyptian, Greek, Roman and medieval cultures, as well as in most Eastern civilizations. Even in non-industrialized societies today, Heilbroner notes, it is often difficult to transform the local peasant population into a factory workforce. Not only do peasants lack an orientation to factory life and the wage system, but they lack the motivation—a motivation that seems utterly natural to us—to work ever harder in order to better their material standard of living. Peasants just don't seem to get it. Comments Heilbroner: "[U]nschooled in the idea of an ever-rising standard of living, [they] will not work harder if wages rise; [they] will simply take more time off." And why wouldn't they? In a culture that doesn't particularly value material possessions, where earning a bigger income will bring no added prestige, they have better things to do with their time than stay late at the factory. What this suggests is that the practice of devoting a huge part of one's life and energy to improving one's material standard—a practice that almost defines our culture—may be rooted more in capitalist traditions than in human nature.

This doesn't mean that primitive or traditional societies didn't take care of their material needs. They clearly did; their survival demanded it. Nor does it mean that people in these earlier societies didn't enjoy and accumulate material possessions. They did, and sometimes their material possessions were extensive, particularly among the ruling elite. But it does mean that most individuals in these societies were not primarily motivated by material gain. They worked hard to provide for themselves or to contribute to the community's overall material production, of which they were entitled to a small part. They were motivated to do so because that was what was required for acceptance in the social order. "Rank and status, compulsion of law and threat of punishment, public praise and private reputation, insure[d] that the individual contribute[d] his share to production," according to Polanyi. The motive of private material gain existed as well, but it wasn't a dominant or even a particularly common characteristic; it tended to be found mostly among those engaged in trade or commerce. "The motive of gain was specific to merchants, as was valor to the knight, piety to the priest, and pride to the craftsman," notes Polanyi. "The notion of making the motive of gain universal never entered the heads of our ancestors."

Rotstein makes the point that in years of teaching Polanyi's ideas in his economic history courses at the University of Toronto, he always found that this central idea was the one students had the most trouble understanding or accepting. This probably reflects the fact that we are so enveloped in a capitalist world, so used to our own way of behaving, that it is difficult to imagine people ever behaved very differently. Thus the economic motive that dominates our way of life seems to us universal. But Rotstein argues that if we look at societies where religion was the dominant force, we see people devoting huge parts of their lives to carrying out tasks related to religion, and we could conclude that humans are basically spiritual. In observing warrior societies, we could end up convinced that humans are above all interested in risking their lives to prove their bravery. "Or," he suggests, "if we observed Iroquois society, we could conclude that it is human nature to collect scalps."

Now let me just interject here that this is clearly part of a much larger debate about human nature. My point is not to imply that Polanyi's position on this, which I have briefly outlined here, is the definitive answer. The scepticism of Rotstein's students is only natural and inevitable. On the other hand, it seems to me that Polanyi is on to something very important when he asks us to discard the lens we are used to—the capitalist lens—and try to look at the world and human history without it. Certainly he cites lots of compelling evidence from history and anthropology to support his contention that traditional and primitive societies revolved primarily around motives other than the endless pursuit of material gain. His observations cast doubt on the certainty with which pro-market enthusiasts today assert as fact that humans are only really concerned with their own material self-interest. Polanyi gives us grounds to challenge that assumption, and raises the possibility that that assumption—so central to the way we've organized our world—might just be wrong.

So here's another way to look at things. *Homo Economicus* is a one-dimensional character who serves a useful purpose in the economics-textbook version of human reality. *Homo's* energetic and cunning pursuit of material gain is necessary for the main plot line of capitalism, and it makes for a compelling cartoon-variety tale. But as a meaningful representation of the human personality and human needs, *Homo Economicus* seems deficient, even fraudulent. If we look at human societies over time and place—not just restricting our view to the past few centuries in the West—we see that the one consistent thing that can be said about humans is not that they are driven to endlessly acquire material possessions; at times, they seem quite indifferent to this goal. The one thing that is truly consistent, as noted as far back as Aristotle, is that they are social. They travel in packs. They build societies. They may go hunting alone, but they return to the tribe's campfire at night. Tom Hanks illustrated Aristotle's point nicely in the movie *Castaway:* even on the best beach in paradise, by himself he's a miserable guy. One suspects that he would remain so even if he had plenty of steaks and lime daiquiris, an endless supply of Gucci shoes and a wrap-around DVD system.

IN OUR OWN TIME, when acquisitiveness is actively encouraged, *Homo Economicus* still seems an inadequate depiction of the whole human personality. While the impulse for material gain is obviously strong today, there are clearly other tendencies in us as well. Many economists would acknowledge that *Homo Economicus* is an exaggeration or a simplification. Even Adam Smith, the eighteenth-century father of classical economics, considered human nature to be more diverse. He devoted considerable space to what he considered human "virtues"—prudence, humanity, justice, generosity, public spirit. "Our sensibility to the feelings of others," he wrote, "so far from being inconsistent with the manhood of self-command, is the very principle on which that manhood is founded." Nonetheless, "neoclassical" economics—the form of economics that has ruled the profession for more than a century—is based on the notion that economic motives are universal and dominant, that humans are primarily motivated by a desire for material gain and acquisition. Given the pre-eminence of the economics profession in our culture, the concept of *Homo Economicus* has had a huge impact on our thinking and our institutions.

It is a central contention of this book that this obsession with the acquisitive motive has resulted in our paying too little attention to other human motives, needs and desires. One that has received far too little attention, for instance, is the impulse for self-protection, which is surely as strong and as basic as the impulse to acquire material things. Both these impulses, at their most basic levels, are aimed at self-preservation. We are clearly driven to acquire the material things we need to survive—food, water and shelter. And the material urge doesn't stop there; we assume that it extends beyond such life-sustaining necessities, and includes a general desire to accumulate possessions. But we fail to pay similar attention to the importance and scope of the self-protective urge. At its most basic level, the impulse for self-protection is what keeps us back from the edge when we're walking on a cliff, or makes us cling to a raft when we're in deep water and don't know how to swim. But presumably, it also extends beyond the avoidance of such immediate life-threatening dangers to include a general desire to protect our interests from infringements by others, and to preserve the natural and social environments that sustain us.

It's not hard to see how this impulse for self-protection can end up on a collision course with someone else's impulse to maximize his or her material gain. In other words, individuals seeking to protect themselves, their communities and their environment can easily find those interests threatened by a person who is pursuing his or her own material advantage. For these individuals, the only effective means of protecting themselves may be to take some kind of collective action in self-defence—action that limits the power of individual greed and acquisitiveness in order to protect the interests of others and the community as a whole. This sort of collective action seems like a logical extension of our basic impulse for self-protection, and it also seems to fit easily with our nature as essentially social animals. Yet for all its apparent naturalness, the urge for collective action has not been accorded the same importance in our society as the more widely recognized impulse to seek individual gain.

Indeed, there is a strong tendency today to dismiss the validity of the urge for collective action. Those celebrating the triumph of the new capitalism—a group that includes our political and business leaders, as well as most of the prominent voices in the media—are quick to reject collective solutions, and often present government, by its very nature, as repressive and a needless drag on the fast-paced, Internet-connected global economy. They advise lock-step acceptance of the "new realities" of private corporate power unchecked by government or any form of collective authority, lest we end up left behind in some backwater port of the global economy. This constant admonition to get on board simply assumes that the new system of liberating individual greed is an appropriate vehicle for human needs, that it is taking us somewhere we want to go. This approach ignores our reality as social beings with deep-rooted instincts to resist threats to our collective interests.

There is plenty of historical evidence of societies that collectively sought to curb individual acquisitiveness. The medieval world considered greed to be a destructive force that could wreak havoc on the well-being of the community. A merchant was permitted to make a fair return—that is, one that would allow him to live in a manner appropriate for someone of his social position—but those who tried to squeeze an extra profit were considered anti-social and even repulsive. Such people, who would be considered smart businesspeople today, were denounced back in the fourteenth century as "enemies both to God and man, opposite both to Grace and Nature." In case there was any remaining doubt about the merits of such people, the denunciation went on to depict them as "Man-haters, opposite to the Common good, as if the world were made only for them." (To which Mitsubishi would now reply: "Not yet, but we're working on it.")

The transformation of traditional societies into our modern capitalist world is in many ways the story of the repositioning of greed and material acquisitiveness in the overall scheme of society—that is, greed's meteoric rise from the status of the dirty scoundrel of human existence to that of liberator and world-class superstar. But in our celebration of greed as the poster boy of our age, and our rush to conclude that its spirit alone shapes us all, we have blotted out a huge part of our history and risk blinding ourselves to a huge part of our present—the desire for collective action to resist the full force of private greed, to seek what Polanyi called "the protection of society."

This impulse to collectively resist the market is a recurrent theme in the history of the past four of five centuries, according to Polanyi. Indeed, right from the emergence of the market economy, about five centuries ago, there was widespread resistance—a story we will return to in chapter five. This resistance has continued in many forms over the centuries. Polanyi argued that true laissez-faire capitalism, in which individual greed is essentially allowed to run loose beyond the reach of social control, only really existed briefly in Britain from the 1840s to the 1870s—and has now been revived, to some extent, in the past two decades in certain parts of the world. Certainly, if we look back at the past five centuries, we are struck by what Polanyi considered a double movement—the implementation of capitalism, but also, each step of the way, the determined attempt of people to come together to protect themselves from the potential damage of newly released market forces. The history of the past five hundred years is the history of the rise of capitalism, but it's also the history of the *resistance* to the harshness of capitalism.

The development of the welfare state in the early post-war period is an important example of this resistance to capitalism's excesses. After the era of fairly free-wheeling capitalism in the early part of the twentieth century, and the disastrous effects of this approach during the Great Depression, there was a clear public sentiment in Western nations in favour of government intervention and market regulation. Although the results varied from country to country, the basic thrust of public policy in the West during the first few decades after the Second World War was towards using the collective power of government to regulate the marketplace and ensure a more equitable distribution of resources among citizens. By imposing higher taxes on the well-to-do, governments were able to redistribute income to those lower down the ladder, and to establish national programs for delivering public services to all. While the post-war system kept capitalism intact, it modified it considerably in the name of protecting the public. There was a widely shared belief that the public interest—as represented by the government—should be given precedence over the powerful private interests that dominated the economic sphere, that ultimately power should rest with the people and their democratically elected representatives. This amounted to what Polanyi described as an attempt to "re-embed" the economy back into society—that is, to make the economy serve the interests of society, not the other way around.

It would be a mistake to overstate the trend towards equality in that early post-war period. There was certainly plenty of inequality, and large corporations were enormously powerful and influential with governments. Popular empowerment had a long way to go. But it would also be a mistake to understate how different the attitudes of policy-makers and the public were in those decades. The trend seemed to be clearly, if slowly, moving in the direction of expanding the democratic rights and sense of economic entitlement of ordinary people—a trend that some in the elite felt angered and threatened by. After all, where would it lead? Would the elite's dominion over the economy and claim to its profits be compromised? When the world economy slowed down in the 1970s, those who disliked the new egalitarian trends saw an opportunity, at last, to move against them.

The attempt to roll back these egalitarian advances is, in a nutshell, the story of the new capitalism. The financial elite has tried to take away the egalitarian gains and the popular sense of entitlement that was achieved during the early post-war decades. To stop this trend towards equality, the elite has sought to strip governments of their power, to return to a laissez-faire approach to the marketplace and to free up corporations—and the rich in general—from the burden of having to transfer what seems to them to be an unduly large part of their wealth to the public purse. Of course, this isn't an entirely "new" capitalism so much as it is an attempt to return to an old capitalism, to create something closer to the unfettered, laissez-faire capitalism that had prevailed in mid-nineteenth-century Britain.

What *is* new, however, is the attempt to establish legally binding international treaties to permanently install this version of unfettered capitalism as the way of the world. This enormously bold step is a bid to permanently "dis-embed" the economy from society—that is, to make the economy and its big corporate players, not the public, the master of things. In many ways, the boldness of the step was prompted by the extent of the egalitarian gains made during the early post-war era. "Never again!" is the unspoken refrain of the new capitalism's advocates, as they do everything they can to discredit those early post-war years, keeping the focus on the evils of "big government" back then and away from the considerable gains that were made by ordinary people in achieving greater access to education, health care and financial security. In place of this, corporations are now to be ensured freedom from restraints on their profit-making. And collective action

aimed at protecting communities and the environment against individual greed is to be curtailed by law.

Given the ferocity of this "new capitalism," it is not surprising that it
has sparked the so-called anti-globalization movement—a radical variation within a long-established tradition of anti-capitalist resistance.

❧

NONE OF THIS IS to deny the power and centrality of greed in our
society. On the contrary, it is to pay it its proper due as a hugely
potent force in human social relations. It is for this reason that greed
merits special attention, although arguably not the veneration that it
receives in our society. Rather, it merits special attention because of
its power to incite behaviour that infringes on the rights of others,
that can wreak serious havoc on the rights of the rest of the community. This right to *protection from* greed is largely ignored, pushed aside.
We are all simply urged to let the greed orgy begin.

Polanyi questions the wisdom of this by providing the powerful
analogy to sexual lust. He notes that sexual desire is one of the most
potent appetites in human beings—and it is precisely for this reason
that just about every society in the history of the world has imposed
rules and restrictions to try to keep the sexual urge from running
amok and destroying the fragile bonds of society. Obviously this
includes restrictions against rape. But it goes beyond this, to include
the whole institution of marriage, which takes many forms but is a
major and fairly constant institution in human societies. What
marriage seeks to do is to confine lust within a social institution,
where its satisfaction will be achieved not on its own, but as part of a
larger set of social relations known as the family, with all the responsibility and emotional commitment that that entails. Polanyi notes
that the family "is never allowed to center on the sexual instinct, with
its intermittences and vagaries, but on the combination of a number
of effective motives that prevent sex from destroying an institution on
which so much of man's happiness depends."

While the institution of marriage is less rigid now than in the past, it is still almost universally observed in some form (even if no longer assumed to necessarily involve a lifelong commitment). Certainly, the norm these days continues to be that people form themselves into couples, and sex is an important part of the relationship, although normally not the only thing going on. This coupling happens usually not out of some religious commitment or legal requirement, but because the participants, and society in general, recognize the enormously disruptive potential of fully unleashed sexual appetite. While many married people might want sexual freedom for themselves, they're often willing to sacrifice it in order to get a commitment that their partner will do the same. It is hard to imagine, outside the glossy, air-brushed world of the Playboy mansion or the TV-show "reality" of *Temptation Island,* a society that encouraged people to believe that their personal sexual indulgence should come before all else, that the world should revolve around their sexual satisfaction— or that this is something Mitsubishi should be working on.

Greed and material acquisitiveness have traditionally been regarded in somewhat the same way—as forces that have the power to destroy the social fabric, and that are therefore best enfolded inside some broader set of human relations. However, the capitalist world that has evolved in the past few hundred years has not only discarded this traditional restraint on greed, but has pushed the material incentive to the very centre of the stage, casting it as virtually the saviour of our civilization. Rather than seeing the material urge as one among many human motives—one with the potential both to encourage work effort and to create social havoc—we've unleashed it, urged it on and celebrated those who have indulged in it most fully.

With the material incentive, one could add, there's an additional danger. While full sexual indulgence may wreak havoc in societies, it probably poses little risk to the broader natural environment. The freeing of greed from social restraint, however, clearly includes the possibility of major environmental damage, a subject we will return to later.

I realize, of course, that in raising concerns about unbridled greed, I risk being thought of as judgemental, or simply as a kind but naive person who probably also believes that nice guys always win in the end. So let me say that I do not mean to pass judgement, and I harbour no illusions about nice guys. (My observation is that the guy in the red Alfa Romeo convertible generally gets the girl.) I also confess to being prone to probably as much greed and lust as the next person.

But that being said, I still feel compelled to ask whether we haven't got seriously off track with our revolutionary approach to the proper positioning of greed in society. I suspect that for most of us, the radical departure of putting greed and material acquisitiveness at the forefront largely goes unnoticed, in part because of our failure to see that other societies have done things differently. (Of course, it's difficult to notice much about other societies when our cultural view is largely restricted to things that happened in the West within the past decade or so, and our understanding of what happened before that is mostly achieved through watching movies like *Gladiator*.) Given this cultural reality, it may be inevitable that negative commentary on the celebration of greed will simply be dismissed as irrelevant, as evidence of a desire to fast-forward to that backwater port reserved for losers in the global economy. Maybe so. Still, I remain so deeply impressed by the profound sentiments expressed in the following passage, written by the late British historian R. H. Tawney, that I wonder if they don't strike a similarly responsive chord in others:

> So merciless is the tyranny of economic appetites, so prone
> to self-aggrandizement the empire of economic interests,
> that a doctrine which confines them to their proper sphere,
> *as the servant, not the master of civilization,* may reasonably be
> regarded as among the pregnant truisms which are a perma-
> nent element in any sane philosophy.

THE NOTION THAT MATERIAL acquisitiveness should be the servant, not the master, of civilization seems so obviously sensible that it would appear to be hard to dispute. And for centuries, this notion was considered self-evident to any thinking person. Left unchecked, greed would break the social bonds of the community, as individuals driven by voracious economic appetites took advantage of others in their quest for personal enrichment. The potential for harm seemed enormous. Human decency cried out against such a system.

Ah, but that misses a crucial point, said some of the early capitalist theorists. The real potential created by unleashing the economic appetites is not that a few people will get rich, but that everyone will end up better off. John Locke, for instance, argued that adopting capitalist modes for agriculture would increase the overall yield of the land. Adam Smith similarly argued that by unleashing individual self-interest, nations would generate more total material wealth. So the community, rather than suffering as a result of the release of individual economic appetites, ends up collectively better off. In other words, by making greed the master, not the servant of civilization—that is, doing the opposite of what Tawney suggested—we all win.

It should be noted that this was a stunningly clever argument, and it had the effect of undermining much of the moral objection to greed. In fact, the argument didn't really deal with capitalism's potential impact on social relations, but it did present a compelling counter-position. Certainly, if greed would lead to improved material conditions for all, this amounted to a positive argument in its favour. Whatever damage it might do to the social fabric, at least it could be said to contribute to the general good in some significant, tangible way.

In fact, this was the somewhat hesitant spirit in which the new system was promoted by its early advocates—as a mixed bag of good and bad whose benefits ultimately outweighed its bad points. Unlike capitalism's more gung-ho advocates today, the early enthusiasts were at least willing to concede some potential problems with the new system. For all his enthusiasm, for instance, Adam Smith had some concerns about capitalism's impact on society. He feared that a heavy focus on commerce and acquisitiveness would introduce a moral and physical flabbiness. "By having their minds constantly employed on the arts of luxury, [people] grow effeminate and dastardly." Smith also believed that capitalism "sinks the courage of mankind, and tends to extinguish martial spirit." As negative as these possibilities were in Smith's mind, they were more than balanced by the potential of an overall increase in society's material well-being.

Thus it was that capitalism got its foot in the door of respectable society. The intellectual breakthrough of the capitalist theorists had helped smooth away the objections to the elevation of greed in the social order. By turning greed into a force for material plenty, they had made a powerful theoretical case that capitalism would improve the economic well-being of all. The only thing they hadn't done was provide any real evidence to prove their case.

ODDLY, THE ABSENCE OF proof turned out not to be a problem. Indeed, more than two centuries later, the lack of proof seems to pose even less of a problem now than it did back then. I am not suggesting, of course, that there's no evidence of capitalism's ability to produce material bounty. That has been amply proven. What I am questioning is the contention that we are all better off as a result, even on a material level. Certainly if we include the whole world—which seems appropriate in the age of the global economy—the case becomes tenuous. We will return to this subject in chapter two, but it is important to briefly note now that roughly 2.8 billion people—almost half the world's population—are living on less than $2 (U.S.) a day, a situation that leaves them in conditions of serious deprivation. Furthermore, the problems seem to be getting worse with the advent of the new capitalism. The latest numbers from the World Bank show that roughly 75 per cent of the world's people actually experienced a *decline* in their real incomes between 1988 and 1993, with the biggest decline in the bottom 5 per cent—the poorest 300 million people, who lost almost one-quarter of their real incomes.

The distinction between capitalism's overall bounty and the adequate distribution of this bounty is surely a crucial one. If the early advocates of capitalism had merely claimed that liberating greed would generate more overall wealth and that this would further enrich the rich, they wouldn't have had such a powerful argument on their side. What gave their argument such force and such power to knock down the deeply instilled moral objections to greed was the notion that their new system was going to benefit *the whole community*. But this claim, as Heilbroner notes, "passes too easily over the question of how widely the gains from accumulation will be shared."

If Smith and the other early advocates of capitalism managed to dance deftly over the question of how the benefits were to be shared, today's advocates have turned this bit of fancy footwork into an art form. Indeed, one of the striking aspects of today's new capitalism is the way its advocates are willing to make the most extreme claims of its advantages. No longer content to pussyfoot around with vague assertions about its benefits, today's advocates portray the juices of capitalism as pure nectar from the gods. It's time to introduce Dinesh D'Souza.

ᕊ

IT'S NOT HARD TO IMAGINE how Dinesh D'Souza landed a job as a research scholar at the right-wing American Enterprise Institute in Washington. There's heavy competition, of course, among analysts pandering to the corporate world, but D'Souza manages to gush about the virtues of American-style capitalism in a way that puts him in a league of his own. "[T]he economic problem has been solved," he breathlessly declares in his recent book, *The Virtue of Prosperity*. "We know how to create wealth. . . . But there is only one way to do it, and that is the American way of technological capitalism."

This sort of triumphant declaration about the wonders of American capitalism is standard fare these days. A recent *Wall Street Journal* editorial suggested that the spread of capitalism globally may in fact be a prerequisite for a world of Christian brotherhood. It went on to quote a religious leader, who said that the difference between Christian teaching and business isn't as great as we might think. It's probably true that a lot of dot-com millionaires feel capitalism has blessed them. And even ordinary folk in the advanced world are reminded that we too share in the bounty; we will all soon have personal digital cellphones that will recognize our voices, help us navigate streets, collect our mail, do our banking and read us the news. It's sometimes hard to sleep at night knowing this nirvana is just around the corner.

Still, it always fascinates me, when I read this sort of literature about the triumph of the market, to see how market enthusiasts deal with the question of the rest of the world. "Short-term inequality remains a problem," writes D'Souza, without explaining his concept of "short term" or hinting at the depth of the problem. "[B]ut is it a problem we can live with?" he asks. After searching his soul for a few seconds, he apparently concludes that we *can* live with it. Of course, inequality always feels like less of a problem to those who don't live in corrugated shacks, which is why sales of D'Souza's book have probably been brisker in Manhattan than in, say, Addis Ababa or Khartoum.

But D'Souza goes on to make a truly extraordinary claim about the benefits delivered by free-market capitalism: "We are living in an astonishing moment in history in which the problem of scarcity, which has plagued our species since the dawn of mankind, is vanishing before our eyes." It's interesting to imagine how a "research scholar" could have reached this conclusion—except perhaps by confining his research to TV sitcoms.

Of course, as noted above, scarcity is not in fact disappearing. But there's a deeper irony in D'Souza's claim. Not only has capitalism failed to bring us to the brink of a scarcity-free world, but in a sense, you could say that *capitalism invented scarcity*—at least as a deliberate method of economic organization. In fact, scarcity is central to the dynamic of capitalism—a point that conveniently gets lost in today's celebration of capitalism's bounty. The flip side of this bounty, this endless feast, is scarcity. As Heilbroner notes: "[W]ealth cannot exist unless there also exists a condition of scarcity—not insufficiency of resources themselves, but insufficiency of means of access to resources." It is this lack of access to resources that obliges the mass of people to work for the few who control the resources, thereby enabling this privileged lot to accumulate wealth. Without this unequal dynamic, there would be no wealth accumulation—the very essence of capitalism. Even Adam Smith acknowledged this central inequality in the system he advocated: "Wherever there is great property, there is great inequality. For one very rich man, there must be at least five hundred poor, and the affluence of the rich supposes the indigence of the many."

This isn't just a theory. It actually happened historically. We will review in chapter five how capitalism emerged as a system by eliminating the kind of traditional rights peasants had long enjoyed, rights giving them access to the resources they needed to live—enough land and tools to eke out their own very modest livings. Capitalism changed all this. The resources that previously furnished them with a livelihood continued to exist, but they lost access to them. Pushed into a situation of scarcity, they became desperate, with no choice but to work for others who now controlled access to the resources. The very essence of capitalism—the accumulation of capital by extracting a profit from the labour of others—was made possible only by depriving the masses of access to what they needed to live. It could be added that the masses weren't happy about the change. Comments political theorist John Gray, "It is doubtful that the free market would ever have been engineered if working democratic institutions were in place."

Thus although capitalism has led to the enormous bounty of riches celebrated by the triumphalists, it has also introduced the concept of scarcity as a basic principle of economic organization. Historically, there were plenty of periods of scarcity, but usually because of an external threat—drought, pestilence or war. The principle that everyone in society should be free from hunger prevailed, according to Polanyi, "under almost every and any type of social organization up to about the beginning of sixteenth-century Europe." It was at that point that capitalism introduced the idea of using scarcity as a *deliberate tool of economic organization*. By intentionally creating scarcity (for the many), capitalism used scarcity to generate wealth (mostly for the few).

With the rise of general material prosperity in the West, capitalist forces have had to move farther afield to find optimum conditions of scarcity. It can be argued that they've simply moved offshore the whole process of imposing scarcity on a country's population in order to transform it into a pool of labour suitable for profit-making. This would mean that the same process that happened in the West, starting about five centuries ago, is now happening on a giant scale as millions of people around the world lose access to subsistence farming. Dinesh D'Souza would no doubt chime in here that, well, those millions of people will all soon be better off as a result—or five centuries from now perhaps they'll be better off, although admittedly there may be some tough sledding along the way. Of course, there are no guarantees; it may be that capitalism simply requires the dynamic of the scarcity of the many to keep generating riches for the few.

Certainly capitalism offers minimal advantages for those without resources. Under the market system, there is demand for a product if a lot of people want it—but that demand counts for nothing if those people have no money. If they lack money, their demand essentially doesn't exist. It will not result in a producer providing a supply of that item—at least not to the people without the money.

This explains why the drug industry is not investing money to develop a cure for a disease known as sleeping sickness, which leaves its victims in a coma. The disease is clearly a serious one—it killed 66,000 people last year and threatens to infect 60 million more—but the only people who are afflicted by it are poverty-stricken Africans with no clout in the marketplace. Interestingly, there is a drug called eflornithine that is effective in lifting victims out of their comas. But drug companies stopped producing eflornithine in 1995 because it was no longer profitable to continue. The drug was still desperately needed, but only by people without money. So, following modern market practices, these people were simply left in a coma. Interestingly, the production of eflornithine was restarted only after its alternate use as a facial hair remover was discovered. Indeed, while there seem to be endless resources to develop products desired by rich Westerners—products to stop hair growth or start it, or to make body parts perform sexual functions more effectively—there is little or no money for products that only poor people need, no matter how desperately they need them.

The plight of AIDS victims in Africa illustrates a different aspect of how the market fails those without money. Of course, plenty of money has been spent on AIDS research, since there are many AIDS victims with financial resources in other parts of the world. And effective treatments now exist, but they cost roughly $15,000 (U.S.) a year—clearly beyond the wildest dreams of poor Africans, who often have incomes well below $700 (U.S.) a year. So, under modern capitalism, most of the 25 million Africans who have AIDS or HIV simply go without treatment. Pressure from consumers in rich nations has recently pushed the drug industry to cut its prices dramatically in poor countries, but the prices are still unaffordable to millions of people. Only strong interventions by governments are likely to improve the situation. The government of Brazil, for instance, has begun producing generic copies of AIDS drugs, enabling the country to offer free universal treatment for AIDS. As a result, in only three years, Brazil has managed to cut its AIDS death rate in half.

But Brazil's non-market solution has met with fierce opposition from the private drug companies. At their behest, Washington even launched a legal challenge to the program through the WTO, withdrawing the challenge only in the last week of June 2001, just as a major UN conference on AIDS threatened to focus world attention on Washington's attempt to prevent dying people from gettting low-cost treatment. Gro Harlem Brundtland, director general of the World Health Organization, has powerfully summed up the situation: "Let us be frank about it: essential and life-saving drugs exist while millions and millions of people cannot afford them. This amounts to a moral problem, a political problem and a problem of credibility for the global market system"—something you'd never have an inkling of, listening to market enthusiasts like Dinesh D'Souza.

It is perhaps understandable that the relatively small group of people who have done spectacularly well in recent years would want to celebrate the triumph of the new capitalism. D'Souza no doubt never dreamt his life would be this good; selling books extolling the virtues of the new capitalism to the corporate elite has proved enormously lucrative. But it is one thing for the market triumphalists to privately celebrate their personal good fortune and quite another for them to make sweeping, unsubstantiated claims in an attempt to convince the general public that the system that has rewarded them so handsomely is also doing great things for others—others who, for the most part, suffer invisibly and silently in faraway corners of the world.

Certainly, the noisy celebration of the market helps divert attention from the fact that market capitalism has not come close to solving the devastating problem of world poverty. I am not suggesting that there is conclusive proof that it won't someday improve things. But as things now stand, the case that capitalism will make the world—not just the West—materially better off has simply not been convincingly demonstrated. Indeed, with almost 70 per cent of the world's people experiencing a decline in their real income in recent years, the opposite appears to be true. The wanton celebration of market capitalism while so many people throughout the world are lacking basic food and shelter seems, if not downright vulgar, at least a little insensitive.

THE EMERGENCE OF THE NEW capitalism in the early 1980s was one of those developments that, you could say, happened just beneath the public's radar. From the late 1940s to the 1970s, capitalism had been subject to considerable restraint, as we've seen. Under this reined-in capitalism, designed by the late British economist John Maynard Keynes, governments asserted a significant amount of control over the economy—an approach that enjoyed widespread support. While there was plenty of discord over specific policies and politicians, there was also, to an extent unimaginable today, popular support for the role of government and a belief in the capacity of government to represent the public's interests and even serve the public good. Before capitalism could be returned to its purer, more rigorous form, this popular support for government, and for collective solutions in general, had to be eroded.

A change that huge does not happen overnight. And it might not have happened at all had it not been for the economic instability—high inflation, high unemployment—that rocked the world economy in the mid-1970s, leaving governments suddenly looking incapable of managing things. This created an opening, a window of opportunity for those who had long wanted to derail this train chugging slowly in the direction of expanded democracy and popular entitlement. It was actually a small group of academics who first started to bring things to a halt. Their work, dating back to the early 1950s, had focused on the idea that government had grown too big in Western countries. Of course, others, both inside and outside of academia, had argued this position too. But these academics, mostly economists, had a theory—a theory that would prove to be highly effective in reshaping the political landscape. Their theory involved our hero, *Homo Economicus,* the chap driven by naked self-interest who is central to economics lore. Their theory took *Homo Economicus* out of the confines of the economic world and plopped him down firmly on the centre stage of society. No longer restricted to the playpen of the economy, *Homo Economicus* was about to go mainstream.

These academics, who became known as public-choice theorists, argued that the same calculating, self-interested approach that shapes human economic behaviour also shapes all other human behaviour. As one of its prominent advocates, Dennis Mueller, explains, "The basic behavioural postulate of public choice, as for economics, is that man is an egoistic, rational, utility maximizer." In particular, the public-choice theorists argued that the public arena of democracy was much like the marketplace, and that voters, politicians and civil servants were not capable of any broader perspective than their own narrow self-interest. This presented a challenge to the prevailing view of government as a force capable of defending the public good.

What the public-choice movement did was provide an intellectual foundation for what was to become, over the next few decades, a massive attack on the very concept of government. The notion that government—even democratically elected government—could in any way represent some kind of broad public interest was seen as fraudulent, since there was no overarching public interest, just a collection of individual desires and preferences. Similarly, the notion of "public servants" operating in the interests of the broader community was dismissed out of hand and replaced with the concept of "bureaucrats," whose only interest was in maximizing the size of their own bureaucracy, and hence their own income and power. Politicians, of course, were dismissed as purely self-serving, and government in general was presented as little more than a public trough that everyone was trying to get their face into.

Of course, we can easily believe much of this. The idea that politicians and political parties serve only the interests of those who donate the most to their campaigns seems dead on the money. Certainly it fits well with leftist critiques of the way business interests are able to dominate the political process. But one can note this reality about Western democracies—and argue at the same time for reforms on campaign finance, etc.—without assuming, as the public-choice theorists do, that things inevitably will be this way, because that's all human nature is capable of. In fact, it seems obvious that countless people have become involved in politics out of some public-spirited zeal. The fact that the reform movements they join often fail to overcome the entrenched power of well-financed special interests doesn't mean that people don't have public-spirited instincts.

The public-choice theorists would have us believe that nobody ever gets involved in government or the political arena out of a desire to accomplish public goals, and that all the products of government— the building of schools, hospitals, roads, libraries, museums, public parks—happen only incidentally, as by-products of someone's desire to advance a personal career. Needless to say, the notion that citizens would voluntarily band together to fight injustice and poverty in faraway parts of the world is incomprehensible to this kind of thinking. This perhaps explains the frequent attempt to dismiss those in the anti-globalization movement as nothing more than a group of self-seeking opportunists—as if there is some kind of money to be made in championing debt elimination for the Third World.

The extreme nature of some public-choice theories can be seen in the rather far-fetched way they explain why the framers of the U.S. constitution enshrined the crucial concept of "judicial independence." The convoluted reasoning goes something like this: if the integrity and independence of the courts could be established, special interests would be unable to bully the courts, so their best hope would be to win over legislators. As a result, the legislators would be able to demand larger campaign contributions from special interests. Hugh Stretton and Lionel Orchard, critics of public choice, comment, "So the politicians who framed the U.S. constitution and the First Amendment are presumed to have provided for judicial independence simply to raise the prices they could thereafter get for their legislative decisions." The absurdity of public-choice theory is captured by Nobel Prize–winning economist Amartya Sen in the following little scenario: "Can you direct me to the railway station?" asks the stranger. "Certainly," says the local, pointing in the opposite direction, towards the post office, "and would you post this letter for me on your way?" "Certainly," says the stranger, resolving to open it to see if it contains anything worth stealing.

While much of public-choice theory seems implausible, its political usefulness appeared to make up for any intellectual deficiencies. When it came right down to it, public-choice theory provided a fabulous vehicle for attacking the role of government. "Public choice theory is, more than anything else, a theory of government failure," explains the sociologist Lars Udehn. "The argument is that government is too big, and public expenditures in Western democracies a gigantic waste of resources." This line of argument quickly found a market among members of the financial and business elite, who had chafed under the growing regulatory control of government and the increasing sense of entitlement among the public. To this corporate crowd, the attempt to discredit government could not have been more welcome. If democratic government could be dismissed as simply an untrustworthy collection of self-interested politicians and bureaucrats, then the huge machine of government, with its power to redistribute income and impose annoying regulations on business, could be greatly scaled back. Government—the sole vehicle for members of the broader public to shape their world—could be rendered powerless, an object of little more than public ridicule.

The financial elite was quick to spot the benefits of the new theory, and the theorists themselves apparently had no objections to their arguments lending support to the cause of the well-heeled. If they hadn't noticed before, they quickly caught on to the fact that their revelations about the untrustworthiness of government could be used to bolster arguments about the danger of majority rule. They could therefore prove a handy tool for those wanting to preserve and enhance the privileged position of the financial elite. Indeed, one of the major focuses of public-choice theory soon became taxation—or more specifically, how to restrict the power of the majority to impose taxes on the rich.

This had long been an area of considerable concern to the elite, who always had a lurking fear that the masses might one day gang up on the small group who enjoyed great wealth. By imposing hefty taxes on inheritance and capital gains, the majority could transfer much of the tax burden away from themselves and onto their wealthier fellow citizens. Public-choice theorists offered a set of arguments to explain why this shouldn't be allowed to happen. Basically, they argued that since there was no broad public interest, only individual preferences, government shouldn't be allowed to make decisions about the distri- bution of resources, because the majority of people would unfairly impose their interests on others. Therefore, there should be constitu- tional protections against majority rule in the area of taxation. And these constitutional protections should not be subject to change without unanimous or near-unanimous public agreement. The practi- cal effect of this would be to hand the rich a veto over attempts to increase their tax burden. Not surprisingly, the public-choice school of thought has found legions of supporters among the upper classes.

With the enthusiastic backing of this influential crowd, the public- choice movement has had an impact that is almost revolutionary in scope. Much of the actual writing of the theorists themselves remains obscure outside the academic world, and with good reason. The argu- ments are sometimes so convoluted and even silly that a thorough airing would probably make them—rather than government—the object of public ridicule. But the public-choice school of thought has managed to provide some apparent intellectual backing for the notion that government is inherently untrustworthy. What has filtered through to the public consciousness—indeed, what has become firmly embedded in the public consciousness—is a profound suspicion and distrust of government. The notion that government is simply an abusive, intrusive force with no higher purpose or beneficial capability has permeated deeply into the popular culture, undermining public confidence in all kinds of policies aimed at distributing resources more fairly or limiting the power of private corporate interests.

The public-choice theorists have essentially provided an intellectual justification for the liberation of greed and material self-interest from social control. By defining greed as the only natural impulse—the one that lies at the root of all human behaviour—they have dismissed everything else as unnatural and artificial, ultimately an illusion or simply wishful thinking. Greed, the public-choice theorists declare, is all there really is. Deep down, we are all that repulsive *Homo Economicus* character that we were hoping we wouldn't be stuck sitting beside at dinner.

In debates in the social sciences, there is always a tension over the issue of what should be defined as natural and what should be defined as the mere product of human conditioning. If something can be defined as natural or innate, we are less inclined to try to change it or modify it, believing that we are dealing with part of the apparatus of nature. How astonishing, then, to think that the greed impulse in humans—long the object of constraints in one form or another in the interests of social harmony—has now been reclassified as natural, indeed as the *only* natural human impulse! Stretton and Orchard note that the public-choice theorists have attempted "to persuade people that material greed is, and will inescapably remain, the single, natural, dominant motive of their political, economic and social behaviour." Such thinking clearly gives a green light to every greedy impulse that is coursing through our veins. If *Homo Economicus* is all there is, or all that we are capable of being, then go for it, man! With the wind at its back as never before in human history, greed is settling in comfortably to a privileged perch atop a luxury schooner cruising the waters of the global economy.

Thus was the modified, more restrained version of capitalism of the early post-war years brought to a screeching halt. Once the public-choice theorists had provided the intellectual underpinnings for the vilification of government, capitalism was easily liberated. No longer would the profit motive be confined by Keynesian constraints aimed at giving the broader public some measure of control. Released from the yoke of government, capitalism could now enjoy a striking new freedom and prestige. No more on the defensive, capitalism could stretch its legs and walk down the street in broad daylight, with a spring in its step . . . and bureaucrats better get out of its way! The new capitalism—cocky, self-assured and ready to take on the world—was born.

THE STAGE WAS SET FOR what's going on now—the redesign of the world's legal and political systems as the tentacles of the new capitalism stretch over the entire globe. With breathtaking speed, all-encompassing international treaties are being drawn up to curtail the powers of government and ensure the worldwide rights of corporations to unlimited material acquisitiveness. Ultimately, the world is being redesigned to accommodate *Homo Economicus*—even though he is, at best, a cartoon character, and at worst, a fraudulent distortion of human needs and aspirations. Never mind. He's coming to a country near you. In fact, to all countries around the globe.

What is involved is arguably the most massive experiment in social engineering the world has ever seen.

CHAPTER TWO

# Remaking the World

IN THE DYING DAYS of his administration, Bill Clinton was still trying to inject some substance into a presidency known best for other things. As the vote recount to determine his successor continued in Florida—with media commentators bizarrely urging an end to the most exciting electoral politics anywhere in more than a century—the U.S. president went overseas in the hope that perhaps some lofty words spoken from afar would help imbue his image with a litte *gravitas*.

Addressing a suitably distinguished crowd at England's Warwick University, Clinton spoke sweepingly of the future and the global economy. While stopping short of saying he felt the Third World's pain, that idea was implicit. But if anyone was thinking that Clinton was veering leftwards now that he was about to lose all power to bring about change, he made it clear that there would be no deathbed conversions. He was still thinking along Wall Street lines. Thus he trotted out the familiar canards of protectionism and isolationism—as if there was a groundswell of people calling for a world without trade.

With his typical flourish and apparently caring demeanour, Clinton managed to make it sound as if the world was divided into two camps—those striving to bring the nations of the globe together and enrich them through globalization, and those hiding in their little corners, determined to suffer alone.

This was reassuring talk for Wall Street. Certainly the business elite likes nothing better than the concept that globalization boils down to more interconnectedness, to pulling the four corners of the earth closer together through increased trade and commerce, all made possible by the wonders of the telecommunications revolution. It likes to portray critics of globalization as go-it-aloners, determined to keep the advances of the twenty-first century at bay and thereby relegate the less developed parts of the world permanently to a primitive state. This business version of reality glosses over a fundamental truth: that globalization is about a lot more than interconnectedness. First and foremost, it's about changing the world, about redesigning it along the lines of the new capitalism, catering to unrestrained private greed.

Needless to say, there is much enthusiasm for this project in the rich countries, at least among members of the business and financial elite. They require that the rest of the world adapt and accept the new rules, and they are highly effective at getting their way. In the future, they insist, it will be the market way—or the highway. You play by the rules of the new world order or you play by yourself, on the sidelines. Once everybody gets that clear, we can all be interconnected.

Clinton's speech was well received. It probably did help deflect the focus from the more salacious aspects of his presidency and onto his deep commitment to transforming the world into a giant U.S.-style market economy—although judging by the level of harm inflicted on the world's people, it's hard to see why Monica Lewinsky would be considered the more damaging legacy.

IT'S PERHAPS ODD TO think of it this way, but Canada got one break in the Walkerton tragedy: the deadly contamination of the Ontario town's water supply, which killed seven people in the summer of 2000, came from cow manure. If the contamination had come instead from, say, a toxic chemical produced by a foreign company, that would have been worse. Then the company might well have sued Canada for hundreds of millions of dollars.

Yes, we are back to the subject of the new trade deals and the far-reaching power they hand over to corporations. But anyone who thinks I am pushing the envelope with the Walkerton example is probably unaware of an actual case with striking similarities. A Vancouver-based company, Methanex, is suing the United States for $1.3 billion. The huge sum involved is the first clue that things are a bit wingy with these NAFTA lawsuits. What injustice could possibly have been done *to Methanex* that the damage is well over a billion dollars?

Well, it turns out that Methanex produces a substance used in the manufacture of MTBE, a gasoline additive that, when it enters the water supply, is considered a health hazard by the state of California. This isn't just a crazy idea on the part of someone who's been producing too many Hollywood movies. The city of Santa Monica, California (pop. 93,000), had to shut seven of its eleven municipal wells several years ago—and they remain shut—after traces of MTBE leached from gasoline tanks underneath service stations into the local groundwater. Even very small quantities of MTBE cause water to smell and taste like turpentine, rendering it unfit for human consumption. Joe Lawrence, assistant city solicitor for Santa Monica, says that the MTBE contamination has forced the city to purchase 80 per cent of its drinking water, at a cost of roughly $3 million a year. Contamination from MTBE also led to the closing of twelve of the thirty-four municipal wells in South Tahoe Lake and other communities along the California coast and central valley. Altogether, more than 3,000 groundwater sites in California have been contaminated by MTBE.

A team of scientists from the University of California, appointed by the state to investigate the potential health hazards, concluded that MTBE causes cancer in mice and rats, and potentially causes cancer in humans. (This conclusion was supported by reports from the U.S. Environmental Protection Agency and the White House National Science and Technology Council.) As a result, California has ordered MTBE to be phased out, and completely banned by the end of 2002.

Under the circumstances, one would think that Methanex officials would count themselves lucky not to be dragged out of the state behind a fast-moving truck. And, in the pre-NAFTA days, they would probably have been relieved just to walk away scot-free. But as we saw in the Metalclad case in chapter one, NAFTA has changed all that.

Now Methanex, not the people whose water was contaminated by MTBE, can claim to be the victim. (Take note, Walkerton.) Indeed, with a new set of legal rights at its disposal, Methanex decided to launch a massive lawsuit under NAFTA's Chapter 11, claiming damages for financial losses it will suffer as a result of California's ban.

Methanex claims that MTBE is not a health hazard, that there is no conclusive proof that it causes cancer in humans and that California should be required to take other measures to contain gasoline from leaking into its groundwater. (Lawrence responds that there is no reliable way to prevent gasoline from leaking into the soil immediately around underground containers. But he insists that such leakage only becomes a problem when MTBE is present in the gasoline because it then moves easily through the soil and into the groundwater.) Methanex has also suggested, in an amendment to its NAFTA suit, that the MTBE ban was politically motivated, arguing that California governor Gray Davis received more than $200,000 in campaign contributions from a company that produces a competing product. But California is not the only state to ban MTBE. At least eleven others have also taken action to phase out MTBE. Are we to believe then that all these state legislatures have been influenced to take action against it due to political donations? So, let's recap quickly: MTBE pollutes the drinking water of a California city, California bans MTBE, and a company that produces a chemical used in MTBE—considering itself the injured party—sues for damages.

Now if it sounds like what everyone involved needs is simply a good shake of the head to get things back in perspective, that may well be true. What's going on here ultimately is a far-reaching power grab by corporations, and so far they seem to be getting away with it. Essentially, they are pushing aggressively to expand the notion of property rights far beyond what is guaranteed in the U.S. constitution, which is already much stronger than what is provided for under Canadian law. Under both Canadian and American law, corporations are not entitled to compensation when government regulations aimed at protecting the public have the effect of making their investments less profitable. So Methanex would not be able to sue for damages or compensation in connection with California's ban on MTBE in U.S. [or Canadian] courts, according to an assessment by William T. Waren of the Harrison Institute of Public Law at Washingon's Georgetown University Law Center.

But NAFTA has created a new international legal tribunal system that appears to offer an expanded notion of property rights for corporations. If a government regulation makes a corporation's investments less profitable, the corporation can argue that this is "tantamount to expropriation"—a concept that is considered grounds for compensation under the rules of NAFTA. In fact, NAFTA doesn't actually define what it means by this concept, leaving it up to individual NAFTA tribunals to decide in each case, and thereby creating the opportunity for corporations to use NAFTA to try to achieve property rights that they do not currently enjoy under U.S. or Canadian law. Corporations are attempting to do an "end run around the U.S. constitution," says Timothy Canova, an associate professor of law at the University of New Mexico Law School.

It's possible, as some people have contended, that the drafters of NAFTA never intended this sort of thing to happen. If so, the problem could be quickly remedied; all that would be required would be a directive from the three NAFTA partners—the U.S., Canada and Mexico—clarifying to the tribunals that corporations are not entitled to compensation when governments take measures in the interests of protecting their citizens. But no such directive is in the works. The Canadian government did take initial steps towards pressing its partners for this sort of "clarification"—but it backed off abruptly in the spring of 2001 after it ran into heavy resistance from the Bush administration. The Canadian government's retreat on this front is not only a serious setback for any hopes of restricting the scope of corporate rights under NAFTA, it also offers an interesting insight into Prime Minister Jean Chrétien.

Chrétien has long tried to portray himself as "the little guy from Shawinigan"—a tough, earthy, street-fighting type. It was this image that allowed him to easily sweep to power after many Canadians had grown to detest the former Conservative prime minister Brian

Mulroney. Mulroney's deferential attitude towards Washington and U.S. corporate power seemed to grate on Canadians. His keenness to please the powerful—captured in that photo op of him singing "When Irish Eyes Are Smiling" with Ronald Reagan—left many people feeling vaguely embarrassed about being Canadian.

But what's fascinating is how Jean Chrétien has managed to get away with a Mulroney-style deference to Washington without being seen in the same grovelling light. For instance, it was barely noticed that in the aftermath of the Summit of the Americas in Quebec City in April 2001, the Chrétien government retreated abruptly from the critical stance it had been taking against the Chapter 11 section of NAFTA. Suddenly, the new tune coming out of Ottawa sounded surprisingly like "When Irish Eyes Are Smiling."

Up until the Quebec summit, Chrétien had allowed his trade minister, Pierre Pettigrew, to publicly express concerns about NAFTA. Like other critics, Pettigrew had singled out NAFTA's controversial Chapter 11 section. And Sergio Marchi, who held the trade portfolio before Pettigrew, had also publicly argued that Chapter 11 had to be "clarified" to "ensure that government's ability to legislate and regulate in the public interest is protected."

The concerns raised by Pettigrew and Marchi were careful, well-measured and in fact awfully mild, given the extent of the erosion of democracy that NAFTA seems to represent. In an op-ed piece in the *National Post* the month before the summit, Pettigrew had supported the notion that the rights of corporate investors should be protected against arbitrary actions by governments. But he went on to argue that some of the NAFTA tribunal rulings seemed to go too far in favouring investors, "often overstepping their authority and taking unusually broad interpretations." This could interfere with the legitimate power of governments to defend the public interest, he noted. "[W]hen investors' interests run contrary to the public interest, public policy—as long as it is openly arrived at and fairly applied—should prevail," Pettigrew wrote. Now this seems like pretty straightforward stuff. It seems likely most Canadians would agree that if it comes to a clash between the rights of foreign investors and the protection of the Canadian public interest, the public interest should prevail.

Pettigrew even pointed to the case of Metalclad, the U.S. company that, as we saw in chapter one, had successfully used NAFTA to sue the government of Mexico after it was denied a permit to build a toxic-waste facility in a Mexican town. When the verdict in the Metalclad case was appealed (and ultimately upheld), the Canadian government intervened in the appeal process to express its concerns that the ruling could limit the capacity of governments to pursue important objectives, like environmental protection. These weren't just theoretical arguments; the Canadian government had already had quite a bit of direct experience facing NAFTA lawsuits from foreign investors—a subject we'll return to shortly. So this problem had received considerable attention inside the government; it had been resolved that something should be done about the wide-open nature of the Chapter 11 provisions. As Pettigrew noted, "Canada has been on the record for many months regarding its intention to find a way to clarify . . . NAFTA's investment chapter."

All this had fuelled hopes that Canada might take on a leadership role in pushing for changes to rein in the sweeping power corporations enjoy under NAFTA. Instead, it was Pettigrew who got reined in. And it all seemed to happen fairly abruptly after Chrétien spent a few days with George Bush at the summit, and apparently got a much clearer sense of how deeply pleased Bush and corporate America were with NAFTA and particularly Chapter 11. Indeed, the U.S. released a copy of a letter, signed by twenty-nine of the largest U.S. corporations and business lobby groups, indicating that they wanted NAFTA's investor protections retained as is and similar protections built into future trade deals.

Chrétien apparently understood his marching orders clearly. Following the summit, both he and Pettigrew fell into line, playing down any dissatisfactions with NAFTA or Chapter 11. Although the three NAFTA trade ministers were scheduled to meet in July 2001— a perfect opportunity for "clarifications" to be drawn up—Chrétien made it clear that Canada wouldn't be pushing for any clarifications. He cheerfully told the House of Commons that Chapter 11 "has been quite positive for Canada." It's not hard to imagine how this sort of enthusiasm on the part of the prime minister might encourage companies to think Canada is a suitable target for NAFTA lawsuits.

Chrétien's retreat has profound implications. Mexico is too weak to challenge the U.S. over provisions in NAFTA, which makes Canada the only partner with enough political and economic clout to push for changes, or at least "clarifications." And if neither country stands up to the U.S. over Chapter 11, the same investor protections will undoubtedly be incorporated into the hemisphere-wide trade deal currently being negotiated—just as the twenty-nine major U.S. corporations and lobby groups demanded.

IT OFTEN APPEARS AS if international trade is something that just sprang up in the past decade, along with the Internet, cellphones and all-night banking. As business leaders and pundits go on about how desperately the world needs new trade deals like NAFTA and the hemisphere-wide Free Trade Area for the Americas (FTAA), the lurking implication is that without them, international trade would pretty much grind to a halt and we'd all be left isolated in some backwater port in an unconnected world.

The truth is that international trade was up and running long before these new trade deals began to appear on the horizon about fifteen years ago. International trade had been a hot topic, for instance, way back in 1944, when the world's leading nations met in Bretton Woods, New Hampshire, to map out the post-war global economy. Under the influence of Keynes, who served as Britain's chief negotiator, the Bretton Woods conference delegates devised an international financial system that would, among other things, seek to promote international trade. And they succeeded; trade flourished in the decades that followed.

In fact, what's new about the trade deals today isn't that they promote trade. What's new is that they promote trade (and investment)—*at the expense of everything else.* By contrast, the delegates meeting at Bretton Woods had more balanced objectives. While keen to promote trade, they also were committed to the principle of democratic governance, and were anxious to ensure that democratic governments would have policy autonomy in the post-war global economy. (Yes, they also created the IMF and the World Bank, but these institutions have turned out very differently than Keynes and the chief U.S. negotiator, Harry Dexter White, had planned.) Specifically, Keynes and White viewed financial institutions and corporations as powerful special interests, and considered it necessary for governments to have sufficient power to regulate and control them in the interest of protecting the public.

The impact of Keynes and White was significant in shaping the post-war international economy in a way that imposed limits on the power of the financial elite. And there was pressure from other nations to go even further in this direction. In 1948, fifty-four countries met in Havana to draft a charter for a far-reaching new agency called the International Trade Organization, which would defend popular interests. Some of the delegations meeting in Havana— notably Britain, Australia and New Zealand—wanted member countries to be required to promote full employment and guarantee labour standards. There were even provisions in the draft charter giving countries the power to expropriate foreign corporate assets— and pay compensation in local currency. This was pushing things quite a bit further than Washington was prepared to go. Besides, the political climate had already changed dramatically from a few years earlier, when Keynes and White had presided over negotiations at Bretton Woods. Keynes was now dead, and White had just been accused by the House Un-American Activities Committee of being a Soviet spy—a charge he vehemently denied up until his premature death later that year. In the end, the Havana charter never became law; although fifty nations signed it, Washington declined to.

But Washington did support an international trade agreement, the General Agreement on Tariffs and Trade (GATT), which was devoted to promoting freer international trade through tariff reduction. International trade—and U.S. corporations, which dominated international trade—thrived under the GATT rules. Interestingly, some

Third World countries also appear to have benefited from GATT, in that it provided for particularly favourable tariff reduction on exports coming from poor countries.

But by the early 1980s, U.S. corporations had ambitious new goals in sight. While tariff walls in general were coming down, many countries were still using some form of tariffs or other government interventions in specific sectors to encourage the development of their own domestic production, rather than always relying on U.S. imports. This was particularly true in the lucrative area of services—including banking, accounting, telecommunications, insurance, advertising, culture and health services. These areas were considered particularly important to the success and vitality of domestic economies, so countries tended to regulate them closely and offer favourable treatment to their own domestic firms. As a result, "services" had not traditionally been included in the concept of international trade, which had focused more on trade in "goods," such as manufactured products or natural resources.

But some powerful U.S. corporations in the services field wanted to change this. They were keen to increase their sales abroad, just as U.S. manufacturing interests had so effectively done in the early postwar decades. This would require knocking down the huge maze of government interventions and restrictions that sought to keep U.S. corporations from dominating key parts of domestic economies all over the world. When Washington tried to get services on the agenda during GATT negotiations held in Tokyo in the 1970s, it ran into a wall of resistance from countries determined to protect their service sectors from U.S. penetration.

A small, determined group of high-powered U.S. executives in the services field, led by the American Express chairman, James D. Robinson, were determined not to take no for an answer and simply became more aggressive in their attempts to open up these foreign markets. Known in trade circles as the "services mafia," this influential group of executives figured out something that proved to be of great strategic importance: Washington would be much more effective in getting its way in trade talks if it was able to divide its opponents, picking them off one by one. Obviously, the U.S. was enormously powerful, but lesser countries were able to resist its demands by banding together and presenting a common front. So, the services mafia reasoned, rather than allowing these countries to gang up on the U.S., as happened at GATT negotiations, Washington would have more leverage if it faced them individually across a negotiating table. By the fall of 1984, the services mafia had been instrumental in getting before Congress a trade bill that gave services the same status as goods and sought to move towards "free trade"—that is, free from government restrictions or interventions. The trade bill also, crucially, included provisions for the U.S. to enter into trade talks, one-on-one, with individual countries. The bill even specified two particular countries—countries that were known for their friendliness to Washington, and were therefore less likely to resist this radical new approach aimed at increasing Washington's leverage; indeed, countries that could be counted on to be fairly acquiescent. Those two countries were Israel, which depended on Washington for its very survival, and Canada.

Getting a deal with Israel proved easy but also inconsequential, given the tiny amount of trade involved. The prospect of a deal with Canada was more interesting, however, and there was additional interest because of Canada's ample energy resources, to which Washington had long wanted reliable access. In fact, the prospect of a trade deal with Canada—with rules for opening up key service sectors, as well as guaranteed access to Canada's oil and gas reserves—was very interesting. And if the deal could serve as a boiler-plate for future trade negotiations with a broad range of countries, then it became even more interesting. In a sense, the deals with Canada and Israel were seen as dress rehearsals for what really mattered—future GATT negotiations, through which Washington wanted to increase its leverage with the whole world.

One problem with the dress rehearsals was that Canada had a long-standing political tradition of opposing free trade with the U.S. Furthermore, it seemed unlikely that the long-time Liberal prime minister, Pierre Trudeau, who was known in Washington for his infuriating nationalism and independent-mindedness, would be easily won over to Washington's transparent divide-and-conquer strategy. Ironically, however, at around the same time that the radical U.S. trade bill was in the works, Canada was in the throes of an election. Although free trade with the U.S. was not on the Canadian political horizon at that point, and was certainly not an issue in that election campaign in the summer of 1984, that changed very quickly after the new Conservative prime minister, Brian Mulroney, took office. Indeed, the services mafia and U.S. trade officials were surprised how quickly the new government warmed to their idea.

It has long been asserted, by officials on both sides of the border, that the initiative for a free-trade deal between the two countries came from Canada. It was striking to me, doing extensive interviews on this subject in the early 1990s, how often and forcefully this "it came from Canada" argument was put forward. It was hard to avoid the feeling that the lady doth protest too much. In fact, it seems that in any meaningful sense, the initiative for a free-trade deal between Canada and the U.S. came from the U.S., with the pivotal role played by James Robinson and the services mafia.

Here briefly is what happened. A group of Canadian businessmen within the Business Council on National Issues had become concerned in the early 1980s about the deterioration of relations between Canada and the U.S., largely as a result of Washington's distaste for Trudeau's nationalistic energy and foreign-investment policies. To ensure that their products weren't shut out of the U.S. market, the Canadian businessmen developed the idea of trying to establish a series of limited trade deals—covering certain sectors and industries—with the U.S. The plan was to model these trade deals after the Canada-U.S. Auto Pact—a trade deal that had been in place since 1965 and had been highly successful, particularly from Canada's point of view. But the Auto Pact was in no sense a "free trade" deal. It was, in fact, the exact opposite of free trade—trade with strings attached. The essence of the Auto Pact was that U.S. auto producers would receive tariff-free access to the Canadian market—*but only under certain conditions*. One condition was that a significant portion of their car production would take place in Canada; essentially, for every car sold in Canada, one would have to be produced here. This meant Canada got a huge auto industry located within its borders, generating tens of thousands of high-paying jobs in auto production. The auto industry and its spin-off industries became the backbone of the thriving post-war Canadian economy.

So it wasn't surprising that the Canadian businessmen would have thought Auto Pact in the early 1980s when they thought of devising new trade deals. The only problem, as we've just seen, was that this wasn't what was on the minds of businessmen and government officials on the other side of the border. In fact, the Auto Pact was regarded very differently down there. It had certainly meant extensive Canadian sales for the giant U.S. car producers. But they didn't like the strings attached. As the mood of the new capitalism took hold, U.S. business leaders felt increasingly comfortable rejecting these sorts of "performance requirements"—government rules that had to be met to win tariff-free access to a foreign market. It all smacked of too much government interference in the economy, too much hands-on management of business by meddling bureaucrats. What the U.S. businessmen wanted instead was guaranteed access to the Canadian market, with no strings attached. Rights with no responsibilities. Free trade, in other words.

The gap between what U.S. business interests wanted and what the Canadians from the Business Council on National Issues had in mind was thus fairly significant—as quickly became apparent one cold winter morning in Toronto, in January 1983. The Canadian businessmen had invited William Brock, the U.S. trade representative, to a 7:30 breakfast meeting to present him with their idea—a series of Auto Pact–style trade deals in sectors like steel and petrochemicals.

Brock, a charming Tennessee millionaire who had spent much of the previous two years travelling around the world pushing the new U.S. trade agenda, was delighted to meet with these enthusiastic Canadians. Certainly their keenness for increased trade with the U.S. was an excellent beginning; this meeting had even been their idea. Of course, their suggestion of Auto Pact–style sectoral trade deals was of no interest, and Brock gently pointed that out. *But wait, my friends,* said

Brock in the finest tradition of bait-and-switch salesmanship, *I've got a better idea*. The smooth, experienced Brock quickly convinced the Canadian businessmen that what they really wanted was not a few Auto Pact–style agreements but a huge, new comprehensive Canada-U.S. free-trade deal. Like the crafty salesman he was, Brock managed in short order to convince the Canadian businessmen that they weren't just interested in that practical new set of tires they had come in asking for—they were interested in a whole flashy new sports car! Within no time, the Canadians had forgotten all about the new set of tires and were looking over with real interest the spanking new Corvette Stingray XKE that Brock wanted to sell them.

Brock had one other crucial suggestion. Like any good salesman, he knew that the most promising sales prospect can be derailed once the customer's wife finds out, particularly when she discovers how her husband has been tricked into wanting what the salesman wants him to want. Accordingly, Brock advised the Canadian businessmen that the idea of a comprehensive free-trade deal with the U.S. could be sold to the Canadian public only if it appeared to come from Canada. "What Brock was saying to us was that . . . politically the impetus had to come from Canada," recalled Alfred Powis, the head of the mining giant Noranda, who attended the meeting with Brock. The clever Brock was essentially counselling Canadian business leaders not only on what to push for, but also on how to push for it. And the Canadians paid close attention. "We threw out sectoral [trade deals] pretty fast," Powis said. "The Americans just weren't interested." Instead, the Canadian businessmen set to work pushing Brock's idea, and they found fertile ground within the Canadian government once the new Mulroney administration came to power in the fall of 1984. It was only a year and a half later that Mulroney and President Ronald Reagan, meeting in Quebec City in March 1985, jointly announced a plan to explore the possibility of a comprehensive free-trade deal between the two countries. And they emphasized that the initiative had come from Canada.

✺

THE NOTION THAT THE INITIATIVE had come from Canada—even though it really hadn't—set the tone for the negotiations, putting Canada in the position of looking a little too eager. The truth was that Mulroney desperately wanted a deal. Having been won over to the cause by Canadian business leaders, and having proclaimed his interest in a highly public manner on a stage with Ronald Reagan, Mulroney became convinced that a free-trade deal with the U.S. was crucial to his own political success. Reagan, on the other hand, had no such concerns. He was certainly keen to please U.S. business interests, and would ensure that his negotiators worked to that end. But if they failed to nudge the Canadians in the direction U.S. business wanted, there would be no political fall-out for him. The rest of the American public paid virtually no attention to Canada, and certainly not to anything as dull as trade relations.

This imbalance in the two positions was reflected in the chief negotiators themselves. Canada put forward its all-time star negotiator— the bombastic and colourful Simon Reisman, who had distinguished himself as a tough bargainer in Canadian eyes by negotiating the Auto Pact. His U.S. counterpart this time around was a taciturn, low-profile trade official named Peter Murphy, whose experience was mostly in negotiating deals with Third World textile producers. In other words, Murphy was used to throwing his weight around, beating up weak little Third World countries that were desperate to get their shirts into the U.S. market and would take whatever deal Washington offered. Canada was in a much better bargaining position but, oddly enough, was behaving a bit too much like a shirt producer.

The eventual deal, known as the Free Trade Agreement (FTA), was enormously contentious in Canada and barely known in the U.S. outside of corporate circles. But inside U.S. corporate circles, there was considerable interest—and delight at what Washington had managed to win. Not only did the U.S. win guaranteed access to Canadian energy resources—something that was to become particularly important by the winter of 2000–2001 with U.S. energy shortages—but Washington got the boilerplate of its dreams. The FTA included major advances in all the key areas important to U.S. business—it opened up services, struck down government intervention-ism, outlawed "performance requirements" and established a whole new set of rights for corporate investors.

Canada, on the other hand, failed to win the one objective that it had always claimed was its central goal: guaranteed access to the U.S. market. The U.S. had never intended offering up such a desirable prize; that would have involved exempting Canada from U.S. trade laws—a privilege no country enjoyed. Murphy had tantalized Canada with the prospect of winning such an exemption, although he had never had any intention of delivering. His failure to produce had ultimately caused an enormously frustrated Reisman to break off negotiations in September 1987. But in the end, Mulroney simply sent in a different team and signed the deal anyway, winning nothing but a "dispute settlement mechanism," which falls considerably short of the dream of guaranteed access.

Within no time, the U.S. was back for more. Having made impor-tant breakthroughs by negotiating one-on-one like this with Canada, it wanted to adopt the FTA as a boilerplate for a broader deal, NAFTA, which was to include Mexico as well. NAFTA actually went further in some crucial areas, establishing even more rights for corporate investors. And NAFTA soon became the boilerplate for multilateral trade deals being negotiated through the World Trade Organization, which had replaced GATT as the overseer of inter-national trade. By the early 1990s, when Washington set its sights on a hemisphere-wide free-trade deal for the Americas, it wasn't surprising that NAFTA once again was the boilerplate. So the services mafia had figured things out pretty well. The divide-and-conquer strategy had paid off nicely, with the Mulroney government's acquies-cence being especially helpful. In fairly short order, Washington had managed to achieve goals that went well beyond improving its trade position. Through the trade deals, it had effectively established a new model for an international economy, with a newly dominant role for corporations.

IT IS STRIKING TO CONSIDER how far things have moved from the heyday of Keynesianism, with its focus on empowering democratic government. The new trade deals do exactly the opposite, limiting the power and autonomy of governments—at least when it comes to exerting control over corporations. Under NAFTA, virtually any attempt by government to impose restrictions on corporations—in the interest of protecting the environment, preserving natural resources, defending public health, ensuring labour rights or culture—can now be defined as a trade barrier. And governments imposing such restrictions can find themselves subject to expensive legal challenges from corporations until they remove these so-called trade barriers.

And it's no defence for a government if it can prove that a health or environmental regulation was put in place for legitimate reasons, and that legitimate procedures were followed. In the Metalclad case, for instance, the actions that led to the denial of a building permit for Metalclad's toxic-waste landfill were all based on legitimate zoning regulations and considerations. When the NAFTA tribunal's decision favouring Metalclad was appealed by Mexico, the judge reviewing the case didn't dispute that the zoning issues involved had been properly handled in Mexico. He noted that *despite this,* the company had a valid claim for financial compensation under the terms of NAFTA. In upholding the NAFTA tribunal's decision, the judge pointed out that the tribunal had defined the language in NAFTA so broadly—as it was free to do—that any government action that interfered with a company's reasonably expected profit amounted to a violation of the company's rights. "The definition is sufficiently broad to include legitimate rezoning by a municipality or other zoning authority," the judge wrote. In other words, even when governments act properly and follow legitimate procedures, and do nothing more than interfere with corporate profit-making, they can be obliged under NAFTA to pay millions of dollars in damages to corporations.

Now one thing seems to leap out here: if the language in NAFTA is so poorly defined as to invite overly broad interpretations, why not define the language more clearly? If we don't want corporations to be able to bring lawsuits against legitimate government actions, why not specify this? This is exactly, of course, what the Canadian government had been planning to do before it got wrapped on the knuckles by George Bush at the Quebec summit. All Canada had in mind was "clarification." As Pettigrew himself put it before he was reined in, "We hope to do this through interpretive notes that would give future tribunals clearer and more specific understanding of Chapter 11's obligations. The NAFTA agreement itself provides for this." The fact that Canada was called off from pushing for this apparently logical clarification suggests that the U.S. government actually wants to keep things murky and therefore open to extreme pro-corporate interpretations. In fact, trade analyst Scott Sinclair argues that this was likely the intention of those who drafted NAFTA; otherwise they would have done the obvious and specified that government measures aimed at protecting the public interest are exempt from NAFTA lawsuits.

It's not hard to see how all this could have the effect of intimidating governments from taking necessary measures to protect their own citizens. "To succeed, foreign corporations need only establish that they would have been able to make a lot more money if only government hadn't put obstacles like zoning bylaws or environmental laws in their way," notes the trade lawyer Steven Shrybman. This explains why Ottawa backed off from its decision to ban a fuel additive called MMT after its U.S. producer, Ethyl Corporation, filed a $350-million NAFTA lawsuit against Canada. Environment Canada had imposed the ban in 1996 because of fears that MMT is a hazard to human health. But after almost two years of preliminary legal manoeuvres in preparation for the NAFTA tribunal hearing, Ottawa apparently became nervous about the possibility of losing the case. Not only would that have been very costly, but it would have drawn widespread attention to the more outrageous aspects of NAFTA and turned Ottawa's support for the agreement into an embarrassing political problem for the Chrétien government. Anxious to avoid this sort of embarrassment, Ottawa settled out of court in July 1998. But the settlement was a total capitulation: Ottawa withdrew its ban on MMT, paid Ethyl Corp. $19 million and even issued a denial that

MMT is a health hazard. Thus, fear of the sweeping powers of NAFTA was sufficient to prompt a sovereign government not only to cancel its own law and pay out millions of dollars, but also to assure the public that something isn't dangerous when chances are it is.

Defenders of NAFTA see no problem with this. The Toronto trade lawyer Barry Appleton has argued that the denial revealed that Canada knew there was no scientific basis for its ban on MMT. I suppose it's possible that Environment Canada simply came to realize the error of its ways. More likely, however, Ottawa changed its tune about MMT for no other reason than to get the company off its back. Ottawa had reason to suspect it might lose the case, largely because NAFTA tribunals are notoriously unwilling to recognize any health risks that aren't yet proven beyond a shadow of a doubt.

But it can obviously take years to amass an overwhelming scientific case proving environmental or health risks. Because of this, it's a basic principle of domestic U.S. and Canadian law that governments can take precautionary regulatory action, if there's sufficient evidence of possible serious harm. In the case of California's MTBE ban, Methanex is also basing its NAFTA lawsuit on the notion that MTBE hasn't definitively been proven to cause cancer in humans, only in rats and mice. Methanex's argument would almost certainly be rejected by U.S. courts, according to the Harrison Institute for Public Law, since government actions to protect the public's health are largely immune from legal challenges, unless it can be proven that elected officials have behaved in an arbitrary or mean-spirited manner. As long as there is a rational basis for banning MTBE—as there appears to be, if for no other reason than it makes drinking water taste like turpentine—then U.S. courts would uphold the right of the elected government to impose such a ban.

If corporations have had little luck striking down environmental and public-health regulations in domestic courts, they are having more luck at NAFTA tribunals. As Shrybman notes, NAFTA tribunals and appellate rulings have tended to reject the precautionary approach that entitles governments to act before open-and-shut evidence of danger is available. This rejection reflects NAFTA's single-minded focus on promoting investment and trade—above all other concerns.

This single-minded focus is reflected in the fact that the people chosen to act as judges on the trade panels tend to be experts in international trade, business and investment, rather than experts in, say, environmental or labour law. There's a certain logic to this; since the trade deals are focused on promoting trade and investment, it would seem natural to have judges that are experts in this type of law. The trade deals have relatively little to say about the environment or labour—even though the decisions the panels make impact hugely on these areas. The actual selection of judges is also interesting, and is subtly biased towards trade and investment, even though it appears at first glance to be quite balanced. It works like this: each panel has three judges, with one chosen by the corporation launching the lawsuit, one chosen by the country being sued and one agreed to by both parties. Technically, any person with legal expertise can be chosen to be a judge; Canada could have chosen the environmentalist Steven Shrybman as the Canadian judge in the MMT case and insisted that the third judge also be strongly sympathetic to environmental concerns. But the company would have never agreed to such a person for the third judge, and without that agreement, the third judge would have been an expert in law, commerce, industry or finance, chosen by the International Center for the Settlement of Investment Disputes, a strongly pro-investment agency operating under the authority of the World Bank. So almost inevitably, two of the three judges in any case are going to be pro-investment types.

The MMT case illustrates the enormous power corporations have under NAFTA to harass governments over laws they don't like in the hope—and apparently realistic expectation—that the governments will back off. Appleton points out that NAFTA tribunals can't actually overturn laws. But who needs the power to actually overturn laws if, as the MMT case reveals, governments will withdraw the laws themselves when corporations harass them with hefty lawsuits—lawsuits that are to be decided by tribunals known to give short shrift to any concerns but trade promotion.

Given the potential impact of what is going on in these tribunals—the effective overturning of laws passed by democratic legislatures—it is particularly striking that the procedures are carried on in such secrecy. They are not open to the public. No transcripts of the proceedings are made available. No group or individual—even those who may be directly affected by the decision in the case—has the right to be represented at the hearings. Most of the decisions about how much information will be made available to the public are left in the hands of the corporations and governments involved. If a corporation wishes the details of its claim to remain secret, it has the power to enforce this. The public is not even entitled to know the outcome of the case, unless the parties involved agree to release it.

All this secrecy would make sense if what was involved was a private business matter between two commercial interests. But that's clearly not the case here. One of the parties is always a government, and what is being challenged is always an action or law that has presumably been taken in the interests of protecting the citizens of that country. And the ultimate result, as the MMT case illustrates, can be the removal of a law, or perhaps the decision to avoid introducing similar laws in the future. All this seems like the very stuff of democracy. And yet, under NAFTA, it takes place not in an open, democratic forum, but in a secret hearing, closed to the public.

One of the striking aspects of the new trade deals is that while they have invested corporations with a new set of rights, they have attached no responsibilities to those rights. Notice how the lawsuits all go in one direction—corporations sue governments for infringing their corporate profit-making rights. A government can't sue a corporation for infringing the rights of its citizens by, say, polluting local drinking water. In fact, a central thrust of NAFTA has been to strip governments of the power to make any demands of corporations at all. For instance, NAFTA bans "performance requirements"— through which governments oblige foreign companies selling in their markets to create jobs in their domestic economies. As noted above, this was the principle behind the Canada-U.S. Auto Pact. But as we saw, performance requirements were outlawed in the FTA. The Auto

Pact itself was grandfathered in the FTA because of its popularity in Canada. A negative ruling by the WTO in the summer of 2000 finally eliminated what was left of the Auto Pact.

Perhaps it seems inevitable that a trade deal would be biased in favour of corporations. But there's really no reason that it has to be. Ottawa trade lawyer Howard Mann points out that NAFTA could have easily been designed differently, in a way that would have given more importance to environmental and labour considerations. For instance, it could have made environmental-impact assessments compulsory in cases, such as those of Metalclad and Methanex, where corporations sued governments to protest environmental restrictions on their products. If an independent assessment concluded that the product posed an environmental or health risk, the company would lose its claim for compensation for lost profit-making opportunities.

Mann also points out that there are other things, even outside the trade deals themselves, that could be done to create more balance and place more responsibilities on corporations. He notes, for instance, that U.S. and Canadian companies are able to escape responsibility for environmental problems they create in other countries. They can be sued in those countries, but their assets there are usually minimal. And domestic law in both the U.S. and Canada does not allow for lawsuits against corporate head offices for problems their subsidiaries have created elsewhere. It was this that prevented the citizens of Bhopal, India, from properly collecting damages from Union Carbide after the horrible chemical leak at its factory there in 1984. Union Carbide was shielded from any lawsuit against it in the U.S., where a court order could have tapped in to the company's massive assets, forcing it to provide some serious level of compensation to the devastated community.

So quite apart from the new trade deals, corporations have long been able to avoid responsibility for their actions abroad. What the new trade deals do is add another layer of pro-corporate advantage by granting investors a powerful new set of rights in their business dealings abroad, without balancing those new rights with any new responsibilities. Howard Mann insists that there would be nothing inherently wrong with a set of investor rights—if they were balanced by investor responsibilities and by equally strong and enforceable rights for other concerns, like the environment and labour. Labour rights could be enforced, for instance, through the Geneva-based International Labour Organization, if key Western nations were serious about taking action against countries violating the internationally accepted labour code. And punishment could be meted out to countries violating environmental laws, if international environmental agencies were given some real teeth through international treaties. The same could apply to violations of individual human rights—as in the case of Maria Sybila Arredondo—if the United Nations Human Rights Committee was given some real powers. All this is possible. But it hasn't happened because Western governments, particularly the United States, have shown no interest in providing real protections for the environment, labour or even human rights. Investor rights alone have been their focus and concern. So, as we saw in chapter one, corporate investors—who include some of the most wealthy and powerful individuals on the planet—have been singled out for a unique level of protection in international law, as if they were some kind of fragile, endangered species needing special shelter.

Of course, the growing power of corporations and diminishing power of governments these days is usually attributed to mysterious forces operating out there in the global economy, well beyond our control. Here's another possibility: governments are less powerful than they used to be simply because we keep signing trade deals that reduce their power and enhance the power of corporations. It's likely no more mysterious than that.

FASTER THAN A SPEEDING horse—or at about that speed—the Canadian postal service used to deliver parcels across the country in the late nineteenth century. It was recognized, all the way back then, that a strong, efficient mail and courier service was necessary if the people of such a huge, sprawling land were going to be able to communicate with each other, which seemed essential if Canada was going to be a country. So considerable importance was attached to the national postal service. And although there have been periods of contentious labour-management strife inside the post office, things have basically worked out pretty well over the years. It is possible today, for instance, to get reasonably fast delivery of a letter or parcel from just about anywhere in the country to just about anywhere else in the country, and at a reasonable price. Canada's postal rates are among the cheapest in the world. In some remote northern Canadian communities, the post office is the only link to the rest of the country and the world.

Canada's postal system came under sharp attack in the summer of 1999. It wasn't that Canadians were dissatisfied with the service or that costs were escalating. (In fact, the post office has been self-financing, operating without government grants, for more than a decade.) The problem lay elsewhere—in Atlanta, Georgia.

At the corporate head offices of United Parcel Services (UPS) in Atlanta, executives have long found Canada's national postal system an annoying impediment to the full implementation of their business plans. The courier business is a highly competitive one, and UPS has been in a tight race, most notably with FedEx, for business all over the world. Canada is simply one of the places it wishes to increase its market share. But one obstacle is that Canada Post's courier business is closely integrated with its mail delivery service, over which it enjoys a monopoly. Therefore, Canada Post can use the same letter boxes, buildings and delivery vehicles—many of them subsidized by Canadian taxpayers—for both mail and courier services. This saves Canada Post money, allowing it to keep its rates low, but making it hard for UPS to compete with it in the Canadian courier market, which leaves UPS executives frustrated. And when executives are frustrated these days, there is one place that they can generally turn—NAFTA. It didn't take long for the UPS legal department to figure out the basis for a NAFTA lawsuit. Faster than a speeding horse, UPS had slapped Canada with a $230-million lawsuit for damages it was suffering due to lost courier business.

I hesitated before deciding to raise the UPS case. In some ways it seems so boring, with nothing dramatic at stake, like drinkable water or breathable air. What we're dealing with here is . . . well, let's face it, postal service. The very phrase seems likely to induce indifference, if not sleepiness. But I've decided to risk it, because the UPS case illustrates a different aspect of the sweeping new powers of the trade deals, and one that could strike at the very heart of programs central to Canadian interests.

Having admitted the lack of excitement that generally surrounds issues related to postal service, I must now contradict myself slightly by pointing out that, while possibly boring, this stuff is not unimportant. For all the reasons that it was important to connect the country back in the late nineteenth century, it is still important to do so today. And yes, telephone, television and the Internet do that too. But actually sending things physically to each other, either through the mail or by courier, is also something Canadians want to be able to do—or there wouldn't be big companies like FedEx and UPS trying to make a business out of offering this service. And while we could undoubtedly count on these big companies to do a bang-up job delivering business parcels between, say, Toronto and Montreal or Vancouver and Calgary, would we really want to rely on them to provide top-notch, affordable service between, say, South Porcupine, Ontario, and Ladle Cove, Newfoundland?

And the fact that Canada Post has managed to blend the two parts of its business—mail and courier—is to the advantage of Canadians. It's convenient, one-stop shopping. You go to the post office with a parcel and inquire about the cost of sending it by courier. If the price is too high, you send it by mail. More important, as noted, it keeps prices low for both services, because the same facilities and vehicles can be used for both. When the private sector does this sort of blending of operations, it's called convergence and everybody thinks it's a good thing. In fact, it's a good thing here too, and without it, it would be difficult to ensure that all parts of a country as physically large as this one could be serviced at a reasonable cost.

Now, it's likely true that this blending of operations gives Canada Post a competitive advantage over UPS. On the other hand, UPS has no obligations to serve the entire Canadian market. It can pick and choose, operating wherever it finds it profitable to do so. In the past decade, it has closed twenty-nine of its eighty Canadian outlets, presumably because business wasn't good enough. In other words, it puts nothing into Canada except what it calculates will be profitable and in the interests of its shareholders. Canada Post, on the other hand, is jointly owned by the people of Canada, and its mandate is to serve our interests. So the question comes down to this: if the blending of operations in Canada Post allows it to keep its costs down, saving Canadians money but giving it a competitive advantage over UPS, why should we care? UPS is essentially arguing that its rights to make a profit in our market should supersede our right as a country to organize our postal service in the way we find most advantageous to ourselves.

But enough about postal service. The real danger about the UPS case is the door it opens. It goes beyond simply challenging the validity of a specific law, as in the Metalclad or MMT cases, and challenges instead our way of organizing needed services, including such essentials as health care and education. Specifically, it raises the issue of whether public programs could be seen as interfering with the private, profit-making rights of foreign corporations, and if so, is that an unacceptable infringement of the rights of foreign investors? It's not hard to see where this could lead. If the UPS case succeeds, will we then face lawsuits from foreign health-care companies, complaining they are at a disadvantage because they have to compete with our medicare system, which uses publicly financed facilities? Would they consider it grounds to sue, for instance, if they have to conduct cataract surgery in private clinics while medicare offers cataract surgery in publicly financed hospitals? Similarly, if a foreign chain of private schools, colleges or universities wanted to set up operations in Canada, could it claim it was at a competitive disadvantage against the publicly supported education system?

If these scenarios sound far-fetched, it should be noted that another trade deal currently being negotiated aims to accomplish the very thing envisioned in these scenarios. The General Agreement on Trade in Services (GATS), actively being negotiated in Geneva under the umbrella of the WTO, is seeking to open up the whole traditionally protected national domain of services to foreign entrepreneurs. This goes well beyond anything James Robinson or other members of the services mafia dreamed of when they first pushed services onto the agenda two decades ago. Now the goal seems to be not just making sure that U.S. companies have the same rights enjoyed by domestic companies in their home markets for services, but also making sure that publicly provided services don't crowd them out. This means that the ability of a country to operate vital public programs may be in jeopardy. Trade critic Maude Barlow notes that those designing the new rules regard publicly funded services— including medicare and public education—as "monopolies," and that their goal is to reduce or eliminate these monopolies so as to increase profit-making opportunities for private business. Trade analyst Scott Sinclair agrees. "The GATS is hostile to public services, treating them as, at best, missed commercial opportunities and, at worst, unfair competition."

But let's not forget why we decided in the first place to provide key services through public systems rather than leave them to the market: because that way we can ensure that important social goals are accomplished. Recall the post office situation. Private courier companies are fine to handle the lucrative parts of the business. But they have little interest in servicing remote communities, so these areas get poor or non-existent service. Similarly, leaving health care and education to the private marketplace will result in fine services for the affluent but leave many others without access to decent services (or in some cases any services at all). While this kind of deficiency is bad enough when it comes to postal delivery, it becomes downright serious in areas like health care and education, which are so closely tied up with human well-being and development.

The far-reaching changes envisioned in the GATS treaty make sense, perhaps, in a world where private profit-making is considered paramount. If protecting the right to make a profit is the highest goal we aspire to as a society, then it follows that all aspects of our society should function strictly according to market principles, with less importance attached to broader social goals aimed at ensuring human development. Such goals may be fine, but they will have to be adapted to the needs of the market, not the other way around. My guess is that the enormous changes lurking in GATS and the other trade deals have come about not because most citizens in the world believe in the importance of private profit-making above all else. I suspect, on the contrary, that it's because most people have little knowledge of what these trade deals are all about—they think they're about trade.

GIVEN THE TIGHTNESS OF the security system, it would be almost impossible to wander by mistake into the World Bank's headquarters in Washington, D.C. But if one did somehow manage to do so, it would be easy to be confused into thinking one had just entered the world's largest charitable organization. No sooner has one entered the vast atrium than one is confronted by concern for the poor. "Our Dream Is a World Free of Poverty" say the large letters emblazoned high up on the wall. A little farther in, past the security, one encounters a life-size statue of a Third World peasant and oxen, with a plaque highlighting the need to stamp out river blindness, one of the many hazards of Third World living. World Bank publications, of which there are an abundance, bear titles like "A Better World for All" and "Hearing the Voices of the Poor," and are full of photographs of the kind of people you never see on TV—except in news footage of disasters. So if the World Bank is in some sense a bank, it certainly seems different from a regular bank. Surely, around the next corner we will encounter ATM machines into which the world's poor can insert their cards and receive instant cash.

Of course, this is not the case. In fact, it would be closer to the truth to imagine ATM machines into which the World Bank (and its sister operation, the International Monetary Fund) can insert *its* card and receive instant cash from the world's poor. That's not far from what happens as the poorest nations struggle to pay the interest on loans they received from the bank and the IMF. Many of these loans were originally made thirty or forty years ago, and the countries have, over the years, paid back massive amounts in interest payments—indeed have repaid the original sums many times over. But caught in the classic debtors' treadmill, they are unable to ever pay off all they owe (which is largely determined by world interest rates, effectively set by the U.S. Federal Reserve). It's interesting to note that the debt payments required of the world's poorest nations are roughly ten times as large (relative to their national income) as the payments the Allied countries felt it was decent to extract from Germany after the outrages of the Second World War.

But almost more important than the lost revenue is the loss of power the debts represent. With the poorest nations deeply in debt to the World Bank and the IMF—which are controlled by the rich Western nations and ultimately by the U.S. Treasury department— the rich Western nations can effectively dictate what poor countries should be doing. Desperate countries must turn to these institutions for loans. And although in principle the loans are "negotiated," what in fact goes on is not really a negotiation in any meaningful sense of the word.

All the power is on the side of the bank and the IMF, so countries accepting the loans must also accept whatever conditions these institutions choose to attach. Their willingness to accept these terms, then, is hardly a sign of their support for the terms. They simply have no other options. If they were to try to find private sources of funding instead, they would almost certainly be turned down unless they had the stamp of approval from the IMF. Thus the World Bank and the IMF enjoy an almost God-like power to dictate what poor countries should be doing. Neither institution has ever been unsure about what these countries should be doing, or shy about putting forward views on the subject. If there's a defining culture within the walls of the bank and the IMF, it is a culture of certainty, of confidence, of faith in solutions. And there is no mistaking what solution the analysts have in mind: the market.

The World Bank doesn't deny its emphasis has been on market-style reforms. "We're not going to apologize for laying what we think is an appropriate emphasis on markets," says Milan Brahmbhatt, a specialist in the bank's Economic Policy Division. Like many analysts at the bank, he is originally from the developing world, in his case India. Holding forth in his small office in the gigantic bank complex, Brahmbhatt sounds reasonable and moderate, and he makes the bank appear at least well intentioned.

Brahmbhatt even suggests he is not really a market purist. He acknowledges that markets sometimes perform badly, and that there is therefore a need for government intervention in the market. He points to the very existence of the World Bank—an institution run by governments—as evidence of the bank's willingness to act as a counterforce to the market. But in fact, the World Bank and the IMF are far from a counterforce to the market. They are just the opposite—institutions devoted to imposing the market system on countries around the world. They are, in many ways, the market's chief enforcement mechanism—a kind of global market police force.

The World Bank and the IMF can be seen, then, as another prong in the apparatus of redesigning the world. While the trade deals are establishing a clear new set of international rights to protect corporate profit-making, the bank and the IMF are working at the other end—whipping the poor countries of the world into shape, restructuring their institutions and laws so they'll be able to provide a fertile setting for foreign corporate investments to flourish. This involves nothing less than redesigning the internal economies of the world's nations along strict market lines, re-engineering these nations economically and socially to fit the needs of powerful interests in the developed world. It's a huge task, but the bank and the IMF are not shy about taking on such a mammoth undertaking. Nor, as noted, are they without clout.

Once again, this is a story of how the highly aggressive new capitalism has replaced the more restrained capitalism of the early post-war period. Although the bank and the IMF were part of the original Keynesian post-war system, they have changed significantly in the past two decades and become a key component in the new capitalism's goal of imposing a much purer market system on the world. Keynes had envisioned the World Bank and the IMF playing a positive role in stabilizing and promoting growth in the world economy. From the early days, however, the U.S. was more interested in using these institutions to assure markets for its exports around the world. Much as it used the Marshall Plan to rebuild the shattered European economies after the war, Washington saw the IMF and the bank as vehicles for channelling funds to Third World countries, to develop those economies and create markets for American goods and investments. Still, despite Washington's clear goals, there was some acceptance within the bank in those early days that individual countries had a role to play in shaping their economies. A generation of analysts within the bank were trained in "development economics," a branch of economics focused on the idea of helping Third World countries modernize their economies. Although the bank's vision of modernization was always restricted to market capitalism, there was a willingness to tolerate some diversity of approaches.

Countries were allowed to develop their economies in ways that weren't strictly market-oriented. They were permitted, for instance, to use government funds to invest in domestic industries, and even to impose tariffs to discourage competing foreign imports. In a sense, this approach was similar to that of the Canada-U.S. Auto Pact, which enabled Canada to ensure that auto production would be located within the country, rather than leaving such an important matter to the automakers to decide. In fact, government intervention in developing and sheltering infant industries has been an effective tactic for decades, even centuries. Britain and the U.S. both protected their fledgling industries for parts of the nineteenth century. And as recently as the 1950s, Japan managed to rebuild itself almost from scratch into one of the strongest economies in the world largely through protectionism, government investment and control over its economy.

But starting in the early 1980s, this tolerance for diversity evaporated. With the more orthodox pro-market approach gaining ascen-
dancy on the domestic front in the U.S., Britain and Canada, the
attitude within the bank towards Third World development changed
as well. Increasingly, "development economics" fell out of favour, to
be replaced with the more rigid, one-size-fits-all, straight-from-the-
textbook market economics. The notion that infant industries could
and should be protected fell into disrepute. What had worked for the
advanced nations of the Western world was now declared off limits to
the struggling nations of the Third World. This had the effect of
locking in the gains of the advanced world, whose industries were
now strong and would be spared the possibility of facing much in the
way of competition from the Third World—except in industries like
the low-wage textile business (which the West was largely willing to
concede to the developing countries). But if there was a benefit to the
West in insisting that the Third World adopt this pro-market
approach, you'd never know it from talking to officials at the bank,
where the rhetoric remains firmly fixed on the pressing need to help
the world's poor.

IT WAS THE PRESSING NEED to help the world's poor that was
supposedly behind the World Bank's decision to hold a major
academic conference in Barcelona, Spain, in June 2001. But with
activists planning to stage protest events to coincide with the conference—and thus the prospect of another scene of clashes between
activists and riot-equipped police—officials at the bank lost their
enthusiasm for the event, and it was suddenly cancelled in late May.
The bank coupled its cancellation announcement with denunciations
of the would-be protestors: "Years ago people used to burn books to
try to clamp down on academic freedom—now they try to prevent
academics from reaching debating halls," said the bank spokesperson,
Caroline Anstey. "A conference on reducing poverty should take
place in an atmosphere of peace, without provocation, violence or

intimidation." The clear message was that it was the protestors who were holding up progress on the poverty front. If only they would lay off their demonstrations, the World Bank could get on with the job of eradicating poverty around the world.

But the bank's notion of how to eradicate poverty, like its general strategy for developing Third World economies, all comes down to the market. The bank and the IMF make it sound as if they offer made-to-measure prescriptions, tailored to address the particular poverty and underdevelopment problems of each country. It's true that their prescriptions are extremely detailed, and that they are drawn up after experts are sent out from Washington to conduct on-the-scene investigations. But it would be wrong to conclude that the prescriptions are based on an intimate understanding of the country's people and their daily struggle for clean water, food and shelter. As more than one critic has pointed out, the prescriptions all bear a striking similarity, and seem quite consistent with the experts having conducted the bulk of their investigations from inside the one five-star hotel that can be found in just about every struggling nation's capital. Having acquainted themselves thoroughly with problems related to room service and the hotel pool, the experts generally proceed to draw up reports highlighting the pressing need for market-style reforms.

So, for instance, the experts who worked on a recent IMF prescription for Ecuador came up with 167 reforms for that small South American country—reforms that Ecuador had to agree to in order to qualify for financial assistance. Under the IMF plan, the government of Ecuador had to fire or otherwise eliminate 26,000 employees from its payroll, and then cut by half the real wages of those remaining. The IMF's plan also required that the country's biggest water system be taken over by private operators, and foreign firms be given access rights to an oil pipeline. Also spelled out clearly was the requirement that the price of cooking gas be raised by 80 per cent; the experts had even gone to the trouble of specifying an actual date for the price hike, just in case any of those remaining civil servants got the idea of introducing more gradually what amounted to a massive hit to the household budgets of Ecuador's many very poor citizens. Not surprisingly, Ecuadoreans responded with street riots in February 2001 after the price hike was implemented. Journalist Greg Palast noted in the London *Observer* that, in all, the IMF's 167 conditions seem "less like an assistance plan and more like a blueprint for a financial coup d'état."

While the details vary somewhat from country to country, a few main themes are almost always present in the IMF's "structural adjustment programs." These include privatizing government enterprises and services, opening up the country to imports and foreign capital flows, shrinking the size of government, reducing labour protections and social supports. And then there's "market-based pricing"—a nice, neutral term that masks the brutal reality of what Ecuadoreans experienced with the dramatic increase in the price of their cooking gas. "Market-based pricing" simply means that the government stops subsidizing basic food items. But such subsidies—on items like bread, rice and cooking gas—have been put in place to counteract serious poverty; they are aimed at making a basic diet affordable, and at preventing widespread discontent and even hunger. When they are withdrawn in order to meet IMF/World Bank demands for lower government expenditures, the result is enormous suffering.

Let's look at something even more basic than bread, rice and cooking gas. If we are considering what people need to survive, it is hard to get much more basic than water. Water is just plain essential to humans; unclean drinking water is a leading cause of death and disease in the Third World. So the way the World Bank and the IMF approach the issue of access to clean water is highly revealing about their priorities and their way of operating. In recent years, both institutions have become increasingly insistent on the need for poor countries to privatize their water systems.

This is consistent, of course, with their pro-market view that the private sector can always manage things more efficiently—a debatable proposition. But equally important from the point of view of the bank and the IMF is the fact that privatization removes water from the financial responsibilities of governments, which are naturally under pressure from their people to provide clean water. Along with privatization usually goes "full cost recovery"—the notion that there should be no public subsidy of water. Like chewing gum or hair gel, water is to be sold by the private sector at market rates.

The needs of the people are all that's left out of this equation. In a breathtaking piece of logic, a World Bank document cites the "willingness to pay" on the part of the people in Ghana as evidence of their recognition of the "health benefits" of drinkable water. It's amazing, isn't it, how people are "willing" to pay huge amounts for things that they need in order to survive! A drowning man will no doubt pay his entire annual income for a raft, thereby showing his appreciation of the health benefits of keeping his head above water through his "willingness to pay." And so it is in the urban sprawl of the Ghanaian city of Accra-Tema, where much of the population can't afford the luxury of piped water and instead must rely on buying water in buckets from private tankers. A daily supply of ten buckets (for a family of five) costs 3,000 cedis; someone earning the minimum wage receives 2,700 cedis a day, and many have no regular employment. So one begins to get a sense of what "willingness to pay" means in Ghana.

Unfortunately, things are likely to get worse as a result of the decision of the government of Ghana, under pressure from the World Bank, to lease the Ghana Water Company to two multinational water firms. A report prepared for the government notes that charges for piped water will have to increase considerably to ensure that the private firms can cover their costs and earn "a reasonable rate of return." The report, prepared in 1999, estimates an increase of 52 per cent in real terms from what was being charged for water in Ghana a year earlier.

The bank and the IMF's insistence on full cost recovery for water systems in poor countries is particularly striking given that Western governments don't insist on such policies in their own countries. In the U.S., for instance, 10 per cent of the cost of water systems is subsidized by federal, state and local governments. The American Water Works Association has estimated that it will cost approximately $23 billion a year over the next twenty years to update ageing water systems. Without government subsidies, this would mean average water bills would double and roughly one-third of Americans would face "economic hardship." So while Western political leaders don't dare to recommend full cost recovery at home because of the hardship it would impose on their poorest citizens, they allow the World Bank and the IMF to insist on it in the most disadvantaged countries in the world, where the poorest citizens already face hardships beyond what we can imagine. An analysis by the Washington-based Globalization Challenge Initiative of IMF loan policies in forty countries in the year 2000 found that the IMF required twelve of the countries—generally the smallest, poorest and most debt-ridden African nations—to privatize their water systems and eliminate or reduce public water subsidies. It is almost enough to make one's jaw drop to think that officials at the World Bank and the IMF would suggest that they have poverty alleviation in mind when they force governments to withdraw subsidies that enable poor people to get clean water to drink. If this is a policy aimed at helping the world's poor, it's interesting to imagine what a policy aimed at *hurting* the world's poor might look like.

Dramatic price increases on basic necessities seem to be a common problem faced by people in the Third World as the IMF reconstructs their economies. Many African countries have been made to devalue their currencies in the interest of encouraging the export of crops like coffee and nuts. A devalued currency makes exports cheaper on world markets, but it also has the effect of making imports more expensive, including imports needed to produce these export crops. This means that only the large-scale farmers, who have access to credit, are able to afford the imported seeds and tools necessary for production. As a result, the well-off farmers in Tanzania, for instance, saw their incomes increase by 279 per cent between 1983 and 1991, while poor Tanzanian farmers experienced income declines over the same period of more than 40 per cent, according to a World Bank study. As one of those farmers, E. Humbo, from the Iringa rural district, explained, "Prices have gone up for everything—improved seeds, insecticides, fertilizers, you name it. At the same time, there's nowhere we can borrow money to pay for these things. . . . I have five children in school and I have to pay school fees for them. . . . This year I won't be able to rent a tractor to prepare my farm, so I'll have to go back to the hand hoe." So much for globalization bringing the benefits of modernity to the far corners of the earth.

Enthusiasts for the new global economy tend to play down or omit the coercive role played by the IMF and the World Bank in remodelling Third World economies. In a column in the *National Post,* for instance, Peter Foster makes it sound as if the only coercion is coming from the "ragtag mob of earnest students, professional activists, power seekers, thugs and scrambled eggheads" who have taken to the streets in recent years to support the concept of "people before profits"—a notion Foster dismisses as completely absurd. "[P]rofits are a measure of the value added to resources by human intelligence, which makes workers more productive, and thus richer," writes Foster. I guess this explains why Mr. Humbo in Tanzania must use a hand hoe.

Foster blames the World Bank for encouraging mushy sentimentality by releasing data showing the extent of the inequality between rich countries and the developing world. Better not to focus on all that since, according to Foster, it has nothing to do with us anyway. He goes on to paint a picture of a benign global economic system that consists of nothing more than companies from around the world interacting and not harming anyone in the process: "A Canadian company, funded with British capital, buys an American product which contains parts made by companies in Germany and Singapore. To ask why Ugandans didn't benefit from the transaction is plainly ridiculous."

But nobody's asking why Ugandans didn't benefit from such a transaction. What they're asking is why Western nations, through their control of the World Bank and the IMF, are insisting that Uganda privatize its water system so that water supply and sanitation services in urban areas "are delivered by local or international private operators." Why, for instance, was it necessary for the Ugandan minister of finance to commit his government to "private-sector management" of Uganda's National Water and Sewerage Corporation, and to guarantee that "cost-recovery policy [would be] operational in most districts" by March 2003? These are among the requirements—along with dozens of others aimed at deregulation, financial sector reform and removal of the constraints on private companies—that have been imposed on Uganda in order for it to qualify for a loan under the World Bank's Poverty Eradication Action Plan—one of the fancy new names for the same old policy of forcing poor countries to behave in ways that benefit rich corporate interests.

THIS RIGIDLY PRO-MARKET APPROACH has now been official policy at the World Bank and the IMF for about twenty years, so it's possible to give at least a preliminary assessment of the results. The first thing that should be noted is how much things have deteriorated in the Third World. As the Washington-based Center for Economic and Policy Research has shown, economic growth has slowed dramatically in virtually every corner of the developing world in the past two decades—which also happens to be the period when the World Bank and the IMF started aggressively pushing their unfettered-market agenda. If we compare the twenty-year period before 1980—when Keynesian-style government interventionism was in vogue—to the twenty years of pro-market policies that have followed, we find that growth was higher almost everywhere in the earlier Keynesian period. (This pattern holds true, although to a less dramatic extent, throughout the industrialized world as well.) In Latin America, for instance, GDP per capita—the standard measure of economic growth used by mainstream economists—grew by 75 per cent in the earlier period and by only 6 per cent in the more recent period.

Consider the case of Mexico, which has been almost completely redesigned by zealous market reformers both inside and outside the country, and is in a "free trade" area with the U.S. and Canada—supposedly the pinnacle of free-market nirvana. Mexico should be a big winner. Yet the country has seen its growth rate fall off sharply since its market redesign began. If growth had continued in Mexico at the pace it was going in the pre-1980 period, Mexicans would today enjoy nearly twice as much income per person. But despite the increase in the number of factories locating in the special *maquiladora* zone in Mexico, real Mexican wages have actually declined since 1994—by roughly 20 per cent.

Elsewhere the story is similar. In the desperately poor nations of sub-Saharan Africa, per capita income grew by 36 per cent in the earlier Keynesian period but has actually *fallen* by 15 per cent in the past twenty years. "These are enormous differences by any standard of comparison," notes Dean Baker, an economist with the Center for Economic and Policy Research, "and represent the loss to an entire generation—of hundreds of millions of people—of any chance of improving its living standards." Even in parts of the world where the last twenty years have been more prosperous—like Southeast Asia— the record of the twenty years before 1980 was still better. Only by separating out East Asia do we see evidence of stronger growth in the more recent pro-market period. (But this is largely due to China, which is notable for its defiance of the dictates of global capitalism.)

Of course, it is difficult to know exactly what caused the slowdown in economic growth throughout most of the developing world after 1980. Likely, a number of factors contributed, including rising oil prices, higher interest rates and, in Africa, the AIDS epidemic. But it would seem almost deliberately obtuse to fail to acknowledge that the downturn in growth also coincides with the abrupt turnaround in the industrial world's attitude towards the appropriate course of development for the Third World, and the aggressiveness with which this new course was imposed after 1980. None of this is meant to imply that things were satisfactory in the Third World under the more modified international capitalism that prevailed before 1980. They weren't. The point of making the comparison is simply to show how badly things have deteriorated under the more rigid pro-market approach of recent years.

Certainly the pro-market reforms introduced in the past ten years in Russia and the nations of Eastern Europe provide a stunning example of the potential dangers. With almost textbook precision, these countries were pushed into adopting a market system—rapid privatization, sudden opening up to trade and capital flows—despite the fact that the countries utterly lacked the necessary laws and institutions to back up the new system. Washington officials like to cite Poland as an example of the success of the market model in Eastern Europe. It's not surprising that they single out Poland; it is the only one of the nineteen countries in Eastern Europe and the former Soviet bloc that has managed to advance its standard of living beyond where it was ten years ago. All the others—from Bulgaria to Belarus to Ukraine—have failed to return to the level of GDP they enjoyed before the arrival of the market economy. In most cases, the results have been devastating. Russia itself has suffered a staggering GDP decline of more than 40 per cent, with the number of poor people rising from two million to almost *sixty million*.

Even the World Bank acknowledges that the past two decades have not produced the results that were hoped for. As the bank's most recent report on poverty concedes, "Indeed, growth in the developing world has been disappointing, *with the typical country registering negligible growth*" (my italics). This is an astonishing admission on the part of the bank that should raise serious doubts internally about what is going on in the name of Third World development. But while the bank is refreshingly candid about the failure of the pro-market reforms, it shies away from taking the logical next step—questioning whether the rigid pro-market approach it has adopted in the past twenty years is the right one.

Instead, bank officials tend to attribute the lack of success to the poor design or execution of the pro-market reforms. As the bank report explains it, "Reforms can go awry when supportive institutions are absent or powerful individuals or groups manipulate the results." No doubt true. But how about also considering the possibility that many of the reforms were a bad idea in the first place, that it is a mistake to insist exclusively on the market? In fact, an earlier draft of the report had been much more critical of bank policies. Written by bank economist Ravi Kanbur, the earlier draft had criticized some of the free market reforms advocated by the bank and the IMF, and argued that social spending and redistributive tax policies were also necessary if Third World countries were going to tackle poverty. These critical sections were missing from the final report, which was published a few months after Kanbur left the bank in June 2000.

Given the bank's insistence on pro-market reforms, poor countries may actually be better off declining loans and avoiding the reforms altogether. That is the conclusion of another bank economist, William Easterly, who has co-written academic papers with IMF deputy managing director Stanley Fischer. In a paper presented to an IMF conference in November 2000, Easterly argued that the poor often end up better off when their governments ignore the advice of IMF and World Bank experts. He pointed to China and India as examples of countries that have refused to follow IMF–World Bank prescriptions, and have had considerable success lifting people out of poverty. "A lot of the countries that have gotten a lot of lending from the IMF and World Bank are worse off," he told an interviewer. "I don't think the record is real encouraging." Easterly also acknowledged that his conclusion "is not the most convenient finding from the point of view of the World Bank's image."

The evidence suggests not only a failure to progress, but also actual deteriorating circumstances in much of the Third World in recent years. Another World Bank economist, Branko Milanovic, says that the real incomes of a majority of the world's people—about 75 per cent—actually *declined* between 1988 and 1993. A good part of this decline had to do with the erosion of incomes in rural Asia and Eastern Europe, according to Milanovic. By contrast, about 25 per cent of the world's people experienced rising real incomes during this period, with some in this favoured group, of course, doing very well. Milanovic says that the result has been a "significant" increase in inequality on a worldwide scale—a development that, he points out, was "rather unexpected."

Here's one way to look at it: in 1988, the richest 5 per cent of people in the world had incomes that were seventy-eight times as big as those of the poorest 5 per cent of people. By 1993, the top 5 per cent were enjoying incomes 114 times as big as those of the bottom 5 per cent. What basically happened, according to Milanovic, was that much of the world's middle class disappeared, slumping down towards poverty. When Milanovic talks about the world's middle class, he is ignoring national boundaries and considering income distribution from the point of view of individual residents of the earth.

So, for instance, a Canadian family with an income of $35,000 to $40,000 a year might consider itself middle class by Canadian standards, but it would be richer than about 98 per cent of the world's population. The "disappearance" of the world's middle class in recent years is in large part due to poor economic conditions in Eastern Europe and Latin America, where the bulk of the world's middle class has traditionally been located. With Latin America experiencing stagnant growth and Eastern Europe experiencing declining growth, the distribution of the world's resources is becoming more unequal. More and more, there is a relatively small upper class, located mostly in the West and in pockets of Southeast Asia, and a growing lower class, located in Africa and parts of Asia but also increasingly in the formerly "prosperous" areas of Latin America and Eastern Europe.

The disastrous results experienced by many of the world's people under the new capitalism have fed the growing anger visible in the anti-globalization movement. While those inside the bank and the IMF have acknowledged some failures, and sometimes have even seemed willing to listen to criticism, they have largely responded by making changes aimed at softening their public image while refortifying the barricades around their besieged institutions. Certainly they haven't wavered from their plans to re-engineer the global economy along strict market lines. And they've been largely successful in keeping protests on the other side of the moat. Only once did a Trojan Horse manage to slip inside the gates—and all the way up to the command tower.

❧

IT'S NOT OFTEN ONE FINDS oneself in the back of a limo in a darkened garage with the chief economist of the World Bank, so I wanted to make the most of the situation. Actually, he was a former chief economist of the World Bank, and the garage was partly lit, but the occasion still had an unusual feel to it. "Can we just have a few more minutes?" he asked the austere-looking driver who had brought us to this odd location in the bowels of a Canadian government building in Ottawa. Permission granted, we plunged eagerly back into the interview.

To the world of international economics, Joseph Stiglitz is what Bruce Springsteen and Madonna combined would be to the world of pop music—a huge, talented, in-your-face kind of star. A year earlier, when he was still chief economist of the World Bank, he publicly defied no less a person than Treasury Secretary Lawrence Summers—easily one of the most powerful people in the U.S. government—and he was rewarded, two months later, with a standing ovation from thousands of his fellow economists at their annual conference in Boston.

Now he is at it again. In the back of the limo, he is freely attacking the IMF for "crazy" policies and accusing the Clinton administration—which he served as chairman of the President's Council of Economic Advisors—of using its economic clout to pressure Third World countries into doing what Washington wants. This kind of dissent from the so-called Washington consensus is rare, to say the least, from such an insider. But what makes Stiglitz a particularly compelling package is that the outspokenness is coupled with awesome academic credentials.

When Stiglitz was a first-year student at Amherst College, his economics professors concluded that they had taught him everything they could and arranged to have him move on directly to the MIT graduate program. After two years there, he went to Cambridge University in England as a research fellow, returning to MIT as an assistant professor. By the age of twenty-six, he was already a full professor at Yale. (Legend has it that his first contract at Yale stipulated that he wear shoes, since his reputation for being indifferent to such formalities had followed "Shoeless Joe" from his graduate student days at MIT.) He went on to teach at Princeton and Stanford. A tireless researcher, Stiglitz has been a pioneer in developing the new field known as the economics of information. In 1979, he won the prestigious John Bates Clark Award, given by the American Economics Association to the economist under forty who has made the most significant contribution to the profession. He is often touted as a future Nobel laureate. So when Stiglitz criticizes the rigid free-market approach of the Washington consensus, it packs a punch.

Stiglitz has described the anti-globalization protests as a "wake-up call" that should alert the developed world to the fact that many believe the global economy is being transformed "for the benefit of the special interests—banks, businesses, and the rich." This may sound radical by Washington standards, but Stiglitz is always careful and informed in his criticisms. He notes that the approach favoured by the U.S. government, and pushed through the IMF and the World Bank, promotes a minimalist role for government and focuses only on the negative effects of government action. He rejects this approach as simplistic, pointing out that most successful countries have become successful through the help of strong government, and that without proper government guidance, markets simply don't work very well on their own. Stiglitz's work on the economics of information backs this up. It challenges the standard belief in the efficiency of markets, and argues that markets are often inefficient because of inaccurate or inadequate information or misplaced priorities, leaving an important role for government in bettering economic conditions.

Raised in a middle-class home in Gary, Indiana, Stiglitz flirted with left-wing ideas at an early age, although mostly through debating and argument rather than activism. His attraction to economics was always linked to ideas about improving the world. "Those of us who entered economics with a touch of the social reformer in us wanted to do something about the wrongs of the world." He quickly discovered that in mainstream economics, issues like income distribution were pretty much on the periphery. "[I]n the intellectual hierarchy which was so plain at MIT, these did not count for much," he notes.

At Cambridge, he found an approach to economics more in line with his own, more geared to trying to figure out how capitalism works and how economics can be used to reduce world inequality. He studied there under the great Keynesian scholar Joan Robinson, with whom he developed a feisty, almost cantankerous intellectual relationship. "She would ask questions like 'What is the marginal product of capital?' and when I came back with the obvious answer (not the answer she wanted, which is that it is not a well-defined question), she would fly off the handle," Stiglitz recalls fondly. Exuberant and intellectually combative by nature, he lapped up the high-powered academic world of Cambridge, revelling in the endless hours of debate and discussion among its "community of scholars."

But Stiglitz was not only oriented to highly technical research and the academic realm, he also wanted to put his ideas in play in the real world. So it was not surprising that after more than two decades at Yale and Stanford, he accepted a position in 1993 on the President's Council of Economic Advisors. This was of course a very different world, as he discovered when he soon found himself at odds with the Clinton administration's policy of pushing Korea to liberalize its financial markets. Stiglitz opposed the policy to no avail, getting a taste for how hard it is to push the Washington steamroller from its course. Still, the real world appealed to him. He stayed on, becoming chairman of the council, and was intrigued when World Bank president James Wolfensohn urged him to come to the bank as chief economist.

In many ways, it seemed like a perfect fit. An Australian-born over-achiever, Wolfensohn was a man of diverse talents; among other things, he had been an Olympic-level fencer and, in mid-life, had successfully taught himself the cello. He was also a savvy, successful and well-connected New York investment banker with an interest in the global poverty issue. Wolfensohn very much wanted to be president of the World Bank, and had lobbied the Clinton admininstration hard to get the position. He liked to think of himself as a reformer, and argued that the bank had to be changed significantly in order to address world poverty. He also knew that he lacked the economic credentials to transform an organization stuffed to the gills with trained economists who were not keen on changing. Stiglitz could be his man—a brilliant, outspoken critic who could give some muscle to the kinds of reforms that Wolfensohn said he wanted to make.

There was lots in it for Stiglitz too. At the President's Council of Economic Advisors, his role had been to provide advice on economic issues for the president, but in fact it was hard to get that advice to the president; the Treasury department controlled the flow of information and generally tried to exclude other viewpoints from reaching the Oval Office. As chief economist of the World Bank, Stiglitz still wouldn't be advising the Oval Office, but he would have more of a bully pulpit to speak out against the prevailing approach to Third World development. Besides, Wolfensohn appeared to share his vision of the neeed for change, and he had agreed to let Stiglitz speak out freely. Ultimately, then, Stiglitz would have enormous freedom and prominence. In many ways, chief economist of the World Bank seemed like the perfect perch for him; it was inside the circle of power, and it offered him the ideal platform to take aim at the Washington consensus.

In fact, chief economist of the World Bank was a job Stiglitz had long aspired to. From a fairly early age, he had set his sights on three big lifetime goals—to win the John Bates Clark Award, to become chief economist of the World Bank and to win the Nobel Prize for Economics. By the age of fifty-three, he had managed to accomplish the first two. Some insiders speculated that an effective assault on world poverty by the bank would only enhance Stiglitz's chances of being awarded the Nobel Prize for Economics, as well as possibly delivering the Nobel *Peace* Prize to Wolfensohn. It seemed that the Wolfensohn-Stiglitz tag team had the potential to bring about important changes at the bank—changes that might even help the world. At the very least, the team promised to shake up official Washington a bit, and bring about some badly needed debate.

But neither man anticipated how these plans would be affected by the political firestorm that swept through Washington in the summer of 1997 as the financial crisis erupted in Southeast Asia. Although the crisis was located about as far from North America as it was possible to be, the "hot money" that sparked it came largely from hedge funds and mutual funds located in the U.S. With the currencies of Southeast Asia plummeting, there loomed the possibility that Asian borrowers might be unable to repay billions of dollars owed to American investors. Furthermore, the crisis was already spreading to other places—huge economies like those of Russia and Brazil suddenly seemed fragile—raising the frightening prospect that the whole international financial system might be unstable and at risk of plunging the world into a global depression.

The response of the IMF, backed up by the Treasury department, was to impose austerity on the countries of Southeast Asia. And yet some, like Thailand, were already lean as a whippet; the IMF's demand for deeper cuts to the Thai government's budget was like putting an anorexic teen on a low-fat diet. To Stiglitz, it was obvious that the overindulgence that needed discipline here was to be found not in government, but among the Western financial interests that had pushed to open the economies of Southeast Asia to foreign capital and then poured in huge sums, mostly in the form of short-term, speculative investments. And there was ample blame to be dished out at the other end, to the Asian bankers and businessmen who had gorged themselves silly on the rich milk of foreign capital, investing these borrowed funds in risky business and real estate ventures.

Stiglitz argued that the Asian businesses and banks should be allowed to go bankrupt, leaving them unable to repay their foreign creditors. This way, the punishment would fall on the private investors—both in the West and in Asia—who had created the problem. Instead, the IMF forced the countries themselves to take over the bad debts. But to repay such huge amounts, the countries had to borrow from the IMF, accepting its conditions of austerity and high interest rates to prop up the currency. The IMF was thus effectively holding the entire population of Thailand and other Southeast Asian countries responsible for what had gone wrong, forcing workers in these countries to accept austerity and job-killing interest rates so that rich Western interests could be fully repaid. What was going on, charged Stiglitz, amounted to "a transfer from the workers [of

Southeast Asia] to the large international banks and other creditors in the U.S., Germany and Japan."

This nonchalance about the rights of Third World workers was endemic to those inside Washington power circles, according to Stiglitz. He noted that the Washington crowd regarded decent wages in these countries as a problem, as evidence of "labour market rigidities" rather than "the fruits of hard-fought bargaining." So the bank and the IMF were often trying to drive wages down—a policy that clearly favoured the interests of capital over those of workers. All this was part of an inability among Washington experts to sympathize or identify with Third World people. Noting the propensity of IMF experts to stay in first-class hotels while completing assessments of Third World countries, Stiglitz suggested that many of the IMF economists seemed to regard themselves as "shouldering Rudyard Kipling's white man's burden."

It's easy to see how Stiglitz quickly got under the skin of the Washington power elite, particularly those at the IMF and the Treasury department. Ironically, Stiglitz had initially believed that he could change their handling of the Southeast Asian crisis. After all, two of his former academic colleagues—Stanley Fischer and Lawrence Summers, for whom he had had great respect and a history of interaction in the academic world—now occupied top-level positions in the IMF and the Treasury department, putting them at the very centre of the team handling the crisis.

In academia, Summers and Fischer had been regarded as independent thinkers. But Fischer, who was now deputy managing director of the IMF, was largely unresponsive when Stiglitz approached him with a harsh critique of what the IMF was doing. Summers, however, was ultimately the more important player. And Summers had even been considered a bit radical at one point, having written an academic paper that favoured capital controls—the type of government restriction on capital mobility that is firmly opposed by U.S. financial interests. After that, Summers had served as chief economist of the World Bank before moving over to the Treasury department, where he soon became deputy Treasury secretary and eventually

Treasury secretary. His quick promotion to the top ranks of the Clinton team had initially brought a stir of excitement in progressive academic circles. It was one of those developments that seemed to suggest that Clinton's boldness was not limited to defiance of the unwritten rules of proper comportment for a president while sitting at a desk.

In fact, it ended up proving nothing of the sort. Summers turned out to be a keen adherent of Washington consensus-type thinking. Gone completely was his former advocacy of capital controls. More disturbing was his apparent abandonment of the intellectually rigorous approach of the academic world—the inclination to probe to the root of an issue and deal with a subject through discussion, debate and reason. Once in power, Summers apparently had no interest in such academic fine points; he seemed to expect people simply to fall in line behind administration policies. "He didn't want any discussion," says Stiglitz. "He used bureaucratic methods to squash debate."

The confrontation between Summers and Stiglitz quickly became public, as Stiglitz was fairly forthcoming in media interviews about his critique of IMF policies. Such outspoken dissent is rarely welcome, but it's particularly unwelcome in the middle of an exploding crisis, where the future of the international financial system seems at risk. The acrimony was only fuelled when in October 1997 Stiglitz gave an interview to the *Economist* magazine in which he blamed the crisis in part on Western pressure to open up Southeast Asian economies to capital flows—a policy Summers had been pushing from the Treasury department. Stiglitz made no mention of Summers, or of the fact that Summers had once favoured capital controls. But the *Economist* pointed out this irony, noting that Summers seemed to have abandoned his old convictions and now appeared content to do Wall Street's bidding.

The suggestion that Summers had abandoned his principles—even though the suggestion came from the *Economist,* not from Stiglitz— added a bitter personal element to the Summers-Stiglitz standoff. Summers appeared to hold Stiglitz responsible for prompting the *Economist* to focus on Summers's dramatic policy about-turn. After that, it seemed to Stiglitz that whenever he spoke to the *Economist,* Summers somehow found out about it right away and protested directly to Wolfensohn before the article was even published.

By now, the driver is growing impatient. And the fumes in the garage are getting to me, as much as I want this interview to continue. What if the controversial former chief economist of the World Bank never makes it to his meeting with Finance Minister Paul Martin, where he is to give Martin his ideas on how to go about reforming the international financial system, but instead ends up asphyxiated in a basement garage, only a stone's throw from the Canadian Parliament Buildings? (In the end, Stiglitz did make it to the meeting—a meeting that had been requested by Martin. As chairman of the G20—set up in the wake of the Asian financial crisis—Martin was keen to hear Stiglitz's analysis of how to avoid such crises in the future.)

Stiglitz resigned as chief economist of the World Bank in November 1999. He left on fairly friendly terms. There was even a farewell party for him, attended by Wolfensohn, and a colleague prepared a "Top Ten List of Reasons Why Joe Really Left the Bank." Reason number three: "After convincing the IMF of the need for capital controls as a prophylactic against hot money, he would move on to reform the Vatican's view on birth control." Reason number two: "To write—as guest expert—the new travel guide for IMF staff, called *First-Rate Hotels in Third-Rate Countries.*" But the number-one reason cited for Joe's leaving the bank surprised no one in the room: "He had just seen one too many 'hot Summers' in Washington."

Stiglitz has always said that he resigned, with less than two months left in his term as chief economist, but the popular view has it that his departure was Summers's decision. Summers, it is widely believed, made it clear to Wolfensohn that if he wanted to be reappointed president of the World Bank, Stiglitz had to go. Given that choice, Wolfensohn apparently had no trouble deciding. One thing is clear: Wolfensohn communicated to Stiglitz that he would have to learn to play by the rules. "If I were to be reappointed, it would not be possible for me to speak out," Stiglitz says in the dim light of the limo, "and I would have to reach some kind of accommodation with

Treasury and the IMF." It might not just have been Wolfensohn whose job was at risk owing to Stiglitz's outspokenness. With huge financial interests at stake, Wall Street was enraged by Stiglitz's open advocacy of capital controls and criticisms of IMF policies. "It was particularly important that he [Summers] show that he had views that were consistent with those widely held on Wall Street," says Stiglitz, finally getting out of the limo and making essentially the same point that had so infuriated Summers when he saw it in the *Economist*.

SUMMERS HAD MADE IT all the way to the job of Treasury secretary. So you could say that he had become one of the most powerful men on earth, if you consider being the vessel for Wall Street's immense power also a form of personal power. With the end of the Clinton administration, Summers took over the prestigious position of president of Harvard University. Undoubtedly, the limos he drives in still end up parked in front of the best addresses in Washington and Manhattan, not in dimly lit basement garages in Ottawa. Stiglitz, on the other hand, could be said to have failed in his quest. He didn't accomplish his goal of stopping the disastrous policies Washington was imposing on countries reeling from the financial crisis. He also failed to change the long-term development strategies of the World Bank and the IMF, with their intense focus on market reforms. It could be argued that his critique didn't go far enough anyway, in that it failed to include the bank which, publicly at least, Stiglitz shied away from criticizing.

Still, it's interesting to ask whether Stiglitz has sparked a rethinking of the Washington consensus, perhaps through his impact on influential players like Paul Martin. Martin is not only chairman of the G20—a group that includes finance ministers of G8 countries as well as emerging nations like India and China—he is also, because of his position as Canada's finance minister, a governor of both the IMF and the World Bank. Yet despite his role as part of the international governing establishment, Martin has made a point of cultivating ties with critics like Stiglitz. "I know Joe well," Martin said in an interview, noting that he considers much of Stiglitz's critique to be valid and that Stiglitz has had an influence on his thinking. Martin also maintains that a rethinking of the Washington consensus is already under way, even at very senior levels. Certainly Martin is not shy about criticizing the World Bank and the IMF himself. "To go into a country and say, as a condition of getting a loan, you're going to privatize, you're going to reform your pension system . . . and here are another forty-five things you're going to do—which no G7 country could do within that short a time period, let alone an impoverished country with a very weak public service—it's just unrealistic and unacceptable. And yet this kind of thing goes on all the time."

Martin is absolutely right that this sort of thing goes on all the time, and it's refreshing to hear someone in his position describe the high-handed tactics used by the bank and the IMF and openly characterize them as "unacceptable." But there seems to be little evidence to support Martin's contention that substantive changes are in the works. Martin concedes that he did not intervene during the Asian crisis—when it might have made a difference—in support of Stiglitz's critique. And while Martin argues, like Stiglitz, that private investors should bear the consequences when their investments go bad overseas, he doesn't rule out the occasional bail-out when necessary for international stability—the same argument used by the IMF to justify its actions during the Asian crisis.

In fact, Martin seems a lot like James Wolfensohn. Both men are cut from a slightly different cloth than the run-of-the-mill Wall Street or Bay Street banker. Both Wolfensohn and Martin have reformist instincts; they seem to share a genuine desire to reduce world poverty. Both recognize that the IMF and the World Bank have failed in this regard. But neither man seems able or willing to push for the kind of big changes that would really turn things around. They talk about the need for the IMF and the bank to focus on social development as well as economic growth, but they cling to the rigid pro-market model of economic growth that has proved so disastrous for Third World countries in the past two decades. Martin

correctly identifies the injustice of the conditions imposed on Third
World countries seeking IMF and World Bank loans. But these
conditions are not imposed for capricious or mischievous reasons.
They're imposed in order to remodel those economies along strict
market lines, in order to make these countries better serve the
needs of Western corporate and financial interests.

It seems fair at least to ask the question: if Martin and Wolfensohn
can see the problems, why don't they use their power to correct
them? If Martin has noticed the unfairness of the conditions imposed
on struggling countries, why doesn't he use his considerable influence
to push for scrapping this "unacceptable" system? Martin suggests that
changing the culture of the World Bank is difficult. While he insists
he's "not trying to blame mid-level bureaucrats," he notes that "if
you've been imposing conditionality for the last twenty years . . . it
takes a lot before that culture shift takes hold." True, but some clear
messages from the top might help things along. Ultimately, however,
it seems that the real problem isn't the intransigence of mid-level
bureaucrats, but the fact that powerful corporate and financial interests are happy with the pro-market way the bank and the IMF are
remodelling the world. Until Wolfensohn and Martin are willing to
take on those key players—and their champions in the U.S. Treasury
department—it doesn't really matter what mid-level bureaucrats
may be thinking.

Still, despite the difficulty of bringing about meaningful change,
Stiglitz's brief confrontation with the powers in Washington had its
value. The only real hope for change lies in enlisting the support of the
public, and that begins with alerting the public to what is going on.
Stiglitz helped on this front. He briefly managed to break through the
impermeable wall of secrecy that surrounds the Treasury department,
the IMF and the World Bank—a wall that prevents the public from
understanding what these institutions are actually up to. By speaking
out strongly and eloquently before being hurried out of his prominent
spot on the international stage, he managed to provide the public with
a crucial piece of information: that the Treasury/IMF/Wall Street
model for development isn't rejected only by protestors wearing

funny costumes or dodging tear gas in the streets. It's rejected too by someone who does path-breaking research in new economic fields and wins prestigious economic awards, and who has seen how the IMF, the World Bank and Treasury operate close up from the inside.

OKAY, SO MOST OF THE world is not doing so well. Here, in the rich part of the world, things at least are sizzling. Right? It's time to take a whirlwind tour through the land of plenty, to check out the state of things at the very centre of the feast.

# CHAPTER THREE

# Loot Bags and the Triumph of the Market

INSIDE A PRICEY LITTLE SHOP in an upscale suburb of Toronto, the "loot bag" has been elevated to an art form. A loot bag, of course, is a bag full of treats given out to children as they leave a friend's birthday party. At this particular store, which is entirely devoted to paraphernalia connected to the giving of expensive children's birthday parties, there is a whole wall dedicated to a display of loot bags and their contents. One has a wide choice of bags containing plastic frogs, miniature battery-operated boats or cars, pop-up toys, glittering face paint, do-it-yourself lip gloss, etc. The bags sell for ten dollars each, or twelve dollars for the more exotic ones. And let's face it, if you're going to spend ten dollars for a run-of-the-mill loot bag, why not spend just a little more and get a high-end bag of trinkets that will make your child's special day just a little more special? So if you're having, say, twelve children to a birthday party, you can easily spend $150 and have covered the cost of only the final few seconds of the party, as the kids walk out the door.

This brutal fact was in the back of my mind as I booked a birthday party for my eight-year-old daughter at an amusement centre known as Chuck E Cheese's—a kind of children's introduction to Las Vegas—which my daughter favoured over having the party at historic Fort York or in a pottery-making studio. The idea of offering the young guests two hours of frenzied arcade and gambling opportunities may seem to have some drawbacks. But on the other hand, I certainly perked up when I heard that in addition to the reasonably priced pizza and cake served on the premises, one could purchase special Chuck E Cheese's loot bags for the phenomenal price of only three dollars each. What a deal! All went smoothly, and I was feeling pretty good about keeping the overall cost of the party at around two hundred dollars, until one of the eight-year-old guests mentioned that the loot bags seemed "cheap."

I felt caught out, mortified, guilty that I'd tried so blatantly to cut corners. Worse, I worried that my daughter would suffer the embarrassment of having a mother who didn't seem to know that a decent loot bag goes for at least ten dollars.

The loot-bag phenomenon is, of course, simply one small example of the explosion of endless new consumer items that have flooded our lives in recent years and become seemingly compulsory purchases in many North American households. This is the flip side of the story of the money not spent on the cure for the African sleeping sickness. While there's lots of demand for a cure for sleeping sickness, but no money in the hands of those with the demand, there seems to be endless money in the hands of some middle- and upper-class North Americans. So corporations have moved quickly to supply items for needs that these people didn't even know they had.

While Christmas was long ago spotted as a big opportunity to sell Christmas-related paraphernalia as well as presents, virtually every other holiday, from Hallowe'en to Valentine's Day, is now marked by stores flooded with consumer items celebrating the event. It seems unlikely that Hallowe'en or Valentine's Day has taken on more significance in our lives, but each has been recognized by corporate marketing departments as a promising growth frontier for new consumer items. In the same way, the needs of dogs and cats are now supplied by a massive pet-food and pet-supplies industry that goes well beyond the basic sort of stuff available two decades ago. Now you can buy seat belts and life preservers for pets, an enormous range of toys and treats, and expensive electronic systems designed to keep your dog within a certain boundary by giving him an electrical jolt whenever he strays outside it.

This proliferation of new baubles and trinkets for everyday life is another side of what the economist Robert Frank has called "luxury fever," and our indulgence in it is closely connected to what Thorstein Veblen called "conspicuous consumption." Frank notes that there has been a huge burst in the marketing of luxury items, and that the kind of perfectly functional gas barbecues or wristwatches made a decade or so ago have now largely been replaced by far more exotic versions of these items—at dramatically higher prices. This isn't just a phenomenon of the very rich wanting ever more luxury, he notes. It may start with that, but it soon has an impact throughout the culture. After a while, it starts to seem normal that people have fully loaded gas barbecues or watches that light up in the dark, work fifty metres under water or are simply encrusted with diamonds—just as it starts to seem normal to spend $150 on loot bags so eight-year-olds won't notice yours are different from the ones given out at the last party.

Let's quickly discard simple moralizing about this sort of wasteful spending. It's true the spending is wasteful—the items in the loot bag are useless and quickly lost, the diamond watch keeps no better time than the plain one, and the exotic gas barbecue is really a help only when you have "guests about to arrive and forty ears of corn left to cook." But it's also true that if these items didn't exist, it's unlikely the money would be spent instead on helping develop a cure for a disease that strikes only in Africa. The problem is not so much with the individual consumption, but with a system that concentrates money in the hands of such a small group of people, and restricts power to those with money.

But let's, for now at least, focus on a slightly different question. Leaving aside the huge moral problem posed by the fact that so many of the world's resources are being directed towards baubles, trinkets and luxury items for the few, let's ask another question that might seem a little easier to grapple with: is all this indulgence making us happier? Are our lives enriched by access to loot bags, massive gas barbecues and glow-in-the-dark, waterproof, diamond-encrusted watches? Is the promise of more exotic material goods the nirvana we have been led to believe it is? Is the elevation of greed to the position of esteem it now occupies in our society bringing us the satisfaction we want?

Before we even attempt to answer these vital questions, it might be useful to get a fuller picture of what's been happening in recent years, in terms of our economic well-being. We constantly hear about how strong economic growth has been under the new capitalism of the past two decades, but in fact, economic growth was actually stronger in North America—and elsewhere, as we've seen—in the two decades before 1980, when a more regulated form of capitalism prevailed. Still, growth has been relatively strong here under the new capitalism. But the huge feast celebrated by the market triumphalists has been attended by a relatively small number of people, even here in the privileged West. Certainly, the rewards of the new capitalism have gone disproportionately to the rich, particularly in the U.S., where income redistribution through the tax system and social programs is minimal. Furthermore, the new capitalism, with its strong emphasis on removing social supports and leaving citizens to sink or swim on their own, has led to a significant decline in economic security—something that most people would consider very important to their sense of economic well-being.

If we look at the standard measure for assessing our economic well-being—the growth of gross domestic product (GDP) per capita—we see a very positive picture. There has been plenty of growth in Canada's GDP per capita over the past few decades, which suggests we are materially much better off than we were in 1970. The picture is so positive, however, because it measures only certain things. It measures the overall amount of economic activity in the country, and then divides this figure by the number of people in the country. So it tells us if the overall amount of income in the country has grown, but it doesn't tell us which income groups are doing well and which aren't. It also doesn't give us any idea of how much economic security people are enjoying.

In order to provide a more meaningful snapshot of the economic well-being of the country, progressive economists have in recent years devised some new methods for measuring economic growth. There are a number of these new indexes, but they all have the same goal—to shift attention from the narrow focus provided by the old index of GDP per capita. For instance, one index developed by the Ottawa-based Centre for the Study of Living Standards tries to measure a broad range of factors that contribute to the overall economic prosperity of citizens, including their personal income and wealth, the amount of economic security they enjoy and the level of economic equality in the society in which they live. This so-called Index of Economic Well-Being is a more subjective measure because the economists who designed it—Lars Osberg and Andrew Sharpe—had to figure out ways to measure economic insecurity and economic equality, and then assess how much weight to assign each factor in the index. But while their index is more subjective, it also seems to present a more meaningful depiction of how well people are actually doing economically.

What is striking is how different our economic well-being appears when it is measured using this new index. If we simply look at GDP growth in Canada, we see a success story—the line on the chart jigs and jags a bit, reflecting recessions, but rises clearly and strongly over time. This suggests that over the past thirty years, we've enjoyed strong economic growth and rising incomes. If we use the Index of Economic Well-Being instead, however, the story is less encouraging. The line on the chart rises much less, and after reaching a peak in 1987, it has actually fallen in the past decade. Today, we are worse off (adjusted for inflation) than we were in 1970.

This reflects, among other things, rising inequality. Although the economy has grown, the benefits of that growth have been more unequally distributed, leading to an overall increase in the level of inequality in Canadian society. This is a significant and relatively new development. For years, Canadian social programs largely managed to counteract the growing inequality of the marketplace. Recent data show this is no longer the case. Not surprisingly, the poor have fared particularly badly. Osberg and Sharpe report an increase during the last decade in the incidence and severity of poverty—a trend that started with the brutal recession in the early part of the 1990s and continued after the recession as a result of cuts to welfare programs, particularly in Ontario. Seeing homeless people living on the streets of major cities has now become as Canadian as over-hyped Olympic bids.

Even more pronounced has been the general decline in economic security, largely due to the significant cutbacks Ottawa made to the unemployment insurance system throughout the 1990s. At the beginning of the decade, 84 per cent of unemployed Canadians received benefits, compared to only 43 per cent by the end of the decade. This has made the economic security of millions of Canadians far more precarious. If they lose their jobs, they could end up on welfare. Osberg and Sharpe also point to provincial cuts that have removed the public subsidy from a number of medical services and drugs. As a result, the financial risks of getting sick have become greater, thereby reducing economic security.

But even this broader index is perhaps not broad enough. A group of researchers in California has developed the Genuine Progress Indicator (GPI), which attempts to distinguish between economic growth that is actually beneficial to people and growth that simply generates economic activity. This is an interesting distinction. If there is growth in economic activity but it leads to deterioration of the environment, are we really better off? Yes, according to the GDP measure. For instance, a spill of toxic wastes that requires a massive and costly clean-up adds to our overall economic activity and pushes up our GDP. But it's hard to see this as an overall gain, when the result is probably some kind of permanent damage to the environment. Any meaningful measure of our overall well-being would surely conclude that we are worse off. So the GPI factors in impacts to the environment. Destruction of the environment is measured as a negative, which detracts from our overall level of growth. Like the Economic Well-Being Index, the GPI—and a Canadian version recently developed for the Atlantic provinces—presents a much less encouraging picture of how we've fared in recent years.

It should be noted, then, that the new capitalism has produced more mixed economic results, even here in the West, than is generally appreciated. Yes, there has been growth in overall GDP, but this is not a very meaningful measure of our economic well-being. The freeing of capital from unwanted intrusions by government—the central goal of the new capitalism—has been a two-edged sword. It can be credited with sparking considerable economic activity, producing particularly massive gains for the lucky few, but it has also led to much more economic insecurity—an insecurity that undoubtedly looms large in the lives of many ordinary people and more than wipes out the relatively small gains in their incomes.

It should be noted that this rising economic insecurity isn't really accidental. It's largely due to deliberate policies aimed at making labour markets "more flexible," that is, making workers less militant in their wage demands. Indeed, an important goal of the new capitalism has been to remove the economic security that workers, through unions and political pressure, managed to achieve in the early post-war period. This economic security took the form of specific job security clauses in union contracts but also, more generally, was reflected in the expanded social welfare system of those decades. Polish economist Michael Kalecki noted back in 1943 that the welfare state had the effect of stripping employers of their ultimate power over their workers—the terror of unemployment. With a relatively strong social safety net under them, workers no longer felt the kind of desperation that the unemployed had felt during the Depression. And this had the effect of making them considerably more demanding—and effective—at the bargaining table.

So with this broader picture in mind, let's return to loot bags, gas barbecues and diamond watches. The question we were trying to explore was whether we are happier or more satisfied now that we are able to accumulate more baubles and gadgets than was ever previously thought possible. Fortunately, there's quite an extensive academic literature, based on surveys conducted in a number of countries over the past half century, examining the link between happiness—or one's subjective sense of well-being—and material gain. One of the findings of this literature is that very low income is directly linked to *un*happiness. It doesn't seem surprising to learn that people who lack adequate food and shelter are overall less happy than those who have these things. It follows, then, that as the incomes of poor people rise, they generally become happier.

But—and this is the interesting part—once a certain threshold of basic material well-being has been reached, there ceases to be much correlation between income levels and happiness. So improvement in a poor country's standard of living can do a great deal to increase the sense of happiness of its citizens. But once a fairly basic level is attained, further material improvements do not necessarily bring more happiness. There is strong evidence to support this conclusion in the academic literature, according to John Helliwell, an economist at the University of British Columbia. He notes that in low-income countries, a 10 per cent increase in income levels makes a noticeable difference in reported levels of happiness. But a 10 per cent rise in incomes in a country with higher income levels will have less impact on happiness, and the same percentage rise in incomes in a very rich country will likely have no discernible effect. Richard Easterlin, an economist at University of Southern California, points to studies showing that despite significant increases in real disposable incomes in the U.S. in the past half century, there has been no increase in reported levels of happiness. This is certainly a provocative finding that seems highly relevant to North America, where we long ago achieved a basic level of material well-being and are now engaged in an orgy of material consumption.

The reason that this unbridled consumption doesn't appear to be making us any happier is that our urge to accumulate material goods is about a lot more than simply acquiring material goods. It's about showing off our possessions, flaunting our success in front of others or simply proving that we are able to keep up with them; it's about positioning ourselves in the social order. In other words, we are back to Polanyi's (and Aristotle's) point that humans are, first and foremost, social animals. "[Man] does not aim at safeguarding his individual interest in the acquisition of material possessions," notes Polanyi, "but rather at ensuring social good will, social status, social assets. He values possessions primarily as a means to that end."

Along these lines, Robert Heilbroner argues that those who seek to accumulate great material wealth are doing so as part of a desire to establish power over others, rather than simply for the joy of having a lot of great possessions. "[T]he drive to amass wealth is inextricable from power, and incomprehensible except as a form of power." So whether a business mogul buys a large mansion to establish himself as a serious contender in the eyes of other business moguls or I hope that an eight-year-old won't notice that the loot bag I bought was below standard, we are both responding to how our acquisition of material goods appears to others. We are both interested, in other words, in what our acquisition of material goods communicates to others about us, in how it positions us in the social order.

Unbridled consumption isn't making us happier, because the overall level of material accumulation in our society is rising; as a result, our personal increases in consumption aren't improving our relative position in the social order. We may be accumulating more, but so is everybody else around us. The standard of consumption just keeps rising; one has to increase one's consumption just to keep up. Thirty years ago, the loot bag hadn't yet appeared on the scene, so children leaving a birthday party didn't even know they wanted one or could look down on a mother who handed out substandard ones. And so it is with all the new features of our higher standard of living. After a while, it is almost weird not to have them. So we must work harder and harder—taking time away from other potentially more satisfying activities like spending time with family and friends or pursuing other interests—just to avoid falling behind (that is, to maintain our relative position in the social order).

There's an interesting study that illustrates the importance of relative social positioning. A person is asked to choose between two possible scenarios. In one scenario, the person will earn a salary of $100,000 a year while everyone else earns $90,000. In the other scenario, the person will earn $110,000 a year, while everyone else earns $200,000. Now, if humans were simply interested in accumulating material possessions for the joy of having them and were indifferent to relative positioning, they would want to earn the larger salary, since it would enable them to buy more goods. But in fact, when asked to choose, a substantial portion of people select the lower salary. While they will be able to buy fewer goods, they will end up with more than those around them, making them feel more important—a feeling that apparently matters more to them than the pleasure of additional consumption. Or, as Karl Marx put it, "A house may be large or small; as long as the surrounding houses are equally small, it satisfies all social demands for a dwelling. But if a palace rises beside the little house, the little house shrinks into a hut."

This isn't to suggest that having more money can't improve one's level of happiness. It can, but primarily if it improves one's status in the social order. Easterlin points out that people with higher incomes than those around them tend to be happier. So if one's income were to increase *while everyone else's stayed the same,* that would generally lead to a higher level of satisfaction or sense of well-being. Again, what matters is relative position. This would seem to offer something of a rebuke to the notion that making material acquisitiveness the central organizing principle of society—as capitalism, and particularly the new capitalism, does—is serving our interests well. "Will raising the incomes of all increase the happiness of all?" asks Easterlin. "The answer to this question can now be given with somewhat greater assurance than twenty years ago. . . . It is no." Easterlin argues that the increased happiness we feel from higher incomes "is offset by a decrease in happiness due to the rise in the average, yielding, on balance, no net growth in well-being."

All this suggests that the feast of material consumption going on in North America today, the endless all-you-can-eat buffet at which we are gorging ourselves, may not actually be delivering us to the state of nirvana we expected. For the small number of new millionaires and billionaires who have zoomed to the top of the pecking order, or have been able to enhance their already favourable position in the pecking order, the new capitalism undoubtedly feels good. Similarly, those who have advanced themselves by serving this new elite— whether by writing flattering books about them, designing clothes for them or offering them personalized tax advice or spa services—are also surely happy with their new-found bounty and the economic system that makes it possible. But for much of the rest of the population, there has been no improvement in their overall positioning in the social order. There's been only a general rise in living standards, and that rise has been a mixed blessing. Yes, it's given them some new trinkets to play with, but it's also obliged them to work much longer hours in order to maintain expectations of ever-rising lifestyles. To this group, it may feel more like a treadmill than a dream come true.

The need to work longer hours is obviously a particular problem for those who don't like their work. This leads to the issue of work and our relationship to it. In the economist's scheme of things, work is simply a means to an end; one works in order to earn the wages that allow one to consume. *Homo Economicus* is willing to make the sacrifice of performing work others want done in order to get at what he's after—money—which enables him to buy the material things he wants. Once again, however, this mechanistic conception of behaviour, while logical, doesn't seem at all adequate to explain the range of human motivations relating to the field of work. Although there is clearly a lot of work done only because of the need to feed oneself or the urge to consume lavishly, there is massive evidence that work is often much, much more.

For many people, work is closely tied up with their deepest sense of satisfaction and fulfilment, and is therefore a positive thing in itself, not merely a means to a larger gas barbecue. Even those who derive little satisfaction from their jobs and work strictly to earn money might well respond very differently if they were given an opportunity to do work they liked, were in control of and found meaningful. Indeed, to return to our subject of happiness, it is interesting to note that there is evidence of a very strong correlation between happiness and challenging, self-directed, satisfying work. Far from the economist's conception that work is nothing more than a means to the end of material accumulation, work turns out to be, for many people, central to their fulfilment and happiness.

Thus once again, the supposedly reality-based concept of *Homo Economicus*—the central assumption in mainstream economics—turns out to be a distortion. *Homo Economicus* is driven by the desire to accumulate materially, and work is for him simply a means to this material accumulation. But as Robert E. Lane has shown, this presents things almost exactly backwards. It seems that material accumulation, beyond a certain basic level, is not the key to happiness—*and work is*. This is certainly a provocative finding, given that our modern capitalist system assumes that we are all, deep down, *Homo Economicus*.

But if greater material accumulation isn't necessarily bringing greater happiness, falling seriously behind in the consumption cycle seems to be a brutal experience in our society. This raises an important point about poverty today. Market triumphalists often downplay the significance of poverty in North America. They argue that while there may be starving people in the Third World, the poor here are doing fine; they're getting enough to eat, indeed are often overweight. These market advocates particularly bristle at the notion that poverty should be a relative measure, and that we should instead be concerned about rising inequality or the widening of the gap between the poor and the rest of society. They argue that as long as people have access to the basic necessities of life—food, shelter, enough clothing to keep them warm—we should have little concern. This argument is sometimes punctuated by a tale of personal experience with poverty as a child growing up in the Depression or in some underdeveloped rural area. And the point is that this material deprivation did little damage; indeed, it perhaps even spurred this individual on to reach the fantastic heights that he later achieved.

It's an interesting argument, and the story of personal experience with poverty undoubtedly makes it more compelling. But it completely ignores the phenomenon discussed above—that one's sense of economic well-being is, to a large extent, a relative phenomenon. So while people may well have lived through hardship—even serious deprivation—growing up in the Depression or in some remote area, these experiences aren't really comparable to the experience of urban poverty today. In those situations, everyone was poor, or at least being poor was fairly normal. So it was common to scrimp and save and do without; there was no social stigma attached to those struggling with financial hardship. When people recount their heart-warming tales of ingenuity in the face of material deprivation—stories about how they had to carve their own fishing rods out of tree trunks or make their own goalie pads out of department store catalogues—they aren't offering a meaningful point of comparison in understanding the experience of poverty today, because all the kids back then were doing the same.

To be poor in North America today is to be painfully aware of the feast going on all around you, a feast to which you have not been invited. It is to have your face constantly pressed up against the glass, watching a magnificent party going on inside. Indeed, in a society obsessively focused on material accumulation, it is pretty easy to feel inadequate if you lack the means to buy what other people consider normal. Of course, some people shun material accumulation out of a commitment to anti-materialism, and they can appear to be principled or eccentric, rather than deficient. But most people living in humble material circumstances are doing so not because they reject the concept of consumption, but because they lack the money to buy the things they want. And this lack of money not only leaves them without material possessions, but also makes them feel left out, not really part of the broader community. So while going without possessions may not be a big deal in some societies, in our highly materialistic society, it is to feel ashamed and disliked and unmistakably branded as a loser. The Vancouver anti-poverty activist Jean Swanson describes the way most people look down on the poor as "poor-bashing."

All this, then, is to try to bring some perspective to the issue of the new capitalism's liberation of greed and the impact it is having right here in our society, at the headquarters of the feast. Since relative positioning is crucial, the greater inequality generated by the new capitalism presumably produces emotional benefits to the few at the top, but emotional harm to the much larger group at the bottom. So, yes, the new capitalism has allowed us to maintain a high level of economic growth (although, as we've seen, not as high as in the early post-war era of more regulated capitalism). But a large share of the gains in recent years has gone increasingly to the small group at the top—an impact that the rest of us are likely to feel more strongly over time, with the continued erosion of social programs.

Furthermore, those gains have come at the price of greatly reduced economic security. And there's reason to believe that the frenzy of material accumulation we've entered into may not even be all that rewarding, as we struggle to keep pace with ever-rising expectations of what the appropriate lifestyle requires. It's possible that buying the ideal loot bag or a really elaborate gas barbecue isn't as much of a high as we've been led to believe. Chalk it up to some deep-seated defect in our nature, but it may be that we're just not as happy with the new capitalism as a perfectly constructed creature like *Homo Economicus* would be.

❧

IT WILL NEVER BE known what went through Jamie Barker's mind as he plunged into the icy waters of the Detroit River on a cold and windy afternoon in late November 2000. The twenty-eight-year-old had been painting the underside of the Ambassador Bridge, which links Detroit with Windsor, Ontario, when the scaffolding under the bridge collapsed and the safety straps that were to prevent him from falling into the hellish waters below somehow failed to work. Several of his co-workers were left dangling by their safety straps, their bodies twisting and turning at the mercy of the winds for well over an hour—plenty of time to contemplate the full horror of those vicious, grey-black waves fifteen storeys below. But they were spared the actual experience of the water, and were off celebrating their rescue and return to dry ground, when it became clear that one fellow worker wasn't among them. Barker's body was never found.

Now, these men were engaging in what I would call risk-taking activities. But interestingly enough, if you do an Internet search for the phrase "risk taking," you get more entries related to investment and business decision making than you do to the potential perils of coming face to face with body-jolting danger. One conclusion could be that in today's global economy, the riskiest thing you can now do is to load up your investment portfolio with too much high-tech or emerging-market stock. Such a view wouldn't be out of sync with the kind of unquenchable enthusiasm about the new age of information that is regularly served up in the media. But it also wouldn't be true—as Jamie Barker and his co-workers above the Detroit River graphically illustrated.

There is plenty of risk attached to manual labour these days. Indeed, the jobs of millions of workers around the world could be considered fraught with considerable risk on a daily basis. That we have come to focus more on the "risk taking" done in the business world tells us nothing about the changing reality of work today, but a great deal about the increasing narcissism and self-absorption of the financial elite. To this pampered minority, the experiences of those outside the elite—whether fellow citizens or those living far away—have all but ceased to exist. This kind of desensitization to the experiences, and suffering, of others is an essential ingredient of the phenomenon of market triumphalism, or the belief that the increasing dominance of American-style capitalism over the past decade has led the world to a higher plane of existence.

Not that insensitivity is a new problem. Certainly, it has long been recognized that history tends to be written by the victors and seen through their moral prism. The past grievances of the victors are thus understood, their suffering is painfully recalled, their need for retaliation and even revenge becomes utterly clear. The grievances, suffering and need for revenge of the losers have none of the same clarity, and are indeed often exorcised entirely from the story or transformed into a tale of ruthless villainy.

It is similar with the triumph of the market. In mainstream Western culture, we don't generally get an analysis of the international situation from those who are, for instance, not getting enough to eat, living in a shack without a toilet, walking miles a day to fetch clean drinking water or contemplating which of their children to offer up to prostitution to support the family. If we did get such a perspective, we could probably expect a different take on things, a

different assessment of what is important and what isn't, of how satis-
factorily the current system is serving the world. I don't think it's
being too provocative to comment on the absence of this perspective
from mainstream culture. After all, it's not as if it's an obscure point
of view. While it may be utterly absent from mainstream Western
culture, it's a perspective that would be quite familiar to the 1.2
billion people, out of a total world population of 6 billion, who live
on less than $1 (U.S.) a day. Or, for that matter, as mentioned earlier,
the 2.8 billion—close to half the world's population—who live on $2
(U.S.) a day. The notion that the new capitalism has brought the world
untold wealth would be devoid of meaning, indeed absurd, to billions
of people alive today.

This is a sobering thought, if one pauses for even a few seconds to
contemplate it. Close to half the world's population is living in what
anybody in the West would consider serious deprivation. This reality
has done nothing, however, to put a dent in the claims of the market
triumphalists. It sometimes seems as if their only response to the
Third World's increasingly desperate condition is to crank up the
volume of the party celebrating the new capitalism. Certainly,
horrific conditions throughout much of the world have done nothing
to dampen one of North America's fastest-growing publishing fads—
books celebrating the triumph of market capitalism.

This literature, produced by economists, journalists and other
assorted commentators, is astounding for its lack of critical perspective—or for that matter, its lack of any kind of perspective. These
commentators seem to consider virtually all outside the realm of
U.S.-style capitalism to be so inferior that it should be swept aside to
make way for the new kingdom. Anything that happened or was
thought about more than ten years ago—before the new capitalism
hit its stride—is considered almost irrelevant. Indeed, destroying
what goes on elsewhere, what has gone on before or any other way of
viewing the world and the human condition is central to the new
triumphalism. The act of destroying the old is even seen as a creative
tonic for the new entrepreneur. "Social systems have to be built that
give entrepreneurs room to destroy the old," writes Lester Thurow,

one of the leading new-market enthusiasts, in *Building WEALTH*.

And building wealth is what it's all about. What has elevated our system above all previous civilizations is the generation of endless wealth, we are told. The proof of this lies in the possibility that a teenager, stumbling upon an idea for a new computer-operated, hands-free toothbrush while brushing her teeth, could be instantly transformed into a dot-com millionaire. Virtue rewarded. Further proof is provided by the cornucopia in America today of something almost unheard of until recently—the billionaire. Creating an environment conducive to the emergence of more billionaires is seen as a goal in itself. It is for this reason that Thurow encourages the destruction of old ways of thinking—because out of the resulting "disequilibrium," he assures us, "billionaires could emerge." Just why we should care is never properly explained. In a society that admires and pays tribute to the endless accumulation of wealth for its own sake, the intrinsic merits of having more billionaires are apparently self-evident.

The emergence of the billionaire, as well as the even more numerous class of some five million millionaires (or billionaires-in-waiting), helps explain the popularity of this new triumphalist cult. These people clearly want to be celebrated, and they are apparently willing to purchase cartloads of books that perform this function, particularly books that convey the message that their new-found wealth signifies something much deeper than luck, connections or good timing. Hence, the demand for this kind of material seems endless, and has created a competition for what the writer Thomas Frank has dubbed the "Most Enthusiastic Pundit"—presumably the one who can go the furthest in extolling the virtues of the new capitalism while stroking the new mega-rich in the most deeply satisfying way. It all goes to reinforce the old adage "Wealth attracts sycophants, and absolute wealth attracts sycophants absolutely."

While there are clearly plenty of strong competitors for the crown of Most Enthusiastic Pundit, it would be folly to ignore the candidacy of Dinesh D'Souza, whom we met in chapter one. Thumbing through a copy of his book *The Virtue of Prosperity*, I was struck by his many fawning overtures to the rich. I was careful not to underline anything, however, owing to my deep determination to return the hardcover volume for a refund so as not to, even in some small way, encourage this kind of semi-pornography. But when I got to chapter ten, my hand could be controlled no longer. Involuntarily, wildly, I underlined the sentence about how scarcity is disappearing before our eyes. It's worth taking another look at it: "We are living in an astonishing moment in history, in which the problem of scarcity, which has plagued our species since the dawn of mankind, is vanishing before our eyes."

Now, to me, this crosses the line that divides run-of-the-mill syco-phantic commentary from something that is almost evil. Certainly, there is plenty in D'Souza's book that would fit comfortably into the first relatively harmless category. He gushes about the bounty of the technological revolution, about the amazing achievements of the new crop of billionaires, etc. This kind of toadying is, it seems, well within the bounds of fair play.

But D'Souza wants to go further. He wants to show that the new capitalism hasn't just been a boon to the new-economy gazillionaires and others of us here in the West. In his quest to be the Most Enthusiastic Pundit of all, he wants to claim that the new capitalism benefits the whole of mankind. Of course, all aspiring triumphalists more or less make this claim, but they usually fudge it a bit, knowing the numbers aren't exactly on their side. So they suggest that the overall improvement of mankind's economic well-being is part of a long-term scenario; if things go well, everybody should end up better under the new capitalism, although of course there are no guarantees. But D'Souza will have none of this eventualism. He wants to be the Most Enthusiastic Pundit, and he wants to be it now. He wants to show that the new capitalism is pushing at the very barrier that sepa-rates mankind from God, that it can accomplish something never before possible in the whole history of our species (going back even farther than ten years, that is).

Hence, we are assured not just that things will work out over time, but that scarcity is "vanishing before our eyes." Why, look—even as we watch—those 2.8 billion people are going to find food on their plates. Look again in a few hours and their shacks will have toilets—and then air conditioning. In a few days, they'll likely have DVD systems and be doing their banking by cellphone.

It's not as if basic information about world poverty is difficult to obtain. From D'Souza's office at the American Enterprise Institute, one can walk to the headquarters of the World Bank—an organization not known for its harsh critique of capitalism but still willing to concede the world isn't exactly poverty-free. To be fair, D'Souza does acknowledge that not everyone is on the fast track to financial ecstasy. But he appears to raise the issue of inequality mostly in order to dismiss it. He argues that "inequality today is largely a consequence of merit." It is hard to imagine a more deeply satisfying way to stroke the rich than with this soothing balm—the rich are rich because of merit, not simply luck; therefore, they deserve the rewards they enjoy. D'Souza is caressing in a way that feels so good. Mmmmm. Please continue. "These are people who start companies and professional practices, take risks and put themselves in a position where the gods of the market can smile upon them. In this sense they deserve their good fortune," D'Souza writes. Don't stop now! Don't stop now! "They are in the position of a runner who has won a race that is open for anyone to enter. What do they owe to contestants who came in behind them? Nothing." Oh, Dinesh, you make things so clear—there's no need for me to feel even the slightest doubt about endless indulgence, about the crippled guy on the street wrapped in a sleeping bag. He had his chance; he bungled the race. This bounty is mine because of merit, because I deserve it. As the L'Oréal commercial says, "Because I'm worth it."

Once again, we have the new capitalism to thank. D'Souza compares this with the old days, when people got rich mostly through inheritance. But he provides no proof to back up his claim that inheritance isn't still the most crucial single contributor to personal financial wealth. Sure, wisely investing what one inherits plays a role, but one is still light-years ahead if one inherits something to wisely invest. D'Souza's contention that today's rich person is simply the winner of a "race that is open for anyone to enter" takes no account of inheritance or how we are equipped as we enter that race. It doesn't acknowledge that some approach the starting line in streamlined Lycra suits and track shoes, with full knowledge of the rules, a determined attitude and a belief in their own abilities, not to mention a close friendship with those setting the rules and choosing the winner. Others, hungry from not having had a meal that day, barely make it to the starting line, don't really understand the purpose of the race or its rules, lack self-confidence and are full of hostility, and are convinced that those officials at the side of the track are actually cops waiting to bust them.

Interestingly, D'Souza rejects even the goal of equality of opportunity, denying that the children of the poor should be given the same chance to succeed as the children of the rich. D'Souza's argument is rather convoluted. Having shown that perfect equality of opportunity can never be attained—because there will always be some parents who provide extra tutoring for their children, giving them an advantage—he then uses this to argue that it is pointless and wrong for governments even to attempt to achieve some degree of equality of opportunity. Now, nobody has ever suggested that the goal of equality of opportunity would require total, perfect equality, so that every child's experiences in life would be identical and all parents would provide exactly the same amount of help at home, and not one bit more. Rather, striving for equality of opportunity is commonly understood—except by those who deliberately choose to render it meaningless—to mean that there would be some effort by government to help those at the lower end come closer to realizing the kind of opportunities available to those at the upper end. Just because perfect equality can't be obtained doesn't mean it's not worth trying to achieve some reduction in the extremes of inequality.

Instead, D'Souza argues, governments should provide a "baseline access to education . . . so that everybody has a chance to develop his or her basic skills." D'Souza never defines what he means by "basic skills." Does he mean just the ability to recite the alphabet and spell one's own name? What is clear is that D'Souza wants to minimize the role for government. He goes on to argue that he would like to see educational access expanded, so that presumably even poor kids could go to college.

But he specifies that the funding of this "noble" goal should be left to the private sector. "At one time only the government could afford to pay for an ambitious social enterprise like this one," he writes, arguing that today we must rely on the rich doing so through philanthropy. D'Souza apparently fails to see two obvious facts. First, the decreased resources of government these days are due not to some act of God, but rather to the deliberate cutting of taxes and dismantling of government encouraged by people like himself. Second, even despite all this cutting, government still has more than enough resources to make a significant contribution to the goal of achieving equal access to education, if that was a priority. Certainly, if we stopped dismantling the power and resources of government and made access to education a priority, we could do a great deal to address the current glaring inequalities. What stands in the way is not the impossibility of the task, but the fierce resistance to it by the beneficiaries of the new capitalism and their fawning chroniclers.

D'Souza soon tires of the whole problem of the poor. "So much for the issue of inequality," he declares. All these disadvantaged kids are cluttering up the exciting story of the new capitalism. D'Souza is clearly itching to get back to doing what comes most naturally to him: praising and stroking the rich. "There is no reason whatsoever for businessmen and businesswomen to feel guilty about being successful," he continues, reassuring any businessperson who, after 239 pages of stroking, is still seeking more. "More than any social type, except perhaps the clergy," D'Souza continues, "the capitalist is, in his everyday conduct, oriented to the task of helping and serving others." So there you have it. The rich aren't just deserving of their wealth, they are the nicest people on earth.

D'Souza's overall contribution to punditry, towering as it is, suffers slightly from his lack of stature. The credential of the American Enterprise Institute is fine—of long-standing pedigree, even if its academic claims are sometimes shaky—but the institute is clearly identified with the right. Ultimately, the celebration of the new capitalism and capitalists in general will be more convincing to a broader audience if it comes from a less clearly ideological source. Hence the enormous value of a pundit affiliated with an institution as trusted and apparently objective as the *New York Times.* Enter Thomas Friedman, a long-time foreign-affairs columnist for the *Times* and winner of two Pulitzer Prizes and a National Book Award. He is described by his publisher, Random House, as nothing less than "one of America's leading interpreters of world affairs." So we're dealing with someone of substance here.

And Friedman no doubt sees his approach as "balanced," in the established journalistic tradition of seeing both sides. The very title of his book, *The Lexus and the Olive Tree: Understanding Globalization,* is meant to convey two essential sides of the story. The olive tree represents home, hearth, community and the human desire for stability and security. The Lexus, on the other hand, represents the zoom-zoom, fast-paced world of innovation, entrepreneurship, the Internet, data criss-crossing the globe at the speed of a nanosecond, etc. "A healthy global society is one that can balance the Lexus and the olive tree all the time," writes Friedman. But if this leaves the impression that we're dealing with the yin and the yang, the good and the bad of what's happening to the global economy, Friedman stops this thinking short by completing the sentence about the need for balance: ". . . and there is no better model for this on earth today than America. . . . It not only can be, it must be, a beacon for the whole world." The U.S., which is synonymous with the Lexus, both to Friedman and to everyone else, isn't a society to be modified or viewed as one side of the story. Rather it *is* the story. It is the beacon, the light at the top of the hill guiding the rest in the dark. Dinesh, watch out! Holding onto the Most Enthusiastic Pundit position isn't as easy as it looks. Friedman's going to wrestle you for it.

There can be no mistake about it: Friedman would make a great after-dinner speaker for any business gathering. The anecdotes of foreign escapades roll easily out of him, and never stray too far from what would interest American businessmen as they devour large steaks. We're not talking here of a grasp of the subtleties of foreign cultures or sensibilities. We get anecdotes of room service at five-star hotels. There is, for instance, a drawn-out story, right at the beginning of the book, of how it took three tries before room service at a top-notch Tokyo hotel managed to correctly satisfy his request for four oranges. The story reveals little beyond how fussy Friedman is and how obliging the room-service waiter was, but it all led to the punch-line about how this was a harbinger of things to come in his world travels for the *Times:* "For I too would find a lot of things on my plate and outside my door that I wasn't planning to find"—like the rude shock of finding oranges that were cut up rather than served whole. Friedman's punchline is the kind of line that works in a speech because it's over with quickly. It seems less suitable for a book, where the reader has the option of pausing for a minute to note what a poor payoff that was for the amount of time it took to get there.

But it does in a way set us up for what's to come in the book—a view of the world through the eyes of a devout American who, despite his extensive travels and access to other cultures, clearly feels most comfortable inside his room at a five-star hotel, which is the closest he can come to being back in America.

Is it just me, or does it not seem almost perverse that "one of America's leading interpreters of world affairs" is someone who doesn't appear to see much of value outside the United States? Foreigners appear throughout the book mostly as buffoonish, corrupt, silly or else hopelessly enthralled with the American way. One could easily conclude that nobody outside the U.S. has had an interesting thought in years—except for those who have fantasized about how to make it to America.

At times, Friedman seems so smitten with the way things are done back home that he gets downright mushy and sentimental. "America, at its best, is not just a country. It's a spiritual value and role model. It's a nation that is not afraid to go to the moon, but also still loves to come home for Little League. It is the nation that invented both cyberspace and the backyard barbecue." At the end of the book, Friedman confesses to wiping a tear from his eye as he witnesses the wonder of his multicultural homeland, where a black man, dressed as Santa Claus, is leading four hundred schoolchildren in singing a Jewish hymn in the town square of Bethesda, Maryland. Comments Friedman: "God bless America."

Friedman's gushing enthusiasm for America could simply be dismissed as harmless sentimentality, material for a heartwarming poem inside a holiday greeting card, if it weren't for its overt political message. At the root of his tribute to America isn't just a fondness for backyard barbecues, Little League games and department-store Santa Clauses. These are all just images used to convey Friedman's belief that American democracy is alive and functioning very well. Sure, America has a few problems, which he deals with in a single paragraph on page 378—making Dinesh D'Souza, by comparison, seem almost to dally over the problem of inequality—and then it's back to bursting enthusiasm for the new order.

The fact that mainstream white kids in Bethesda apparently have no problem with a black man dressed as Santa leading them in the singing of Hanukkah tunes is Friedman's snapshot way of communicating that after all is said and done and it's time to wrap up the book, this is the image he wants to leave us with, and it tells us that everything's working pretty well in America. Does Friedman think this image in some significant way captures the state of racial affairs in the U.S.? Is the experience of that jolly African American in the Santa suit a meaningful depiction of life for millions of blacks in the U.S.? Would there be perhaps other snapshots—from the South Bronx or Anacostia or any maximum-security jail—that would give us a perspective less harmonious and inclusive, and less likely to bring a tear to his eye and to leave his reader feeling pretty damn good about America?

And we are supposed to thank the new capitalism for the vibrancy of American democracy. In fact, Friedman's ultimate theme is that the new capitalism isn't just about everybody—or at least a few people—getting rich; it's about democracy. While D'Souza focuses on how exciting it is to have so many rich people living among us, Friedman comes across as the more serious commentator because he appears to be interested in something more substantive than the mere accumulation of huge vats of money. Friedman is interested in democracy. His joy at the new world order is based on his claim that never before has the world enjoyed such democracy. The fall of the Berlin Wall becomes a metaphor for "the fall of walls everywhere"— by which he means the free flow of capital around the world, as if restrictions on capital mobility are the only impediments to human liberation. The free mobility of capital, according to Friedman, has ushered in an era of the democratization of finance, technology and information that has left citizens around the world empowered, or even, as he puts it, "super-empowered."

It's hard to get a handle on Friedman's concept of democracy. He seems to confuse it with large numbers of people. He points to the familiar statistics about the growth in the number of people investing in the stock market, either directly or indirectly through instruments like retirement plans. And he treats us to the usual raft of anecdotes about how we are all now so focused on the minute-by-minute changes in our stock portfolios that we can barely go to the bathroom without needing an update when we return. We're reminded that couples can now "trade from their bedroom through an online broker," making us wonder how in the world people ever managed to find things to do in their bedrooms late at night before they could go on-line and make stock transactions. But while Friedman is correct in saying that more people are now involved in the stock market, this is hardly proof that finance has been democratized.

Democracy means government by the people. For finance to be democratized, it would have to be in some way more representative of or more responsive to the people. But there's no evidence that all these ordinary investors have any more power over the economy or how the markets operate. While democracy is based on the principle of one person, one vote, the market recognizes no such concept. One's empowerment in the marketplace is more closely based on one dollar, one vote—a very different idea. While one person, one vote gives the same number of votes in a national election to a firefighter with a few Microsoft stocks in her pension plan as it does to Bill Gates, obviously the firefighter doesn't have the same number of votes as Gates does at a Microsoft shareholders' meeting.

Yet Friedman goes so far as to suggest that in the era of the new capitalism, power is so widely diffused that there's no one in charge any more! He constructs an elaborate imaginary scene where the secretary of the U.S. Treasury—a person widely understood to be Wall Street's point man in the White House—doesn't even have a phone on his desk any more because, as Friedman says, "there's nobody to call." This is one of those take-your-breath-away lines that one encounters from time to time in the writings of the new triumphalists. Like D'Souza's claim that scarcity is "vanishing before our eyes," the suggestion—even in a fabricated account—that the man entrusted to defend Wall Street's interests in the West Wing is just operating out there on his own, that power is now so widely held that Wall Street has no more clout with him than any other street in the republic . . . well, how is one to respond? If we were able to get a log of phone calls made from the Treasury secretary's line, could we not expect there to be more calls made to the president of Morgan Stanley, Merrill Lynch or Citibank than to, say, that nice couple making on-line trades from their bedroom in the middle of the night? What can be said about such disingenuousness?

Friedman himself notes that there are basically two types of market players in the new economy—first, the financial types, including "currency traders, major mutual and pension funds, hedge funds, insurance companies, bank trading rooms and individual investors," and second, the multinationals, like "the General Electrics, the General Motorses, the IBMs, the Intels, the Siemenses." In other words, it's mostly big financial interests and big industrial interests. Sounds pretty much like the old days. All those new "ordinary" investors, who are betting their little nest eggs on the dream of getting rich or at least avoiding spending their retirement in a trailer park, are now out there too.

But does holding a few stocks give them any real power? If so, please explain how. To suggest that they are part of a newly empowered experiment in democracy simply doesn't square with the facts. More people may be investing than ever before, but control over financial assets has actually become more closely concentrated. So in terms of empowerment—that is, of real control over major assets in the economy, not just the "empowerment" of being able to buy and sell a few stocks on the Internet—the new "ordinary" investor has made no discernible progress. If Friedman is thinking of some psychological or emotional empowerment these people now have, he should be more explicit. Without some explanation, his use of words like "empowerment" and "democratization" has the effect of rendering these concepts meaningless. If there are more stores to shop in or they stay open longer, are we empowered? If more people have pimples, are we experiencing the democratization of acne?

But Friedman insists that these days we are not just empowered—we are super-empowered. By this, he means that the Internet and other technological breakthroughs have made it possible for ordinary people to "act directly on the world stage." By way of example, he points to "a few guys" who are so empowered they almost brought the world financial system crashing down. Of course, these particular guys, he acknowledges, were the ones running the hedge fund known as Long-Term Capital Management, which was managing an enormous amount of money on behalf of some of the richest people on the planet. And the "few guys" included two Nobel Prize–winning economists. So not exactly ordinary guys playing with computers in their basements. Furthermore, it may be that such "super-empowered" individuals wield enormous power largely because we have failed to take steps to regulate their activities. In this era of deregulated financial markets, we have allowed hedge funds to operate virtually without scrutiny, despite the fact that their actions have the power to cause chaos in the world economy. Political scientist Adam Harmes argues that it would be possible, with international co-operation, to regulate hedge funds. But Friedman opposes such regulation, insisting that markets should be left to discipline themselves. Instead, he advises: "Fasten your seat belts . . . Because both the booms and busts will be coming faster. Get used to it." While Friedman wants tough international action to combat terrorism, he insists that no such international action is possible or even desirable when it comes to reining in the power of capital. This hands-off approach allows super-empowered hedge fund managers to play fast and loose with the financial security of people all over the world.

Friedman cites Jody Williams as another example of a "super-empowered" individual who used e-mail to organize opposition that led to the world ban on land mines. This was certainly a significant achievement, but impressive individuals have always been able to use their personal talents and efforts to bring about change, using whatever communication technology was available to them at the time. No doubt, Martin Luther King would have made use of e-mail had it been around in the 1960s, but even without it, he was able to have a considerable impact on history, as were Che Guevara and Joan of Arc, who also lacked e-mail addresses and Web sites.

So Friedman's super-empowered individual turns out to be just the same old rascal or hero who happens to be using the latest technological equipment. The more interesting question is whether the Internet breakthrough will change the nature and scope of available information enough that the broader public could be meaningfully exposed to differing ideological perspectives, rather than having everything presented through the lens of mainstream capitalism. Could the Internet, for instance, inform a general audience to the point that it could read Friedman's book and be constantly struck by his deep ideological biases? This is theoretically possible. At this point, however, there's little evidence it's the case. The same huge players who dominate public debate in the real world are buying up control of much of the Internet, making considerable progress in their bid to limit our use of cyberspace to the ultimate shopping experience.

Friedman would undoubtedly be chagrined to see the Internet used to subvert the new capitalism, which he's hell-bent to sell to us. Indeed, not only is Friedman a gung-ho American patriot, but he's unabashedly on the side of America's financial elite—all those guys the U.S. Treasury secretary would be phoning, if only he had a phone. Friedman repeatedly points enthusiastically to the ease with which American owners can fire their workers as one of the secrets to success in the new economy. Ronald Reagan's decision to fire all the striking air-traffic controllers in 1981 is lauded by Friedman as the single most important event in tilting the balance of power away from workers and towards management, thereby opening the way to the proper functioning of the new economy.

Friedman's argument is that if workers are easy to fire, then employers will be more likely to hire them in the first place. The less responsibility you put on an employer to treat a worker decently, the easier you make life for an employer, and this, it is said, will induce him to hire more people. The logical extension of Friedman's argument is the trashing of all labour laws, since anything that defends the rights of workers—minimum wage laws, workplace safety restrictions, the right to unionize—puts something of a burden on the employer. Having to worry about whether a worker could complain about dangerous conditions on the job might indeed cause the employer to hesitate before hiring someone. On the other hand, if you're the worker, you might like having a few laws that protect you—or as they say, "empower" you—in your dealings with someone who inevitably has considerable control over your life.

The question of which system works better for the worker in the long run is one that reasonable people could debate. If we even just confined our focus to the U.S. and Canada, we could try to assess whether workers are better off economically today, in the era of the new capitalism, or were better off thirty years ago, when unions were stronger and there was more pro-labour legislation. Friedman doesn't bother with any evidence, however. If he did, he would be obliged to acknowledge that the real median wage in the U.S. today is no higher than it was in 1973, and that the real wages of the bottom 20 per cent of workers declined by 9 per cent between 1973 and 1997. Whatever. Friedman just states his position that things are better now that employers have more power—a position that is indistinguishable from that held by corporate and financial leaders.

Friedman's prose is full of anecdotes of ordinary people—like the couple trading on-line from their bedroom, or another couple, holidaying in Utah, who were forced to use a pay phone to call their broker when the modem connected to their motor home went on the blink. But for all these folksy tales, Friedman clearly has the perspective of a Wall Street magnate. Indeed, judging from who gets quoted most often in the book, he seems to have spent most of his time talking to Larry Summers, who was then U.S. Treasury secretary but nevertheless seemed to have had plenty of time on his hands to talk to Friedman. (As Friedman notes in the acknowledgements, "more than a few ideas in this book were sparked by some insight Larry tossed off in one of our off-the-record brainstorming sessions.") Indeed, one gets the impression that when Summers was wondering if there was anyone out there to call, Friedman popped into his mind as often as any Wall Street honcho. Of course, from Wall Street's point of view, this was time well spent by the Treasury secretary. Friedman's book is, after all, a fabulous vehicle for Summers and Wall Street to make their case for the new capitalism, to deliver Wall Street's message with all the charm of Friedman's easy, anecdotal, after-dinner style, backed by the prestige of a newspaper that is the very bedrock of respected opinion in America.

So this makes things really tough. But if you were to put Thomas Friedman in a straight one-on-one against Dinesh D'Souza for Most Toadying, Obsequious Pundit Alive Today—my God, you'd have to call it a tie.

✸

THUS NOT ONLY HAS GREED become the central organizing principle of society, but it has also come to be regarded as a moral triumph, inextricably linked to human liberation. *Homo Economicus* has been crowned and given the seat of honour at the banquet. From the giddy heights of this celebratory feast, it's worth reviewing how we got here and what's been given up—or forcibly removed, and from whom—along the way. It's time to look at capitalism through a completely different lens. Let's leave Friedman and D'Souza fussing over the guests at the head table and return to Karl Polanyi.

# CHAPTER FOUR

# Love and Revolution in Red Vienna

*Vienna, 1922*

THE ARRIVAL OF THE young woman with the long, dark hair was a matter of considerable interest to the other guests at the Schwarzwald *pension* on the outskirts of Vienna. In fact, the arrival of any young woman would likely have been of considerable interest to the lonely group of Hungarian exiles who now made the dilapidated old *pension* their home. But this young woman was of particular interest. After all, she had been imprisoned by the Hungarian government in 1918, and months later, she had been liberated from prison and carried through the streets of Budapest on the shoulders of giddy revolutionaries, some of whom now lived in exile in Vienna and even frequented the Schwarzwald *pension*. At the tender age of twenty-three, she had revolutionary credentials that were already impeccable. She was also rather pretty.

For the exiles who lived at the *pension* or came regularly to eat at its large open kitchen, this was the first sighting of the almost legendary Ilona Duczynska. Petite and well-mannered, she had an almost angelic quality, a feminine gentleness, a kindliness about the eyes. "She is the most moving creature of God amongst men, birds, butterflies and tiny flowers," was the way one of the exiles, the poet Bela Balazs, described her in his diary. But there was also in her manner a poise and self-assurance, and above all a sense of purpose, that was striking. To the destitute exiles who talked fervently of

Budapest and revolution every day over a hot bowl of soup, there was something impressive, even awe-inspiring, about this fearless young woman.

The émigrés were badly in need of inspiration. Having toppled the weakened rightist regime that had led Hungary through the long, unhappy years of the Great War, they had lost power almost as quickly and unexpectedly as they'd gained it. Escaping into exile in Austria, they now felt confined and frustrated, looking back longingly to the glorious days of the revolution and debating endlessly what had gone wrong. The presence of Ilona Duczynska in their midst seemed to provide an energizing spark. The talk around the table at the *pension* seemed just a little more animated after her arrival, the claims of revolutionary heroism just a little more exaggerated.

Ilona herself had just returned from Moscow, where the Russian revolution, unlike the Hungarian one, had survived the assault from Western forces at the end of the war. The exiles listened eagerly to her stories of Moscow, of how a successful revolution really worked, of the horrible repression of their former comrades inside Hungary. Unlike many of the men, she felt little need to emphasize her own heroism or importance to the revolutionary cause. She was always, unfailingly, more committed to the cause than to elaborating on her role in it. There were probably few at the table who even realized that she had shown considerable courage only a few days earlier; crossing the border into Austria from Russia under an assumed name, she had smuggled among her belongings a tube of toothpaste stuffed with diamonds, which she'd delivered to a Hungarian Communist leader in Vienna to help keep alive the cause that these men gathered around her at the *pension* had fought for.

There were also probably few of them who didn't wonder what it would be like to make love to such a woman. Although talk of women's emancipation was in the air, and some young women now spoke and acted far differently than their mothers had, there were certainly few young women who approached Ilona Duczynska in terms of independence of spirit and action. There was something intriguing about that spunkiness. It would surely take a man of extraordinary courage and moral strength to master such a creature. Balazs, the poet, imagined himself to be just that sort of man. "She is a primitive little saint. I love her very much," he wrote in his diary. "I am afraid she might fall in love with me."

Balazs had every reason to think he would be the man of Ilona's dreams. He was used to the attention of women and to occupying a dominant position among the exiles. As a celebrated poet and dramatist, he exerted a kind of moral force and was treated by the others with a certain deference. In the endless hours of debate over theoretical issues and political strategies, Balazs was always a powerful force to contend with, a leader around whom the failed revolutionaries tended to rally. Certainly the other exiles took his side against the somewhat older man at the *pension* who, despite sickness and depression, regularly challenged Balazs's fervent revolutionary ideas. Balazs was at his best when he mocked this older guy for failing to take up the revolutionary cause, indeed for standing by on the sidelines and criticizing it while others bravely risked their lives.

But Ilona ended up not falling in love with Balazs. No one was more surprised by this than Balazs himself. Still, he was willing to forgive her for this failing. What was harder for him to take was his growing suspicion, only a few weeks after her arrival at the Schwarzwald *pension,* that this extraordinary woman, this firebrand of impeccable political pedigree, this "most moving creature of God" was falling instead for Karl Polanyi, the sick, depressed older man who hadn't lifted a finger for the revolutionary cause.

ILONA DUCZYNSKA HAD BEEN radicalized at an early age. Her father, probably more than anyone, was responsible for that. Certainly it was her father, Alfred Duczynski, who profoundly shaped her attitude towards the world.

Most people found nothing particularly impressive about Alfred Duczynski. A largely self-taught engineer, he was seen as a bit of a gadfly, a would-be inventor who was unlikely to rise much above his position as a mid-level railway official. But to Ilona, the only child in the family, he was a person of immense talent and inspiration. His departure for America when she was only seven to try to develop some of his aeronautical inventions seemed simply part of his restless and inventive spirit. He had always had a rebellious streak, which he displayed by rejecting religion in favour of science and dabbling in anarchist ideas. Ilona absorbed his ideas and attitudes. When he died suddenly and unexpectedly in the New World so far away, she was devastated.

Under normal circumstances of the time, Alfred Duczynski's death would have left Ilona and her mother in the arms of her mother's family, the Bekassys, who belonged to the Hungarian gentry. This should have meant an elitist life for Ilona, but the Bekassys had never taken to their son-in-law, whose family belonged to the impoverished end of the Polish gentry. While Ilona and her mother were provided for on a modest basis by the Duczynski family, their relations with the Bekassy family continued to be strained.

This only reinforced Ilona's distaste for the gentry life—a distaste she had felt from an early age. It was certainly difficult to visit her mother's relatives without being confronted with the grinding poverty of the uneducated masses who toiled in the countryside. That poverty formed a backdrop that seemed almost invisible to those living pampered lives behind the walls of their manors, but it was never invisible to the outsider Ilona. She associated her mother's family with a mindset that was shallow and staid and locked in the past—the very sort of thinking that her father's scientific mind had rebelled against. After her father's death, Ilona felt these feelings harden within her. By the time she turned ten, she had come to the conclusion that she would always be "against the world."

As a young adolescent, she mostly withdrew into herself, avidly reading epic Russian novels, which seemed to capture her sadness and disappointed idealism. She regained some sense of direction only in her late teens, when she met Ervin Szabo, a prominent and respected leftist intellectual whose anarchism reminded her of her father. For the first time, her sense of alienation from society started to take a definite shape; in socialism, she began to find a sense of purpose, a channel for her rebellious idealism.

That sense of purpose was greatly intensified when she went to study engineering at Zurich's renowned Polytechnic University. More interesting to her even than her scientifc studies was the political world she could watch at close quarters. With the war raging throughout Europe, Zurich had become a haven for left-wing, anti-war dissidents from all over Europe and Russia. Among other well-known political émigrés, Vladimir Lenin himself was often seen working in Zurich's well-stocked Bibilothek für Soziale Literatur. Although Ilona was sick much of the time, suffering from bouts of tuberculosis, she thrived on the political mood of the city. She was deeply inspired by the Zimmerwald conference, an international socialist event held in Zurich in September 1915, which produced a radical anti-war manifesto. Regarded as treasonous by governments fighting the war, the manifesto charged that the international working class was being used as cannon fodder in a clash between imperialist powers, and it called on all soldiers and workers to stop participating in their national war efforts.

Energized in a way she had never been before, the eighteen-year-old Ilona dropped out of school, hid a copy of the outlawed Zimmerwald manifesto in her suitcase and headed back to Hungary with the intention of beginning a socialist revolt against the war.

If she had any doubts about her new direction, they evaporated after she paid a visit to her favourite aunt once she was back in Hungary. While Ilona had never felt comfortable in the aristocratic milieu of her mother's family, she did have fond memories of her aunt reading German classics to her as a child and walking about with her in the gardens of the family's once-grand country estate. But now, after Ilona's enlightenment in Zurich, this gentrified life seemed more alien than ever. She arrived to find police guarding the entrance to the grounds. Inside, despite the bloody trench war raging through-out Europe, a country ball was in progress! Her aunt, dressed in a fairy-tale costume and carrying a parasol, scampered about beaming and bantering with the guests. Ilona fled the manor with new conviction that revolutionary socialism was the only answer.

Her mentor, Ervin Szabo, tried to direct her towards moderate activism, encouraging her to join a progressive intellectual group at the University of Budapest known as the Galileo Circle. But she found the group rather uninspiring, lacking in the highly directed political activism that had captured her imagination in Zurich. Inspired by a political assassination in neighbouring Vienna, she came up with the idea of killing the Hungarian leader, Count Istvan Tisza, who was staunchly opposed to any kind of peace effort. She took a pistol from the house of a family friend, apparently with the intention of proceeding with her plan. But Tisza ended up resigning before she got a chance to kill him. Thwarted on the assassination front, she linked up with a few activists on the fringes of the Galileo Circle and formed a small group of "revolutionary socialists." Despite knowing that discovery would mean certain imprisonment, the group proceeded to print up leaflets urging soldiers to mutiny.

Ilona thrived on the clandestine activities, feeling more alive and full of purpose than ever before. She even had a lover now—a fellow conspirator in the revolutionary socialist group by the name of Tivadar Sugar. A clever, headstrong young man, Tivadar was "like a flame" whose passion lit up her life. Together, they walked hand in hand along the riverbank, threw anti-war leaflets over the high fences of munitions factories and military barracks, and organized a workers' peace demonstration that was to parade defiantly down the main street of Budapest. Life had become a fast-paced mix of high-risk conspiracy and late-night lovemaking. But it all came abruptly to a halt in January 1918, when the police rounded up the members of the fledgling revolutionary movement. Ilona and Tivadar found themselves in jail.

Despite the austere conditions in jail, Ilona and Tivadar, the ringleaders of the group, remained unbroken and even defiant. When her defence lawyer suggested to Ilona on the stand that she was really a reformer, not a revolutionary, she corrected him: she was a revolutionary. Tivadar and Ilona were convicted of high treason; he was sentenced to three years in jail, she to two. But her sentence proved

short-lived. With the victorious Allied army approaching in the fall of
1918, the Hungarian monarchy could no longer rule, and it handed
over control to a coalition headed by the popular liberal democrat
Count Karolyi. With soldiers ripping the royal insignia off their
uniforms, a frenzied crowd in front of the parliament buildings
declared "the People's Republic of Hungary." Ilona and Tivadar were
soon liberated from their jail cells, hoisted onto the shoulders of jubi-
lant comrades and carried triumphantly through the streets of
Budapest.

Despite the difficulty of the situation, the Karolyi regime pressed
forward with great speed to bring in some astonishing reforms. Most
ambitious was its massive land-reform program, under which huge
estates were to be divided up among the peasantry. Karolyi's inten-
tions were serious: within a week of introducing the land reform, he
allowed his own massive estate to be carved up and handed over to
landless peasants.

The boldness of the moves provoked a strong reaction from right-
wing factions, including some groups that showed early signs of
Nazism in their attempts to pin the blame for Hungary's difficulties
on Jewish reformers. Meanwhile, on the left, there was impatience
with what was seen as the overly moderate approach of the new
regime. With the increasing polarization between extreme right and
left, it was actually the Allied powers that inadvertently pushed
Hungary dramatically to the left by demanding the further surrender
of significant chunks of territory. Karolyi concluded that the only
hope of avoiding such devastating territorial losses was to turn to the
new Soviet regime in Russia for support. Thus it was that Count
Karolyi—a deeply refined and dignified man who had been born into
a traditional aristocratic family—made the second astonishing move
of his life. Only a month after happily handing over his entire estate
to impoverished peasants, he willingly relinquished control of the
national government to a revolutionary governing council, which had
the stated aim of creating a dictatorship of the proletariat.

This was joyous news to Ilona Duczynska. By this point she was
separated from Tivadar, their relationship having lost its momentum

during the months of jail-time separation. She quickly volunteered to serve the new Communist-dominated government, headed by the former Hungarian journalist Bela Kun. She was immediately dispatched to Zurich on a secret mission, which required her to adopt a false identity as a French governess. Once again she was back doing what she loved—carrying out clandestine operations on behalf of revolutionary socialism.

∾

THE NEW COUNCIL WASTED little time in introducing measures that went considerably further than the liberal-democratic reforms tried by Karolyi's government. Within a few weeks of taking power in March 1919, the revolutionary council embarked on a course of action that went beyond anything attempted in Soviet Russia at the time. In a sweeping series of decrees, the new government national- ized all major factories, mines, transportation companies and credit institutions. It also seized apartment buildings and made it illegal for a single person to occupy more than one room or a family to occupy more than three rooms. And land reform—which under the last regime hadn't gone much further than the divvying up of Karolyi's own estate—was now relaunched with enthusiasm. There was almost no aspect of Hungarian life that was beyond the reformist zeal of the new authorities. Theatres, for instance, were brought under the control of the Committee for the Communization of Theatres, presided over by Bela Balazs. The committee quickly drew up ambi- tious plans to use the nation's theatres to re-educate the masses. As part of this, Balazs launched a program of "fairy-tale afternoons," in which actors would perform fairy tales—with a Communist message—in primary schools throughout Budapest.

Although many of the measures were popular with the destitute urban poor, the new regime soon came to be widely regarded as dogmatic and dictatorial. But once again, the actual fall of the govern- ment was caused by outside forces—this time by a massive invasion of Romanian troops from the east and Czechoslovak forces from the north. With these foreign armies marching towards Budapest, Kun and his comrades fled to political asylum in Vienna in early August 1919—just a little more than four months after launching their revolution. Some of the luckier ones, like Bela Balazs, ended up in the welcoming arms of Eugenia Schwarzvald, who generously opened her *pension* to the fleeing socialists.

In Zurich, Ilona learned of the fall of the revolutionary government and immediately went underground. Seizing an opportunity to go to the mecca of revolutionary socialism, she travelled by train to Moscow, crossing through hostile territory under the guise of a deaf-mute relative of a Russian family. In Moscow, she soon volunteered for a mission to smuggle diamonds into Vienna to support the Hungarian exiles as they plotted their return to power. (Her Russian bosses instructed her not to give the diamonds to Bela Kun, who was seen as somewhat unreliable. Instead, they told her to deliver the precious stones to Gyorgy Lukacs, who had served in Kun's government and, as the son of a bourgeois banker, was considered more likely to be responsible with money.)

Having delivered her cargo as directed, Ilona found her way to the Schwarzwald *pension,* where it was arranged that she would stay. After years of underground political networking, she was at home in these informal sorts of living arrangements and found the group of exiles congenial, except for the pompous Bela Balazs. Although stout and short in stature, Balazs had a constant stream of lovers, in addition to his second wife, Anna, who was unusually tolerant of his philanderings. Still, his latest highly public fling with a Danish writer in Vienna had apparently left Anna threatening to divorce him. Determined not to lose her, Balazs had solemnly promised his wife that after just one more week with the Danish woman, he would end the affair. During their final week together, Balazs and the Danish woman collaborated on a short confessional novel about infidelity, which they published under the title *Beyond the Body: The Diary of a Man and a Woman."* As he elaborated in his diary: "I, the most sensuous of men, regulate my life purely in accord with the pull of spiritual attractions, which have nothing to do with my sexuality." *Beyond the Body* had just been

published and was attracting curious attention in the émigré community when Ilona arrived in Vienna. From her first evening at the
*pension,* she was conscious of Balazs's wistful glances in her direction,
but there was no doubt in her mind that she wanted to confine their
interaction to the realm of revolutionary politics.

Ilona also knew Karl Polanyi by reputation, and had little expectation of liking him. She knew—and was not impressed by the fact—
that he had started the Galileo Circle and had established it as nothing
more than a kind of progressive debating society. After all that had
happened in the past couple of years, Ilona had little patience for this
sort of purely intellectual approach to politics. She soon learned,
from the conversation at the *pension,* that Polanyi had also been an
outspoken critic of the revolutionary governing council during its
brief time in power.

But what struck Ilona most about Polanyi was how depressed and
unwell he seemed. He appeared to be at least a decade older than his
thirty-three years, with the gaunt and wasted look of someone who
has suffered too much for too long. It was hard to imagine that this
was the same man who was reputed to be such a powerful orator; he
seemed too discouraged and broken in spirit to appear on a public
platform. He had the air of someone who looks back on life, rather
than forward to it. He appeared to be suffering from some kind of
ongoing inner torment that made him, for the most part, withdrawn
and almost indifferent to the world around him.

None of this prevented him from being drawn into political and
philosophical debate with Balazs, and Ilona watched these debates
with increasing interest. Balazs obviously enjoyed puffing himself up
by portraying Polanyi and his fellow Galileists as weaklings who lacked
the guts to fight for their convictions. These sorts of thoughts had
certainly crossed Ilona's mind too during her long months of imprisonment for her activism, while the Galileo Circle had continued
its timid anti-war debating exercise. Still, it quickly became clear to
her that Balazs was pretentious and superficial. By contrast, Polanyi,
despite his physical and emotional frailty, possessed an intellectual and
moral rigour that was fierce, uncompromising and compelling.

Apart from his debates with Balazs in the *pension* kitchen, Polanyi kept mostly to himself, spending long hours in his small room, reading or writing. His only other contact seemed to be with Janos Lekai, a young exile suffering from incurable tuberculosis, to whom Polanyi acted as something of a mentor. Ilona sometimes joined Polanyi by Lekai's bedside, and they would take turns reading to the sick young man. Polanyi, it turned out, loved a wide range of literature, and had been deeply influenced by Russian writers, particularly Tolstoy. But perhaps what really struck a chord in Ilona, as they sat together in Lekai's room, was her discovery that Polanyi's withdrawal from the world was part of a deep and lasting pain he had felt for more than a decade, ever since the death of his father.

BORN INTO AN ASSIMILATED Jewish family from northern Hungary, Mihaly Pollacsek, Karl Polanyi's father, had studied engineering in Zurich and Edinburgh. He developed a lifelong affinity for British political values, as well as Scottish-style puritanism, with its emphasis on strict morality, self-discipline and personal integrity. Returning to Central Europe as a railway engineer, Pollacsek met Cecile Wohl, an unsophisticated Russian-born girl with a bohemian streak, who was working as a jeweller's apprentice in Vienna. Mihaly and Cecile married and soon began a family, which would eventually include six children.

With the railway boom in full swing in the 1880s, it was an excellent time to be a highly trained railway engineer. Pollacsek moved the family from Vienna to Budapest, which was being transformed into a Parisian-style capital with lovely wide boulevards and grand public parks and buildings. Railways connecting Budapest to other major centres were an essential part of the expansion, and Pollacsek found his services in high demand. Now operating as an independent contractor and railway entrepreneur, he became part of the city's rising Jewish bourgeoisie. The family was soon living in grandiose style, occupying a whole floor in a magnificent building on the prestigious Andrassy Street, in central Budapest, and spending summers at its villa on the hills just outside the city.

But for all their affluence, the Pollacseks for the most part failed to adopt the behaviour of upper-class Hungarians. They had little contact with members of the Hungarian gentry or the newly prominent Jewish elite. (Although Mihaly Pollacsek kept his Jewish name for himself, he later changed the surname of his children to the more typically Hungarian Polanyi.) The family also showed little interest in the refinements of formal dress or habit of other upper-class Hungarians. Cecile displayed a complete disinterest in the dictates of respectable grooming and comportment; she cropped her hair short, dressed her now perpetually overweight form in loose-fitting clothes and usually had a cigarette dangling from her mouth. Apart from the classy address, there was little emphasis in the family on material indulgences. Cecile was almost hostile to material goods, and Mihaly remained committed to self-restraint and personal responsibility. For all his puritan strictness, however, it should be noted that Mihaly was adored by his children. He put great effort and attention into raising them, and successfully imparted to them his devotion to liberal political values that were not widely shared by the Hungarian elite, such as democracy, human rights and the emancipation of women.

Of greatest importance in the family was the rigorous education of the children. Up until adolescence, they were educated at home, in a demanding daily regimen that began at 7:00 a.m. with a cold shower, a simple breakfast and an hour of Swedish gymnastics. This was followed by long sessions with private tutors, whose lessons included mathematics, Greek, Latin, French and English—in addition to the Hungarian and German that were regularly spoken around the home. The appreciation and discussion of literature, art and philosophy were very much part of the children's lives; from an early age, they read Goethe, Schiller, Racine, Corneille, Milton and Shakespeare. Athletics, including the important Hungarian sport of fencing, were also emphasized as a route to rigour and self-discipline; each child had a horse or a pony and received equestrian training from a member of the royal army.

Karl Polanyi, born in 1886, was the third child. He thrived in this intense atmosphere of love, learning and striving for excellence. In addition to the rigorous regime of study and athletics, there were also occasions when he'd be allowed to accompany his father on business trips. Usually it would happen just as his father was heading out the door; Mihaly would turn around and, barely able to suppress a smile on his usually stern countenance, select one of the older children to come along. These wonderful adventures could involve riding horseback all day along the Danube to inspect a stretch of railway construction or travel by overnight train to some far-off European capital. These treasured outings with his father were among Karl's favourite early memories.

This almost idyllic childhood continued until Karl's early teens, when a severe economic downturn brought a halt to Mihaly's flourishing railway business. He probably could have staved off bankruptcy if he hadn't resolved, as a matter of honour, to pay back his creditors in full. Although the family was still far from poor, the privileged life of Karl's childhood was gone. The Pollacseks had to leave their spectacular apartment, move into reduced circumstances in the city and give up their governesses and tutors, as well as their villa in the countryside. Furthermore, the older children, including Karl, had to contribute to the family income by tutoring, as well as taking on primary responsibility for educating the younger children. Worse, their father was now often away, obliged to take on assignments wherever he could find them, and these trips were no longer exciting short adventures that the children could accompany him on. The frequent absence of Mihaly transformed family life, which up until this point had revolved mostly around Mihaly's close relationship with the children and his personal supervision of their education and development.

But the financial setbacks were only a prelude to the real family tragedy, which occurred six years later when Mihaly Pollacsek died. Karl was nineteen at the time, in his first year of studying law, for which he had already developed a strong distaste. The financial burden of caring for the family now rested more heavily than ever on Karl and his older brother. With some financial help as well from their uncle, a

successful Budapest lawyer, the family survived without great material hardship. But the emotional chasm left in the lives of the children
was immense and, in the case of Karl, never really overcome.

For Cecile, the changes ushered in a new life. She had never quite
been comfortable in the role of managing a substantial bourgeois
household; indeed, the task had mostly overwhelmed and disheartened her. With the family's more modest apartment, she started to
assert herself and indulge in her own love of intellectual discourse.
Over the years, her living room became a kind of literary salon,
where intellectuals, literary figures and artists came together for
witty conversation and serious discussion. Cecile herself became a
central participant, admired by many for her cleverness, charm and
scope of interests. She was well read in Marx and Nietzsche, and kept
up on the latest intellectual developments abroad, including the
psychoanalytic movement. It wasn't long before the Saturday afternoon gatherings in her living room attracted the leading figures on the
Budapest intellectual scene.

Although the intellectuals who flocked to Cecile's salon had been
heavily influenced by Western political thought, they also flirted with
ideas that were considerably more radical. Socialism and Marxism
were treated very seriously, and were seen as the most promising
alternative to the repressive semi-feudal system of the Austro-
Hungarian Empire. At Cecile's salon, one could get up to speed on
the latest thinking from the more advanced revolutionary circles in
Russia and Germany. The salon was almost a clearing house for the
latest trends in radical thought. For the Polanyi children, it was hard
not to get caught up in the ideas that were constantly under discussion in the family living room. The eldest, Laura, in addition to being
renowned for her great beauty, was a feminist who was in the
vanguard of women attending university in Budapest. The next child,
Adolf, was a committed socialist who was one of the founders of a
socialist student group on campus and later served at a minor level in
the Bela Kun government.

Like his two older siblings, Karl was attracted to socialism. But his
attraction was always more theoretical and intellectual than activist.

His introduction to the world of socialist ideas had actually come
earlier in his life, by way of a family friend, Samuel Klatschko, a well-
to-do entrepreneur who married Cecile's best friend. Klatschko was
a free-spirited intellectual-adventurer who had run away from his
strict Russian family at the age of fourteen. In his many years wandering abroad, he had worked as a cattle herder in America and a photog-
rapher in Paris, where he became close to the early leaders of the
Russian revolutionary movement, especially Leon Trotsky. In Vienna,
Klatschko became a key figure in moving revolutionaries in and out of
Russia. The Klatschko household was like a second home to the
Polanyi children in their early years in Vienna. There, a young, impres-
sionable Karl Polanyi experienced not just a warm, inviting home full
of culture and music, but also a revolutionary atmosphere quite
exotic and different from his father's strict puritan world.

Klatschko was a mentor and teacher to all the young Polanyis. But
while brother Adolf and cousin Ervin Szabo eagerly soaked up his
lessons on underground activism and the tactics of revolutionary
movements, Karl was primarily inspired by the revolutionary ideals
and vision. It was as a law student that he first found a way to express
the political and philosophical interests that Klatschko had inspired in
him. Polanyi became involved in a student effort to defend a progressive law professor from physical attacks by right-wing students.
Having successfully repulsed the attacks, the group of progressive
students felt such a sense of camaraderie and intellectual kinship that
they wanted to stay in touch. They decided to form themselves into a
group called the Galileo Circle, which would be free in spirit, dedicated to decency, learning and teaching, above the fray of politics and
committed to reaching out to those in poverty. The principles were
very much Polanyi's, and he was chosen the group's first president.

The circle developed into an institution of sorts at the university, a
rallying point for students who were opposed to the intellectually
stifling regime of privilege and clericalism that dominated Hungarian
society. There was much talk within the circle about socialism and
socialist ideas. But Polanyi was above all—as a student and later in
life—interested in challenging accepted orthodoxies, in relentlessly

taking apart and destroying the accepted dogmas of the day in order to bring people to some new awareness. Thus Polanyi's approach was always one of slight detachment. Certainly, he wanted to change things. But he wanted to do so not by forcefully imposing another system, but by exposing what was wrong in the assumptions of the existing order. The activist side of the Galileo Circle was thus oriented not towards political agitation, but rather worker education. Polanyi himself was deeply involved in the circle's extensive efforts to teach illiterate workers to read and write, as well as to think critically.

Polanyi's involvement in the Galileo Circle brought him into a lively world of intellectual activities. He soon discovered that he was an effective speaker who could motivate a crowd with his passionate oratory. He also began writing analytical articles for left-leaning Hungarian journals and became part of an editorial collective operating the Galileo Circle's own journal, *Szabadgondolat* (free thought). His interests spanned politics, philosophy and literature, sometimes in combination. In an essay called "The Drama of Historical Materialism," Polanyi brought a Marxist analysis to the plays and essays of George Bernard Shaw.

Polanyi's intellectual life was beginning to flourish, but his emotional life remained depressed. After finishing his legal training, he practised law at a junior level in his uncle's firm, but he only grew to hate law more and more. It wasn't simply the dull, technical nature of the subject that Polanyi found offensive, but also the notion that a lawyer should be able to argue any position, regardless of its merit or truthfulness. He wanted to expose lies, not spin them for personal gain. He longed to do something else, but because of the heavy financial responsibility of contributing to the upkeep of the family, he felt honour-bound to stay. By his late twenties, he was trapped in a world he deeply disliked, with no clear path out. Oddly, his escape came only through the horrors of war.

In 1915, at the age of twenty-nine, he was called up for active duty to serve as a cavalry officer in the Austro-Hungarian army. The grim conditions on the Galician front in the winter were hardly conducive to improving his state of mind. The joyous experience of human tenderness and learning that had been such a part of his childhood now seemed impossibly remote, part of a world that had utterly vanished. His copy of *Hamlet,* which he carried in his breast pocket, was by now well dog-eared. The Shakespearean play spoke to his sense of despair and his feeling of failure, of hopeless inaction. He read it over and over; the beauty of its language and the power of its insight into human frailty offered him the only solace he could find from the death, cold, hunger and destruction all around him. Eventually, war injuries—coupled with a kind of nervous breakdown—delivered Polanyi from the war front to a hospital bed in Budapest in 1917.

With the war heading to its tumultuous end by the fall of 1918 and Polanyi mostly recovered, he became involved once again in political commentary and now even political action. Polanyi helped Oscar Jaszi, a respected leftist, establish the Radical Party, which became a key force in the Karolyi coalition government. But Polanyi worried about the growing strength of the Communist Party, which was exerting enormous pressure from the left. In his writing and public speeches, Polanyi underlined the difference between the socialism of the Radical Party, which was based on democracy, and that of the Communists, who sought simply to transfer power from the old elite to a new one. Even so, when the Karolyi government arrested a number of leading Communists, Polanyi denounced the detentions as wrong, heavy-handed and unnecessary.

The fall of the Karolyi government and its replacement with Bela Kun's pro-Soviet regime represented everything Polanyi had feared. He spoke out critically against the new regime, attacking it for concentrating too much power in the hands of the state. But he also volunteered to serve under it, spending three months in the People's Commissariat of Social Production. And when an uprising among rightist soldiers at the national military barracks threatened to topple the Communist government, Polanyi sided with the Communists, even sent a message to his old friend Gyorgy Lukacs—now a senior Communist official—that he would join the party in solidarity against the attempted rightist insurrection and the threat of foreign invasion. Just when being a Communist had become possibly life-threatening, Polanyi had signed up.

But while Polanyi had no trouble choosing between the Communists and the ultra-right, he was increasingly disturbed by the Kun regime—and by the very nature of Communism itself. It wasn't difficult to see the potential for tyranny in a system that handed extensive powers to a small elite, and then considered any actions carried out by that elite morally justified. But Polanyi's critique of Marxism went beyond the obvious potential abuses of the Soviet-style system. To Polanyi, the problem with Marxism was much more fundamental and was rooted in Marx's basic conception of human nature, which, Polanyi argued, was really quite similar to the conception of human nature found in capitalist ideology. Both Marxism and capitalism were based on the assumption that the desire for material gain was the overriding instinct in human behaviour.

Of course, Marxism and capitalism advocated radically different systems. Supporters of capitalism argued that this individual impulse towards acquisitiveness could be harnessed to benefit all of society. Marx rejected this upbeat conclusion, arguing that the capitalist system primarily benefited the owners of capital. But Marx accepted the notion that material gain was the central motivating factor in human behaviour. And he saw the struggle to improve material conditions as the driving force that pushed human society through an inevitable process of evolution, from feudalism to capitalism and eventually to socialism. Thus while they ended up proposing vastly different ways to organize society, Marxism and capitalism were both based on the idea that human beings are driven essentially by economic or material urges. In both systems, *Homo Economicus* was the central character.

Polanyi rejected this concept that humans are basically prisoners of their economic motives. Yes, the human body has certain basic physical needs, and meeting these needs is of paramount importance to all humans. But to extend this into a theory that effectively trivializes or diminishes the importance of all other human motivations is to seriously distort the human personality, Polanyi argued. He saw this kind of "economic determinism" as greatly underestimating human potential, and even stripping humans of their essential human quality— their capacity for honour, decency and moral responsibility. To note that humans often fall short in these areas is not to deny that they have the potential. This potential is a central and dynamic force in human society; it is the driving force behind all attempts at social betterment and human progress. By ignoring it, Marxism and capitalist economic theory had reduced human beings to little more than economic automatons, ultimately stripping them of their humanity and freedom.

Above all, Polanyi rejected the notion that people were victims of forces beyond their control, powerless to shape their own destinies. "There never existed a more absurd superstition," Polanyi wrote at the time, "than the belief that the history of man is governed by laws which are independent of his will and action"—a view that Polanyi saw as essential to Marxism. Polanyi deeply believed that humans had the capacity for moral vision, and that this capacity—not the impersonal forces of economic conditions—could lead them to build a better social order.

After three months of the Kun regime, Polanyi was convinced that Communism represented an obstacle to the kind of human betterment he profoundly believed to be possible. Deeply disillusioned and disheartened, he left Hungary in June 1919, following Oscar Jaszi into voluntary exile in Vienna.

At the Schwarzvald *pension,* where he was lucky enough to find accommodation, Polanyi slipped back into the depression that had haunted him during the war and before. It was only heightened by the presence of the bombastic Bela Balazs. The brief week Balazs was gone with the Danish woman had been one of the most peaceful at the *pension.* Now, with the arrival of Ilona Duczynska, Balazs's need to display his mental jousting seemed to increase, his revolutionary rhetoric to grow a little more flamboyant. Polanyi considered it to be only a matter of time before Ilona, like the others, fell into Balazs's camp, and likely into his bed.

But it soon became clear that Ilona was not like the others. She was a very unusual person, utterly lacking in pretense or affectation. It also, in very short order, became clear that she deeply believed in the possibility of human betterment, of improving the world. That was a belief Polanyi shared, although in recent months he had felt almost too weak from depression to think much about the world, let alone about improving it.

But those ideas now came trickling back into his mind, recalling some of the most powerful feelings and thoughts from his past. The task of improving the world had been presented to him as a moral duty by his father, as an idealistic dream by his mentor, Samuel Klatschko, and now as an exhilarating source of inspiration by Ilona. The impulse to improve the world was at the very core of her being, pulsing through each energized vein.

Together, Polanyi and Ilona read to Janos Lekai, and after their patient fell asleep, they would stay by his bedside, talking of Tolstoy late into the night. And gradually, as Polanyi noticed in Ilona's eyes something that wasn't there when she talked to Balazs, he felt, for the first time in almost two decades, a yearning once again to be connected to the world.

WITHIN MONTHS, KARL AND ILONA were a couple, and his dark, brooding depression had lifted. After interminable years of war, failed revolution and unhappiness, Polanyi now found himself living in what almost seemed like an impossible dream. Ilona's presence filled up his life, imparting a kind of raw energy and activism that revived his idealism. She was changed too, although in her case the change was perhaps less obvious. Although she would always remain committed to revolution, she absorbed from Karl a healthy scepticism about Communist leaders and their exercise of power. Before long, she had even published an article in an underground paper attacking the Communist Party for centralizing power too much and for encouraging violence as a means to social change—an argument that was a bit of a departure for someone who once had plotted an assassination. The article did not go unnoticed in Moscow; she was soon officially expelled from the party.

Oscar Jaszi invited both Karl and Ilona to work for him at a journal he edited for exiled Hungarians. They eagerly accepted. By the spring of 1923, Karl and Ilona had married and moved into an apartment in a working-class neighbourhood in Vienna. In June that year, their daughter, Kari, was born.

On a political level, Polanyi suddenly found himself in much happier surroundings as well. After living through the discouraging experiment with revolution in Hungary, he and Ilona were now in what was the closest thing to a socialist paradise. The city of Vienna—or Red Vienna, as it was popularly and proudly known—was a social-ist oasis in the middle of capitalist Europe. While Austria elected right-leaning federal governments, the municipality of Vienna over-whelmingly supported the Social Democratic Party. This was signifi-cant since Vienna, with a population of two million, had the constitutional status in the 1920s and 1930s of a virtually autonomous city-state. The socialists in Vienna enthusiastically used this power to transform the city into a deliberate showpiece of redistributive social justice. So while conservative forces backed by business and the Catholic church maintained control over the rest of Austria, the Viennese socialists boldly went their own way. They overhauled the Viennese tax system, imposing steeply progressive income tax rates and additional taxes on anything that could be construed as a luxury—carriage horses, dogs, liquor, restaurants, servants (one was allowed tax-free) and most forms of bourgeois entertainment.

These heavy taxes, dubbed "tax Bolshevism" by the more affluent classes of Vienna, allowed the municipal government to launch an ambitious program of social welfare that went well beyond what was available anywhere else in the world. It was all the more amazing, considering that it was carried out against a background of almost total economic breakdown, mass poverty and unemployment. Despite all this, the city established an extensive network of free nursery schools, kindergartens and day-care centres, which provided free lunches and school supplies. It established health clinics and special treatment centres for the many afflicted with tuberculosis. And in its most ambitious venture, it tore down slums and replaced them with attractive low-rise housing developments that provided a vision of a socialist urban landscape, complete with libraries, youth centres, bathing houses and dental clinics. The developments were often massive in scope—the Karl-Marx-Hof included 1,325 apartments—but they managed to provide appealing public and private space. While the apartment units themselves were small, they were bright and cheerful and all looked out on an extensive and attractive network of shared playgrounds and courtyards.

All this was wildly popular with the large and highly organized working class in Vienna, which was committed to socialism and to strong trade unions. There were more than half a million dues-paying union members in the city, and their lives revolved around their union and the Social Democratic Party. They bought their bread at a socialist co-operative, belonged to socialist cultural and recreational groups, lived in municipally owned housing, enjoyed strong labour protections on the job and sent their children to summer camps run by their unions. Labour Day parades filled the city's huge public boulevards; red flags were everywhere. In Vienna, it was possible to live one's life in what seemed like almost a completely socialist world. One could even avoid brushing up against capitalist exploitation at death: a socialist co-operative offered basic, no-frills burial services.

Ironically, the socialist stronghold of Vienna was also home to some economists who later played a pivotal role in pushing the Western world firmly back into the arms of capitalism. Ludwig von Mises and Friederich von Hayek, in particular, were prominent members of what became known as the Austrian school of economics—a school known for its fierce defence of free-market ideology. During the heyday of Red Vienna in the 1920s, von Mises railed against the socialist experiment from his position as secretary of the Viennese chamber of commerce. He also taught at the university, but as a Jew, he had little chance of serious advancement in the anti-Semitic academic world.

Although he was a voice in the wilderness in Red Vienna, von Mises found a sympathetic audience for his attacks on socialism at the chamber of commerce. In fact, von Mises's arguments were highly sophisticated and went well beyond simply raging against the "tax

Bolshevism." He argued that socialism was essentially economically irrational because it lacked a proper means of determining the price of goods. In a free market, von Mises noted, the price of goods was determined by supply and demand. Consumers would pay for the goods that they wanted. The amount that they were willing to pay signalled how much they valued a good. This was the information producers needed in determining what to produce. The price of goods was thus a vital signal that made it possible for the most efficient use of resources—that is, producing what consumers wanted at a price they were willing to pay.

Socialism, on the other hand, lacked a free market and therefore had no way of determining prices. Instead, prices had to be imposed by central planners. But this meant it was impossible to see what people wanted and therefore to know what should be produced; in other words, there was no way to make economically rational decisions that would make the best use of available resources. Of course, von Mises could not have picked a much worse venue for his attack on socialism than Red Vienna, which even its opponents acknowledged was an efficiently run operation. Von Mises himself didn't deny that Red Vienna was a tightly run ship, but he argued that it could succeed only because it was a small city in a huge, capitalistic continent, so it could freeload economic calculations from the broader free-market environment surrounding it.

Von Mises and his young research assistant, von Hayek, would go far in economic—and other—circles one day with these arguments, although they made little headway at the time. Among the increasingly strong and organized working class, as well as among the intelligentsia of Vienna, socialism was widely considered to be the wave of the future, the humane replacement for brutal, nineteenth-century-style capitalism. Polanyi, while he shared the view that things were evolving in the direction of socialism, nevertheless took the arguments of the Austrian school seriously. Von Mises was laying down a powerful intellectual challenge, predicting that owing to its lack of free markets, a socialist economy couldn't really work effectively. The issue struck Polanyi as profound and important, and he spent a lot of time pondering it. Indeed, he spent several years conducting a private seminar for interested students in his home in an attempt to come up with an answer to the very question that von Mises and the Austrian school had posed. He also published a provocative rebuke of von Mises in the prestigious German academic journal *Archiv für Sozialwissenschaft und Sozialpolitik*.

Polanyi began his article with a concession: von Mises was right; it was pretty well impossible to make meaningful economic calculations in a centrally planned economy. This would seem to have conceded the whole argument; without meaningful economic calculations, the long-term viability of socialism seemed questionable. But Polanyi was willing to concede no such thing. He immediately went on to declare that it was wrong to assume that socialism had to involve a centrally planned economy. This was a bold argument that, right from the beginning, set Polanyi apart from most of the socialist thinking of the time. Polanyi was wary of too much centralization, whether on political or economic matters. He had little faith that a small, unelected group, no matter how well meaning, could run things in the public interest. He was too strong a believer in human freedom and individual choice to agree to the surrender of that much power to a central bureaucracy.

But how could an economy be managed, if not by central planners or by the "invisible hand" of the marketplace? Polanyi's solution was to distribute power among a number of institutions in society, which would separately represent the interests of consumers and producers, with prices being negotiated between the two. (It should be noted that in Polanyi's model, producers are not corporations but the workers and the craftsmen who produce goods. These workers and craftsmen are, of course, also consumers. So the institutions representing consumers and those representing producers are really representing different aspects of the same people. Polanyi argues that as a result, there should be some basis for resolving differences.) In addition to these groups, Polanyi's model of a socialist economy included a body, called the Commune, which would represent the interests of the community as a whole, and which again was made up of individuals who were both producers and consumers. Polanyi's idea aimed to retain some of the dynamic effects of a competitive market economy for the purposes of setting prices, without surrendering power to the market.

At first glance, Polanyi's system seems bizarre. Having so many different institutions sharing economic power seems awkward and inefficient. But Polanyi's system is similar to the way modern democracies separate *political* powers between the legislative, the judicial and the executive branches. In the U.S., for instance, political powers are divided among the Congress, the Supreme Court and the White House. The idea is that the three separate branches will provide checks and balances against the abuse of power by any one branch, thereby safeguarding the public. Polanyi had, in effect, tried to accomplish the same checks and balances *for the economy*—an intriguing idea.

While Polanyi's economic model is more complicated than a market economy or a centrally planned economy, the same could be said of the political separation of powers. It would be far more efficient, in terms of getting things done, to have no separation of political powers. Imagine how quickly the White House—or the central government in any modern state—could get things done if it wasn't slowed down by opposition from Congress or the courts. But in the political sphere, we willingly sacrifice expediency in the interests of a more balanced distribution of power and protection from potential abuse. Strangely, in the economic sphere, we seem less willing to distribute power more widely, even though there is also reason to fear the concentration of too much power in the hands of individual players.

Polanyi's economic model also attempts to overcome a related flaw inherent in the market economy. The "invisible hand" of the marketplace might seem to be the perfect vehicle for working out prices on the basis of supply and demand. But in fact, the economic calculation the market makes is a flawed one, according to Polanyi, because it leaves out a crucial factor—social costs. In other words, the market considers only the bare costs of production, including the costs of labour and capital, without allowing for the extra costs of providing adequately for the needs of all members of the community. For Polanyi, these social needs are essential, and any economic system that leaves them out is not providing properly for society, nor is it giving a full economic accounting.

Indeed, Polanyi's emphasis on the primary importance of meeting social needs puts him outside the parameters of mainstream political debate today. In today's debate, the efficient operation of the market is regarded as essential, and the debate between left and right generally revolves around how much importance should be given to the secondary issue of meeting social needs, with the right wanting very little emphasis on social needs and the left wanting somewhat more. The left often bases its defence of the importance of meeting social needs on the grounds that doing so will actually enhance economic efficiency, as the highly productive social-welfare economies of Scandinavia show. (In fact, there's considerable merit in this position; there's a lot of evidence to show that investing in public health care or education isn't just more equitable, it's also more economically efficient.) Still, by making the defence of social needs contingent on the enhancement of market efficiency, the left is staying within the parameters of the debate established by the right. It is implicitly accepting the right's position that the market's efficient operation is the first and foremost goal. All else must fall in line behind that.

But Polanyi would reject the limited nature of this debate. He would start by rejecting the notion that the efficient operation of the marketplace is the required starting point. For him, the starting point is the well-being of society. He would have liked the concept of an index of economic well-being—rather than a measure of simple economic growth—although he would have insisted that even this broader concept wasn't broad enough. For Polanyi, the well-being of society included the material well-being of all members of society, as well as the cultural, ethical and moral development of the whole community. By this measure, we have things fundamentally backwards today: we let the needs of the economy dictate the nature of our society, while we should let the needs of our society determine the nature of our economy.

Polanyi argued that human motivation is more complex than the way it is presented in market theory. Humans are motivated not only to secure their own physical and material well-being, but also to live in strong, cohesive and just communities. This other side of human nature is simply left out of market theory, which makes the economic calculations of the marketplace of limited value. He argued that any meaningful economic calculation has to include social costs, which add an additional burden. Rather than trying to hide this burden or ignore it, Polanyi actually wanted to highlight it, to draw our attention to it. Only by doing so, he argued, will we become conscious of the strength of our moral will, aware that we are not only physical beings, but moral beings as well.

Whether or not Polanyi's economic model could have worked, it contains some compelling ideas. His insistence that socialism be based on human freedom—not centralized control—sets him clearly apart from the thinking that led to disasters like Stalinism and the Soviet repression of Eastern Europe after the Second World War. For Polanyi, there can be no true socialism without freedom, and anything else is not worth considering. Furthermore, his system of economic accounting also hints at themes that have become central to the more recent concept of "sustainable development" (that is, the notion that economic growth must take place in ways that are compatible with the protection of the natural environment and human communities). Like the movement for sustainable development, Polanyi accused the market system of failing to take "social costs" into account in its unconditional dedication to economic growth. By measuring success purely in terms of the speed of growth of GDP, the market system failed to factor in the simultaneous destruction of the environment or the rise of inequality that might result.

Above all, Polanyi wanted to challenge the notion that the market economy represented the only rational way to organize society. He wanted to show that it was both desirable and possible to give the social dimension of society precedence over the economic dimension. Later, he would do some of his most important work demonstrating that this desirable state of affairs—the supremacy of society over the economy—was not some bizarre idea, but rather the basic way that societies had organized themselves throughout most of human history.

❧

IT WAS JULY 1927, and Karl and Ilona were on holidays with their four-year-old daughter, Kari, at a resort north of Vienna when their idyllic world started to fall apart. Ilona first heard the news on the morning radio broadcast: tens of thousands of angry workers on the streets of Vienna had set fire to the Palace of Justice to protest the increasing threats from the right to Red Vienna and the socialist cause. Dozens were dead after a bloody clash with police. Almost instinctively, she rushed back to the city and witnessed first-hand events that would eventually lead to the end of a free Austria, as well as her own peaceful, happy life there.

It was a dramatic reawakening. While Ilona had never lost interest in politics, she had been lulled into a temporary tranquillity during the preceding few years. Her life had been almost completely transformed from her near-vagabond existence as a roving revolutionary. With her happy marriage to Karl and the warm, supportive community of Red Vienna all around her, she had returned to her studies and become preoccupied with her own small personal world.

Karl too had felt almost overwhelmed by the positive turn of events in his life. He was one of a small group that wrote and put together the respected mainstream weekly *Oesterreichische Volkswirt*, an Austrian equivalent of the *Economist*. While he was considerably to the left of the others who made up the editorial board, he commanded great respect for the scope of his knowledge about foreign events, and he was soon promoted to senior editor, in charge of world affairs. He would arrive at editorial meetings with a briefcase full of clippings from dozens of international newspapers; the sheer scope of his knowledge and persuasiveness of his arguments led him increasingly to dominate the weekly sessions. When the magazine's publisher went out of town, he left Polanyi in charge.

The events of July 1927 marked the beginning of problems for Polanyi at the *Volkswirt*. The publisher continued to have confidence in him and his grasp of international events—particularly the rising tide of Fascism in Germany and Italy. What had changed was the relationship of the magazine to the Austrian authorities. The freedom of speech that had been considered a basic democratic right in post-war Austria was no longer guaranteed. The rightist Austrian government made it clear that free speech was now a conditional right. Polanyi continued to write articles and commentaries that were clearly anti-Fascist, but increasingly his voice stood out in isolation, and the magazine became more visible in its dissent.

This turn to the right was in keeping with events in nearby European countries, but it was still something of a shock, given the different state of affairs in Austria. The Austrian working class was much stronger, more organized and committed to political action than the working classes of Germany and Hungary. At the end of the war, the working class had actually been in a strong position to seize power in Austria. As the war effort had collapsed, leftist elements within the Austrian imperial army had formed into clandestine groups and gained control over the vast Vienna arsenal, with its massive store of weapons. These clandestine groups thus had effective military control over what was left of Austria, and some wanted to use this sudden power to declare a workers' state, as the working classes had done in Russia and Hungary. But the established tradition of Austria's Social Democratic Party was more moderate, and the unions and workers in Austria had long looked to the Social Democrats for leadership. As a compromise, the Social Democrats agreed to the establishment of a parliamentary democracy, but they maintained the clandestine groups as a private army, now known as the Schutzbund, for the purpose of defending the working class from possible counter-revolution.

It was an odd arrangement, to say the least. Throughout the 1920s, a coalition of right-wing and Catholic parties managed to keep the

Social Democrats from actually holding power in the Austrian Parliament, but the Social Democrats remained the single most powerful and popular party in the country, and held power, of course, in Vienna. The party's enormous power and prestige was reflected in the fact that it continued to maintain the Schutzbund—a trained military force of some eighty thousand men, double the size of the official Austrian army—which openly carried out military drills throughout the country.

The nation's military weaponry remained in the arsenal, with an explicit agreement between the Social Democrats and the elected government that the arms were exclusively for the defence of the republic, and were not to be removed from the arsenal except by mutual consent. Crucially, the Schutzbund, which answered directly to the Social Democratic Party, maintained full control over actual access to the arsenal. Indeed, only a handful of senior Social Democrats and Schutzbund officials even knew exactly where the weapons were stored within the massive compound. This arrangement gave the Viennese workers a feeling of some security as they charged ahead in the bold adventure of creating Red Vienna. But it was also a situation that many in the country, particularly the increasingly militant rightist forces, found intolerable, and they grew impatient to smash the power of the Social Democratic Party and the working class itself.

The first challenge to the private military power of the Social Democrats came in the spring of 1927, when steel-helmeted troops from the Austrian army entered the arsenal, met no resistance and proceeded to remove trailer trucks full of armaments over a period of several hours. A crowd of angry workers gathered in front of the arsenal and demanded the action be stopped. But in a taste of what lay ahead in the coming years, the Social Democratic leader, Otto Bauer, declined to act. An important threshold had been crossed. The line long drawn in the sand by the Social Democrats had proved to be no line at all. Within weeks, a Schutzbund parade marching through the sleepy Austrian town of Schattendorf was fired on by members of a pro-Fascist paramilitary group known as the Heimwehr. A crippled war veteran and an eight-year-old boy marching alongside his father in the parade were killed. The killers were arrested, tried by jury and, at 10:00 p.m. on July 14, fully acquitted. The next day, as Ilona learned from the radio, Vienna erupted.

Once again the Social Democrats proved utterly unwilling to use the Schutzbund to defend the working class. The events in Vienna started as a peaceful mass demonstration against the acquittals, but things turned ugly after the protestors set fire to the Palace of Justice. Police opened fire into the largely unarmed crowd, killing eighty-five people, seventy-five of them members of the Social Democratic Party. A mass funeral for the seventy-five socialist victims was organized by the city of Vienna, with workers carrying their fallen comrades down the tree-lined city avenues before laying them to rest in a special place of honour in the city's main cemetery. There were bitter calls for revenge and an enormous, city-wide outpouring of grief. "I have had to attend many funerals which made news," wrote the *New York Times* correspondent G.E.R. Gedye, "but I hope I shall never see anything as terrible as the mass funerals of the seventy-five Socialist victims."

The right was emboldened, and grew more aggressive and violent in its attacks. It was further buoyed by the sudden and dramatic rise of Hitler in neighbouring Germany. Yet still, the Social Democratic leaders failed to act. Despite the strong public support they enjoyed and the growing calls within the party for some show of armed resistance from the Schutzbund, the party leaders continued to waffle and back off from confrontation. By March 1933, with Hitler now in power in Germany, any remaining pretence of democracy in Austria was finally destroyed. The rightist government suspended the Austrian Parliament and proceeded to rule by decree. In one of its first measures, it outlawed the Schutzbund. Still the call to arms failed to come.

By now, the situation for Polanyi at the *Volkswirt* had become untenable. As the situation in Austria deteriorated, he had tried to push the magazine to take a clear stance against what was happening, but the rest of the editorial board was reluctant to criticize the increasingly authoritarian regime. Polanyi's sympathy for socialism and for Red Vienna—which had been evident from the start—was now perceived to be a problem, and he began to feel unwelcome at the magazine. There was talk of a shortage of funds to pay his salary. This rejection felt all the more acute because there had been such camaraderie, such mutual respect among the editorial team. Within a few months of the suspension of Parliament, Polanyi quit the best job he had ever had and left to live in exile again, this time in England—and later, at least partially, in Canada.

Ilona stayed behind in Vienna with their daughter, Kari. Ostensibly, Ilona remained in Vienna because she was studying to complete her doctoral dissertation in physics, but the truth was that since July 1927, she had become obsessed again with politics. She sharply criticized the Social Democratic leaders for their failure to act, even putting out a small newsletter calling for a much stronger response to the rise of Fascism in Austria.

In the end, the rank and file of the Schutzbund took matters into their own hands. In February 1934, Schutzbund members in the city of Linz spontaneously opened fire on Heimwehr troops trying to seize their weapons. News of the resistance electrified working-class districts of Vienna, and local Schutzbund fighters rushed to take up positions in hundreds of designated areas. As the Heimwehr troops rallied in the capital, Schutzbund fighters searched desperately in the huge arsenal for the hidden cache of arms. But, unbelievably, they couldn't find them; the few local commanders who knew the whereabouts of the weapons had all been arrested. The Schutzbund fought with what arms they had, concentrating on defending housing complexes in working-class neighbourhoods. But with virtually no leadership or serious weapons, the great Schutzbund resistance was reduced to a few pockets of hopeless, bloody defiance. Most of it was over within a day. A few determined groups, cut off from food, water and ammunition, managed to hold out for three days. The first armed resistance to European Fascism had largely sputtered to defeat.

For Ilona, watching the events from her lab in the university's physics department, there was a terrible sense of helplessness. Only days before, she had made a last-ditch, desperate visit to the home of Otto Bauer, begging him to call the Schutzbund into action. But Bauer saw her as nothing but a disloyal troublemaker and dismissed her pleas. Even worse was the aftermath, as Ilona watched her friends and comrades being rounded up. Almost eight thousand Schutzbund fighters and sympathizers were arrested, and fifty-six men and three women were hanged. Within weeks, Ilona sent Kari to England and went underground herself, using the name Anna Novotny, and was actively working with the remnants of the Schutzbund, which had reconstituted itself as an autonomous underground movement.

With the clerico-Fascist forces fully in control, any political activities now had to be done in utmost secrecy. This meant, among other things, that it was difficult for the Schutzbund to keep in touch with the workers of Vienna. It was here that Ilona felt she could make a contribution, by making use of her knowledge of physics and engineering. She pulled together a small, trusted group of close friends and relatives with engineering skills. Meeting secretly in the evenings over a period of several months, they built a radio transmitting device so they could bring news of the Schutzbund to the demoralized workers of Vienna, and also encourage others to join the new underground movement.

The plan was to broadcast a message on the same wavelength as official Radio Vienna, during the three-minute interval in programming just before noon each day, when nothing but the gentle ticking of a metronome was normally heard. The range of Ilona's transmitter was limited, but the idea was to move it to different locations each time, to enable it to reach various working-class sections of the city. Moving it around would also reduce the chances of detection. With police and Heimwehr members now patrolling working-class districts, watching for any suspicious activities, each transmission would have to be done from a safe location and be carried out quickly and efficiently, before authorities could track down the source. Despite the obvious dangers involved, there was no shortage of apartments offered.

So with their homemade transmission devices tucked inside a box of sanitary napkins, which was carried inside a briefcase, the group gathered, one by one, in the chosen apartment. They quickly assembled their transmitter, and at the last moment, a young Viennese worker arrived to read the message, which Ilona had prepared. The group waited nervously for the low ticking of the metronome, and then the speaker launched into his script. Throughout the surrounding neighbourhood, a voice could distinctly be heard over the sound of the metronome: *"Hallo, hallo, hier spricht der Sender des Schutzbundes!"* As soon as the message was over, the text was ripped up and flushed down the toilet. The machine was dismantled, the devices put back in their hiding spot in the briefcase and the group left, one by one.

There were five broadcasts in the course of a month, each one from a different location. The messages clearly had some impact: there were reports of the pirate broadcasts in Viennese newspapers, and the police searched the surrounding area each time, looking for the perpetrators. It's possible that the messages brought some comfort into working-class apartments during those grim days in Vienna. It's also possible that they helped the Schutzbund's efforts to reconnect with the workers after the failed 1934 uprising. (The Schutzbund continued to operate clandestinely until the middle of 1936, when it was effectively swallowed up by the newly emerged Austrian Communist Party. Some twelve hundred Schutzbund fighters made their way to Spain to fight Franco's Fascism in the Spanish Civil War, and others later joined the French and German resistance during the Second World War.)

If nothing else, the radio broadcasts were small acts of defiance, carried out by Ilona and the others at great personal risk. With Hitler's shadow extending over Europe, Ilona left Vienna in 1936, joining Karl and their daughter in England.

KARL HAD FOUND WORK as a teacher for the Workers Educational Association, an academic adult-education program operated by Oxford University. It provided him with a modest living and an introduction to English economic history. Polanyi was also pleased to be working again in the field of adult education, as he had with the Galileo Circle in Budapest. But the Oxford program was less political; it focused on worker self-improvement, rather than on giving the working class the "intellectual and cultural equipment" to transform society. To Polanyi, the education of the working class should involve more than simply equipping them to get ahead in a capitalist society; it should empower them to change that society.

And certainly, in the case of the British working class, there was a lot of work to be done on this front. The lack of a strong working-class culture was something that Karl and Ilona found very disturbing about Britain. The British working class not only lived in poor conditions, but seemed relegated to a distinctly inferior status. In marked contrast to the high material, political and cultural standards achieved by the workers of Red Vienna, British workers lived deprived, down-trodden and demoralized lives. Certainly, to Karl and Ilona, Britain lacked the charm, passion and decency of Red Vienna. Before Fascism had destroyed it, Red Vienna had been an amazing experiment in which public-spiritedness and a sense of community had been harnessed to build a surprisingly inclusive, egalitarian society out of the ruins of war. With far fewer resources than were available in Britain, the citizens of Vienna had created a society that met the basic needs of its people, and then some.

The poor condition of the British working class and the class-ridden nature of British society struck Polanyi as being curiously at odds with the official story of Britain as the birthplace of modern rights and freedoms. To be sure, British political freedoms were impressive—all the more so in contrast to the Nazi oppression that was spreading across Europe—but the common people of Britain didn't seem empowered and thriving, as the common people of Vienna had. In British lore, the people had risen up centuries ago against a too-powerful monarch, fought a revolution that clipped the monarch's wings and established a parliamentary democracy devoted to the rights of the individual. But as Polanyi looked deeper into British history, he became convinced that one could regard what followed the revolution as a triumph of rights and freedoms only if one concerned oneself mostly with the rights and freedoms of a small elite group of merchants and property owners. This elite had used its new-found power in Parliament above all to transform Britain into a market economy, thereby opening up for itself new economic opportunities, as well as guaranteeing for itself economic rights that had previously not existed.

But for hundreds of thousands of other people in Britain, the rise of the market economy had been a hellish experience. For the common people, the transition had involved the seizure of their most basic rights and freedoms. These rights and freedoms—which had been essential to their survival—were simply ignored, denied, trampled and revoked.

It seemed to Polanyi that here was a further important omission from the official triumphal tale—the enormous popular resistance that accompanied the transformation to a market economy. Although uneducated, the common people of Britain had clearly understood that their rights were being taken away, and they resisted bitterly and with whatever means they had available, from generation to generation, over a period of centuries, from the 1500s through the 1800s. In that intense resistance, Polanyi saw the same anti-market, communal spirit that had been the source of inspiration for Red Vienna.

All this was central to the question that increasingly came to interest Polanyi: what was man's true economic nature, and therefore what kind of society best suited human needs and aspirations? According to market theorists, humans were driven by greed and material acquisitiveness, and a market economy was simply the best vehicle for expressing this true nature. But if greed and acquisitiveness were so central to human needs, and the market economy was the expression of this nature, how was one to account for four centuries of resistance to the coming of the market economy? Why did so many people resist so ferociously and for so long something that was apparently designed to set them free?

The story of that resistance undercuts the sense of celebration surrounding the rise of the market economy, which is probably why we hear so little about it. Oliver Cromwell's battles and the tales of the Glorious Revolution are indelibly imprinted on Western minds as part of the story of the triumph of rights and freedoms. But we rarely ask, Whose rights? Whose freedoms? In the powerful words of the eighteenth-century poet Oliver Goldsmith, who sided with the common people in their battle against those taking away their rights, "[They] call it freedom / When themselves are free." Certainly the fact that we know little about centuries of resistance against the coming of the market doesn't mean that the resisters were any less passionate, or that the rights they sought to defend were any less "natural" than the rights imposed by the victorious merchants and property owners who gained control of Parliament. It's probably just that the resisters haven't had the enthusiastic chroniclers to laud their efforts and hype their cause, as the victors have had. The resisters were simply, in E. P. Thompson's memorable phrase, people who were "of no importance to anyone but themselves."

IT WAS IN ENGLAND that Polanyi researched and developed the themes that would become the basis of his most important work. Published in 1944, *The Great Transformation* is the story of the rise of—and the resistance to—the market economy. That same year, Frederich von Hayek, the disciple of Ludwig von Mises, published his book *The Road to Serfdom,* which is a fierce attack on socialism and Communism, and argues strongly for the market economy and private property.

Both books are, in their own way, masterpieces. The fact that Hayek's was widely celebrated and became a kind of Bible of our times, while Polanyi's has been largely ignored in mainstream circles, tells us nothing about the merits of the two books, but a great deal about what the dominant class wanted to hear.

# CHAPTER FIVE

# Behind the Hedge

IT MAY BE HARD for us to imagine fully the terror that can be caused by the sudden appearance of a regular garden-variety hedge. Yet there was almost nothing else that put more fear into the hearts of the common people of England in the fifteenth, sixteenth, seventeenth and eighteenth centuries. For these common people—mostly small tenant farmers living a pretty marginal existence—the large prickly hedge might just as well have been a steel barricade topped with barbed wire, because the effect was the same. It meant that they were suddenly blocked from entering the huge expanses of field and stream from which they had, as long as they and their parents and grand-parents could remember, retrieved all the necessities of life. All of a sudden, sometimes overnight, the presence of a quickly transplanted hedge could signify that they were without any means of feeding themseves and their families, that they would soon be obliged to join the vagabond poor.

This was the stark, horrifying reality faced by hundreds of thou-sands of people over three or four centuries as Britain was trans-formed into a market economy. What was going on is usually referred to as the enclosure movement, which was really the first wave of privatization. The semi-communal society of the Middle Ages was being transformed into a society built around the notion of private property. In practical terms, this meant that land that had been avail-able in some way to all or most of the community was suddenly cut off from public use and available only to its wealthy owner. This "common" land had amounted to roughly one-third of the land in England; it included vast tracts of pasture, as well as huge forests and marshes often referred to as wastes. The term is misleading, however, since these wastes were full of wildlife and natural resources of great value to the people.

Any history of Britain will recount the importance of this transformation for the improvement of agriculture and for Britain's development into a huge exporting power. But let's, for a moment, follow the small farmer as he or she—women were very involved in the work of the farm—walks down the well-worn path of knee-deep mud, leading a couple of large oxen, to find a hedging hawthorn bush suddenly spreading across it. On the other side of that thick bush lies everything the farmer needs. To begin with, the oxen are hungry and thirsty, having just spent the day pulling a heavy wooden plough through the thick earth of the farmer's field, which could range in size from a few acres to several dozen. Oxen are amazing creatures, capable of putting in an honest day's work with little slacking, but their huge bodies require, at the end of the day, large amounts of grass and water. The only way small farmers are able to keep their operations afloat is by providing their plough beasts with copious amounts of grass to graze on and a stream to drink from. This system had worked for centuries because small farmers had access to a large stretch of "common" land—the same land that had just disappeared forever behind that damn hedge.

Also behind the hedge was much more that farmers—as well as craftsmen and small merchants from the village—needed and had previously had easy access to. Behind the hedge lay ample acres of pastureland for their cattle to feed on, as well as the wastes, where they could scavenge for wood for fuel or for making repairs to their homes and barns. Their little cottage-like houses could be almost entirely constructed with material found in the common land. There was always plenty of bracken, heather and rushes to make thatched roofs. By gathering up dead wood and new sprouts of willow branches and rolling them together with clay, farmers could make a kind of plaster for walls and fences. Stones and slate were always useful, and sometimes peat moss and coal could be dug out of marshy or flooded land. There was also plenty to eat here. And tenant farmers and villagers enjoyed "gleaning" rights—that is, the right to gather up any corn, or what we would call grain, left in the fields after harvest. And fruit and berries growing on trees were plentiful, as were fish in the millponds and rabbits and deer darting through the woods. Indeed, there wasn't too much the resourceful fifteenth-century farmer needed that wasn't found somewhere out there on the common land.

All this gave the common people a fair degree of independence and freedom, surprising as it may seem to attach these words to people living in such humble circumstances. Although their lives were simple and hard, and their standard of living minimal, they enjoyed access to a treasure trove of natural resources that allowed them to meet their basic needs. As a result, notes the historian R. H. Tawney, these fairly poor people were able to "exercise that control over the conditions of their lives which is the essence of freedom, and which in most modern communities is too expensive a privilege to be enjoyed by more than a comparatively few." The loss of this access to the common lands was therefore accompanied by a real sense of lost freedom, a sentiment captured in contemporary verses like this: "Enclosure came and trampled on the grass / Of labour's rights, and left the poor a slave."

Now, "common" may be a misleading term. It's not that the land was some kind of huge free-for-all playground where anybody could do anything. In fact, it was a tightly regulated space available only for specified uses. But these uses served the interests of a large number of people in the local village and surrounding area, and had been recognized from time immemorial, sometimes by actual legal title and sometimes by long-established tradition. The system that determined who enjoyed what rights was actually quite complicated; there were simple grazing rights (with the type of animal specified and the number of each animal permitted; pigs, for instance, were not usually permitted on the common land because they were deemed to eat too much). In addition, there were rights known as "common of estovers," which meant the right to take essentials like wood from the common land, or "common of turbary," which meant the right to dig below the common land's surface in search of fuel.

All these rights had derived from feudal times, when they had been granted to the villagers in exchange for performing services and duties for the feudal lord, such as helping out with his crops at harvest time or taking up arms in times of war. These rights, over the centuries, became firmly entrenched and widely accepted as part of the legal code of the country. An important legal principle, embodied in something called the Statute of Merton, had established back in 1235 that lords who enclosed land for their private purposes were required to ensure that sufficient common land remained to enable tenants to exercise their traditional rights. That statute was re-enacted in 1549, and the courts continued to recognize the principle of "user rights" on the common land.

But if the rights to the common land can be traced back to some real or imagined concession made by a feudal lord, in practice the villagers of the fifteenth and sixteenth centuries were pretty well managing the use of the commons on their own. Since everyone's livelihood was so heavily dependent on proper access to the common land, the villagers worked together to guard this precious resource, vigilantly preventing anyone from taking more than he or she was entitled to. If a farmer dared to slip an extra cow onto the common or, God forbid, a hungry pig, the rest of the village would protest. There were regular meetings in which the village people worked out problems of this sort, readjusting regulations for the common land for common advantage and improvement, perhaps arranging to rent out an extra bit of pasture on behalf of the community. As Tawney notes: "In practice, the whole body of customary tenants are found managing their commons on a co-operative plan."

The co-operative way a village operated can be seen in the response of the village of Wootten Basset, a small borough in Wiltshire, to a particularly nasty enclosure of a huge tract of common land in 1555. The local people had long enjoyed rights to the two-thousand-acre common land of the manor, until the property was inherited by a mean-spirited new lord, Sir Francis Englefield. Sir Francis decided to enclose the property to provide better grazing for his extensive herd of sheep, leaving his tenants only one hundred acres of the original two thousand for grazing and other rights. The devastated community got together and carefully apportioned among themselves the crucial grazing rights to the small remaining common land. "[T]o the Mayor for the time being two cowes feeding, and to the constable one cowe feeding, and to every inhabitant of the said Borough, each and every of them, one cowe feeding and no more."

What is most striking about the Wootten Basset case is the communal approach the villagers took to the management of the common land. Even after suffering the catastrophic setback of losing nineteen-twentieths of what they had previously enjoyed, they decided to divide what remained in a highly equitable manner. Some fifty years later, when disaster struck this little village again, they once again hung together, and clung to their sense of common entitlement. This time, the grand-nephew of the despicable Sir Francis, apparently dissatisfied with his great-uncle's taking of virtually everything the villagers had, enclosed the one hundred acres of land that the villagers had been forced to get by on for the previous two generations. The villagers together petitioned Parliament "to enact something that we may enjoy our right again." The grand-nephew responded by launching a number of lawsuits against the tenants. As the lawsuits dragged on endlessly without resolution, the grand-nephew's sheep and cattle grazed undisturbed on the contested bit of turf, while the plough beasts of the villagers grew thin and weak from lack of nourishing grass. Eventually, with their beasts withering away and their legal bills mounting, the villagers were driven into bankruptcy.

Their strong communal sense, like the strong sense of rights, has its roots in the feudal era. One of the striking aspects of the feudal age is the entirely different approach to the notion of private property. Today, private property is the foundation of our economic system, and much of our legal system is designed to protect our right to enjoy the use of our property and to enable us to accumulate more of it. But the medieval approach to property was more communal, and more conditional on the rights of the community as a whole. It wasn't that people then didn't have private property. They definitely did, and there were clearly huge inequalities between the holdings of the elite and those of the rest of society. Still, property rights were more qualified; ownership of land came with plenty of strings attached. Ultimately, these strings had to do with the performance of duties that were considered to be one's necessary contribution to the community.

Of course, we just encountered this same principle above, in the case of the farmers who enjoyed certain rights to the common land in exchange for duties and services performed for the lord of the manor. This concept—that property rights were conditional on service performed—permeated all levels of medieval society. The lord of the manor didn't fully own the land any more than his peasant farmer did. Rather, he held on to it and benefited from its produce in exchange for performing duties for the king, such as raising an army when necessary and meeting obligations at court. Even the king, in theory at least, had obligations. The medieval historian Bede Jarrett argues that there was an explicit "social contract" in the Middle Ages that obligated the king to behave in a certain manner in exchange for enjoying the allegiance of his people and a handsome share of the nation's wealth. The thirteenth-century philosopher St. Thomas Aquinas made this point when he argued that the public would be justified in rising up against a king who went beyond the proper bounds, because "by his non-observance of that fidelity to which his own kingly oath committed him, he has not observed his compact with his subjects." Fear of torture or imprisonment might well have discouraged subjects from testing this right, but the notion that the king had obligations to the people was nevertheless a justification for his control over the kingdom and its resources.

While the king and the lords certainly got the better end of the deal, they were still subject to the notion that all property came with obligations attached, and that those obligations involved performing some kind of service for the community, contributing in some specified way to the "common good." Thus while private property existed, it wasn't simply something to be privately enjoyed. Rather, it was part and parcel of a function one performed in society. It was perhaps more accurate to think of property as being "held" rather than "owned." In a sense, property didn't really belong to any one person; it ultimately belonged to the whole community. Jarrett describes the medieval attitude towards possession as "reducing all ownership of property, whether house or cattle or arms or castle or land, to mere conditional use." He goes on to note that the basic principle of medieval society was that "the means of production remained in the hands of the community."

This is a striking notion, with overtones of Communism, and it lies at the very heart of medieval thinking. Unlike our society, where the individual is deemed to come first, in medieval society the community came first—after God, that is. So while medieval society was based on the notion of the supremacy of God, what came next in line after God was the whole human society created by God. This society was not seen just as a chaotic assortment of individual beings. Rather, it was an ordered community, and everyone had a place in it, as well as a responsibility to contribute to its overall well-being.

Society was often likened to the human body—a functioning mechanism that required the co-operation of every different part, each performing its own function and ultimately making possible the operation of the whole. A little muscle in the finger, a piece of the lining of the stomach, a blood vessel leading to the brain—each had to perform its individual task for the proper functioning of the body. This metaphor of the human body, with each part doing its essential task—a metaphor that was constantly invoked in religious writings from the twelfth to the sixteenth century—certainly helped medieval religion justify a society riddled with inequality and exploitation. Every little piece was a vital part of the whole, and the whole was God's plan. But this thinking also reveals something else that is significant and too often forgotten about the pre-market medieval world: there was a deeply embedded notion of community and the interconnectedness of human society.

We will come back to the peculiar nature of this medieval mindset—peculiar at least to us—but first let's return to the poor farmer confronted with the hedge as the market economy starts to

establish itself. The farmers and villagers fight back with every
(limited) means they possess. They pursue legal actions, often pooling
their resources; they appeal to Parliament in the later years, even
though Parliament is often the source of their troubles. But above all,
they fight back with spirited, spontaneous and often pathetic attempts
to physically re-open the common land, using their crude farming
tools to hack through hedges, rip out fence posts, fill in ditches, poach
fish or game from suddenly restricted lands or do anything else necessary to restore access to what they feel is rightfully theirs. There are
extensive legal and administrative records of these anti-enclosure
protests taking place over a wide swath of England over the course of
many centuries. In some cases, they involved perhaps only a farmer or
two and their families cutting down a hedge in the middle of the night
or filling in a ditch where a hedge is about to be planted. But they also
included hundreds of rowdy and sometimes violent "riots," and even
several large-scale revolts.

What was clear in all of these protests was the strength of feeling
and sense of violation on the part of those losing their rights. In one
typically bitter feud that raged over two generations, for instance, the
villagers of Finedon, Northamptonshire, were enraged when, in
1509, the lord of the manor, John Mulsho, enclosed their common,
as well as a crucial raised path that allowed them to pass between two
connecting fields and that they had regularly used for village proces-
sions. There was much litigation on both sides, and a local commis-
sion settled on a compromise that obliged Mulsho to keep some of the
common land open for part of the year. In 1529, his enclosures were
removed by order of the sheriff. Following that, a number of farmers
decided to chop up Mulsho's gates and gateposts. Some sixty rowdy
villagers arrived on the scene to dig up the roots of the hedges so that
they couldn't grow back. For eight days, the villagers continued with
their protest, hooting and shouting against the enclosures and defiantly ringing the village bell. Mulsho responded by seizing their
cattle. The protestors then broke into his pound to set their cattle
free, even turning the animals loose on one of Mulsho's lush pastures,
where the hungry beasts made quick work of the tall grass. In subse-

quent litigation, the villagers were ordered to replant hedges that had been removed illegally. They did so, only to organize another riot to rip them down.

Many of the protests were larger in scale. In June 1535, four hundred people forcibly removed the enclosures erected by the unpopular earl of Cumberland at Giggleswick, on his estate in Craven. This resulted in indictments against eighty-two of the rioters. Within a month, in an apparent response to the Craven situation, anti-enclosing riots broke out in Lancashire, Westmoreland, Cumberland and Northumberland. Five months later, there was rioting against enclosures in Galtres Forest in East Yorkshire. Another more extensive wave of anti-enclosure rioting broke out in 1548 and continued the following year. Increasingly, rioting seemed to involve large groups that went from village to village, urging others to join them in widespread destruction of enclosures. To discourage such large, roaming bands, it was made a treasonous offence for twelve or more people to band together for more than an hour. If the rioters kept their numbers below twelve (three to eleven was specified) and worked quickly, they could get away with being charged only with "riot and maintenance," a misdemeanour punishable by a mere one year in prison.

But the harsh laws did little to discourage the protests, which picked up in number and intensity in response to the more aggressive enclosure actions on the part of landowners by the end of the sixteenth century. From the early 1500s to about 1625, there were anti-enclosure riots recorded in every county. In the Midland Revolt of 1607, there were a number of riots with more than one thousand participants, and sympathetic riots occurred across the countryside. They also became bolder in format. In Ladbroke, Warwickshire, in 1607, a band of four hundred protestors, led by a "captain" on horse-back and a piper, openly marched in military-style formation as they advanced to the task of levelling hedges and pulling out hedge roots.

Not far away, an enclosure dispute in Welcombe, near Stratford-on-Avon, managed to drag in William Shakespeare a few years later. Shakespeare, by this point a celebrated success near the end of his life,

had invested some of his money in shares in revenue-producing properties from the Welcombe estate, owned by the local proprietor
William Combe. When Combe decided to enclose his open fields and
turn them over to sheep pasture, he assured Shakespeare there would
be no reduction in income from his shares, and Shakespeare offered
no objection. But the town of Stratford was strongly opposed, and a
number of townspeople appeared on the scene in time to fill in the
newly dug ditches where the hedges were supposed to go. One of the
diggers, Thomas Greene, was a friend of Shakespeare's, and some
Shakespearean scholars believe the bard ended up playing a heroic
role in defending the rights of his fellow townspeople. They argue that
notes made at the time by Greene reveal that Shakespeare, once he
fully understood the situation, indicated he "was not able to beare the
enclosinge of Welcombe," thereby providing Greene's band of diggers
with a powerful celebrity endorsement for their cause. Greene's
notes are apparently a little ambiguous, however, and it's also possible
that it was Greene himself who couldn't bear the enclosure, and the
playwright was content to know that his money was secure.

These tales of anti-enclosure resistance, which are representative
of hundreds and hundreds more like them, shed light on the depth of
attachment people felt for the common land, and their keen sense of
violation at losing access to it. With that loss, life changed dramatically for the vast number of farmers and craftsmen who made up the
ranks of the common people. The choices at this point were incredibly bleak. One option was to try to disappear into the still-immense
spaces of forest and wastes that were not yet developed, build oneself
a makeshift shack and hope to eke out a primitive existence in
hiding, poaching the occasional deer or pigeon from the parks of the
nobles. Needless to say, the punishment for anyone caught doing so
was harsh—castration for poaching the king's deer, for instance. One
could try being a mobile vagabond, hoping to sell one's services as a
pedlar, palm reader, card player, singer, actor or minstrel, or
performing any other service that was in high demand. However,
even if one were able to earn a penny or two entertaining a crowd
with card tricks or palm reading, this sort of vagabond existence was

not permitted. A series of measures known as the settlement acts came down heavily on this form of homelessness, calling for vagabonds to be flogged. In London, there were whipping posts every few hundred yards to deal with the problem of people begging on the street.

Such harshness reflected not only a clear lack of sympathy for the plight of those who had lost their rights, but also the fact that the propertied classes had other plans in mind for this newly idle group of people. The conversion to the new market economy required more than land enclosures. It also required the services of this motley crew of would-be pedlars, palm readers, actors, forest squatters and beggars bleeding at the whipping posts. The market economy desperately needed all of them. The propertied classes had managed to secure their own rights to private ownership, but they now needed someone to do the work so that they could strip off the surplus value created and turn it into profits for themselves. It was simple: no wage labourers, no profits. This of course helps explain the distaste of the rich for the "idleness" of the poor, their contempt for all those dirty, lazy men hanging around the whipping posts. The usefulness of the poor was not lost on the rich. "We hardly have poor enough to do what is necessary to make *us* subsist" (his italics), noted Bernard Mandeville, an eighteenth-century philosopher. "It would be easier, where property was well secured, to live without money than to live without poor; for who would do the work?" Or as Lord Goderich succinctly put it in the nineteenth century: "Without a class of persons willing to work for wages, how are the comforts and refinements of civilized life to be procured?"

Of course, the desire of the propertied classes to have the poor's labour didn't mean they were willing to offer wages that were sufficient to live on. It seemed that they had no intention of paying such wages. One landowner, Sylvanus Taylor, complained that he had trouble finding workers to perform a day of heavy labour, since the idle poor considered his wage offer insufficient to live on and would "as good play for nothing than as work for another." The poor had a point. If they were unable to eke out a subsistence existence on what they could make in wage labour, perhaps it was better not to work, to take their chances in the woods or the fields, where they could "play," or at least remain somewhat in charge of their own lives.

Hence the need for some strict punishment to discourage "the most damnable vice of idleness." In 1530, a law specified that any beggar found outside his local area was to be "sharply beaten" and then flogged back to his home town (where, presumably, he'd get a job). Under a statute that came into effect some twenty years later, during the reign of Edward VI, any vagabond or other poor person without a job could be made a slave. In 1559, this law was beefed up to include the new provision that even once an employee's term of service was completed, he was not permitted to leave the local area without permission.

Despite these punitive measures, the poor still didn't take to wage labour as readily as the rich had hoped. Hence more clarity and discipline in the law seemed required. The Statute of Artificers in 1563— during the reign of Elizabeth I, who today enjoys a reputation as a just and far-sighted monarch—tried to set things straight. This brutal statute makes it clear that when market incentives failed, the state had no reluctance about forcing the poor into wage labour in the then new economy. It called for forced labour for anyone either under thirty or unmarried who had been trained in a craft. Any other males between the ages of twelve and sixty were required to work as farm labourers. The only exceptions specified were "gentlemen born" or those attending university, which only gentlemen born had the resources to attend. Furthermore, once in this wage labour, one was obliged to stay. The Statute of Artificers went on to specify that anyone leaving a job without permission would be whipped and considered a vagabond—which meant one could be enslaved and also branded, so as to be easily spotted as a troublemaker. Anyone forging a letter from an employer granting permission to leave was also subject to whipping.

All this suggests that the transition to a market economy, far from being a liberating experience, was in fact the opposite for the majority of people. One could argue that the descendants of these people—

or at least many of them—have fared well as a result. But that's another matter really. Certainly, people throughout history have chosen to make sacrifices in the hopes that their children would be better off somewhere down the road. But that isn't what we're dealing with here. We're dealing with people who were not given any choice, who did not elect to suffer themselves in order to make a better life for their children. (In fact, it's clear that they thought their children would be worse off as a result of the change, that it would leave their children deprived of the traditional rights they and their forefathers had enjoyed. And at least over the following generation or two, they were undoubtedly right. We'd have to go several generations forward before we saw much improvement.)

But once we take away the argument that it was all for the best *in the long run*—a conclusion based on a number of arbitrary assumptions about what might have been—we are left with the simple reality of what happened to the particular people involved. And it certainly seems hard to believe that having one's livelihood taken away and then being forced, under threat of whipping, into below-subsistence wage labour would be anyone's idea of "freedom." It also seems obvious— and necessary—to acknowledge that the transferring of property to the exclusive use of one individual removes it from the use of others. And this would seem to raise a question: what about the rights and freedoms of those others? Are they to count for nothing? If a pasture or a woodlot that is providing sustenance for a large number of people is enclosed for the use of one individual, are the common property rights of all others not extinguished? It's hard not to hear Oliver Goldsmith's words jingling somewhere in the background: "[They] call it freedom / When themselves are free."

The notion that the market economy brought rights and freedoms to the people is clearly one encouraged by those who benefited from it. The group that did benefit—and that went on to prosper, and to interpret history—was the landowning class, as well as a new class of merchants and entrepreneurs. After rising against Charles I in the English Civil War, which led to his execution in 1649, they were able to win a new set of legal protections that clearly established private property rights and brought an end to the king's power to arbitrarily interfere with their property. No longer would it be necessary, as it had been in the past, for a landowner to curry favour with the royal family to secure his estate and ensure there would be no arbitrary interference in its safe transfer to his heirs. Henceforth it would be law—not the whims of the king or his cronies—that would determine one's right to property.

But while these new property rights were a great boon to the wealthy upper classes, and also benefited some yeoman farmers who could establish property claims, the lower orders lost ground, since the traditional rights they had enjoyed were simply eliminated along with the system of feudal tenure. And this was no oversight. All the changes were deliberately and carefully put in place by the new Parliament, which consisted of people elected exclusively by members of the propertied classes. (The two bodies of Parliament corresponded to two sets of property owners—the House of Lords representing the titled propertied class who generally had immense land holdings, and the House of Commons, representing the untitled propertied class, whose property holdings were of varying but still substantial size.)

And to underline the importance it attached to the changes, Parliament reconfirmed its new approach to property rights in 1660, when it accepted the return of Charles II as monarch under restricted terms. At that time, Parliament reconfirmed the abolition of feudal tenure and also the establishment in law of private property rights. The parliamentarians also reconfirmed—so there could be no mistake about this equally crucial point—the elimination of the traditional "common" rights, on which the lower orders had previously relied so heavily.

All this may seem inevitable, part of the march of history towards progress, although it's interesting to note that it didn't necessarily seem so then. Tawney makes the point that, at the time, nothing seemed more inevitable than the rise of the peasant farmer, whose life was clearly getting better and better! In the early days of the revolution, it had seemed to many as if this trend would simply continue.

There had been real hopes among the lower orders that the uprising against the king was going to result in the establishment of a more egalitarian system—a notion that was often encouraged by rebel leaders in order to keep the common people willing to fight in the rebel army. Specifically, there were expectations that bringing an end to the absolute power of the monarchy would lead to the restoration of "common rights." Some groups had organized to press for this result. The Diggers and the Levellers, for instance, were ordinary folk who saw the overthrow of the king as a chance to enhance the power of all the people, not just rich people. The Levellers wanted to level the playing field for all. The Diggers, it will be no surprise to learn, believed that everyone should have the right to dig and plant on the common lands.

This dream of reviving common rights is reflected in the views of the Digger leader, Gerard Winstanley, who argued that bringing an end to the despotic powers of the king was just the beginning. "[K]ingly power is like a great tree spread. . . . That top bough is lopped off the tree of tyranny . . . but alas oppression is a great tree still, and keeps off the sun and freedom from the poor commons still." Winstanley insisted that the next step was for Parliament to "give consent that those we call Poor should Dig and freely Plant the Waste and Common Land for a livelihood. . . .We claim our freedom in the Commons."To Winstanley, the private property rights the rich were establishing for themselves amounted to a kind of theft that permitted them to "lock up the treasures of the earth from the poor."The Diggers envisioned a revival of traditional common rights—without the dominance of king and landowner that had been part of the system in the past. In other words, they wanted to preserve the communal aspects of traditional society while rejecting its repressive, hierarchical structure. Now there's an appealing idea.

This perhaps seems like a utopian fantasy, but it might not have been as far-fetched as it sounds. It should be remembered that roughly one-third of the land in England at the time was common or waste land—that is, land that was already effectively administered for common purposes by local townships and villages. It was this land that the Diggers wanted made available for the common people to cultivate—land that was already largely available to them. In other words, it was those in the propertied classes who wanted to change things radically by gaining full control themselves over otherwise shared property. By contrast, the common folks who made up the ranks of the Diggers simply wanted to reaffirm and strengthen their claim to what they already had access to. Winstanley justified their case by arguing that the land should belong to those who labour on it, and that only through one's labour does one acquire a claim to the land. This argument about labour being the root of property rights is later echoed in the works of John Locke, although with very different results—a subject we will return to in the next chapter. For Winstanley, the vision was clearly one of a society of small stakeholders, each entitled to enjoy nothing more than the fruits of the land where he personally laboured.

Of course, things didn't turn out this way. When kingship was officially abolished on March 17, 1649, Winstanley and his fellow Diggers were disappointed—although probably not surprised—to discover that the declaration of England as a free state and a "commonwealth" didn't actually mean that the wealth would be shared in common. By the early months of 1650, groups of Diggers had decided to proceed without parliamentary approval, establishing little communal colonies on the waste lands, where they were busy digging and planting. At least ten such colonies were established in central and southern England, and the local gentry and clergy called for army intervention to eject the squatters. Convinced that the Diggers represented a dangerous idea, the government responded in April 1650 by driving Winstanley's Digger colony out of Cobham Heath, and taking similar steps against the other Digger colonies soon afterwards. The unarmed colonies put up little resistance. Still, their easy suppression by the new forces of private property probably had little to do with the level of popular support for their different approach, and a great deal to do with who had the guns. Had the common people been better organized and armed, the result could well have been different.

In fact, the triumph of the propertied interests wasn't necessarily inevitable. Nor was their new system of private property the only possible model for development. As the historian Brian Manning has noted, "[T]he central issue of the 1630s and 1640s, and of the English Revolution . . . was to decide whether the landlords and big farmers or the mass of the peasantry were to control and develop the wastes and commons." The real issue wasn't whether there would be development or no development, but who would get to do the development and who would benefit from it. No doubt the market enthusiasts will assert that the propertied classes alone were capable of doing the development—a plausible assertion, but one that, like so much else they assert, remains unproven and probably unprovable. Tawney counters that those who opposed enclosure weren't necessarily averse to the kind of consolidation of properties that is considered essential to improved agricultural cultivation; indeed, this sort of consolidation had been going on at a more gradual pace for a long time without causing problems, and would no doubt have continued to do so, allowing cultivation to continue to improve. "What aroused alarm, and produced rioting and legislation," according to Tawney, "was a movement the distinctive feature of which was that it was initiated by lords of manors and great farmers . . . in short, by the wealthiest and most powerful classes, and that it was carried out frequently against the will of the tenants, and in such a way as to prejudice their interests."

So the notion that the choice was either the reforms advocated by the propertied classes or nothing is undoubtedly painting the picture too black and white. It might be more accurate to say that the propertied classes were able to improve cultivation *at a faster pace* by ruthlessly seizing control of the land. (Similarly, it's true today that development can move ahead faster by ignoring people's rights.) But what was the price that was paid for that extra speed? Who paid that price, and who received the benefits? Karl Polanyi argues that if the propertied classes had been able to move faster still with their enclosure plans—as they desperately tried to, only to be blocked by the Tudor and early Stuart monarchs—English society would likely have suffered much more serious damage. The transition to a modern economy in England was made socially bearable, says Polanyi, only by the fact that the enclosure movement was slowed down considerably from what the propertied interests wanted. An even slower pace, with much more recognition of the rights of the common people along the way, would likely have worked out better still—if we are considering more than the interests of the powerful few.

Taking away the peasantry's rights to the land was the first and most crucial step in setting up a modern market economy. But it certainly wasn't the only one. Stripped of access to land and its natural resources, and pushed into wage labour, the formerly self-sufficient peasant still had a ways to go before he or she could become the true *Homo Economicus* envisioned by the theorists of capitalism. Also necessary was the unleashing of greed and acquisitiveness. This part surely promised to be easy. After all, these traits had always been present in the human personality. So a transformation to a society that based its economic system on greed and acquisitiveness should be effortlessly accomplished; it would presumably involve nothing more than the removal of the rigid restrictions on private profit-making that had been imposed by the oppressive medieval system. Yet, oddly, the transformation didn't turn out to be easy. As in the move from common to private property, there was plenty of popular resistance. Once again, those being liberated showed a strange lack of enthusiasm for their liberation.

AT FIRST GLANCE, THE "food riots" of the seventeenth and eighteenth centuries appear pretty straightforward. They started, not surprisingly, with hunger. Despite the remarkable improvement in agricultural methods and production in these centuries, the price of bread frequently rose to levels that made it unaffordable to most ordinary people. And bread was what these people lived on; it made up the bulk of their diet. Paying for bread was what their daily financial struggle was all about. By working twelve hours a day, six days a week, a weaver or a cobbler or a miner hoped to earn enough to provide the family with an adequate supply of bread. The cost of the family's bread consumed close to half of its income; when that cost went above half its income, the squeeze became acute. Hungry and desperate, they would pick up a cudgel, a large wooden spoon, a horn or some other artifact they found lying around, start hooting and hollering, and along with neighbours also hooting and hollering, parade through the cobblestone streets of the town in what historians call a "food riot."

These kinds of spontaneous outbursts were surprisingly common, and were particularly prevalent and vigorous in the years 1709, 1740, 1756–57, 1766–67, 1773, 1782, 1795 and 1800–1801. Historians have long attributed them to simple hunger, which undoubtedly was the driving factor. But E. P. Thompson, in his masterful, detailed study of the phenomenon, noticed something more.

Let's look at what happened, for instance, when a group of food rioters stopped a wagon full of wheat being driven through the town of Handborough, Oxfordshire, in 1795. A couple of women in the crowd eagerly climbed aboard the wagon and boldly pitched a few sacks of grain onto the road. Now, 1795 was a very bad year for grain prices. And despite the abundant fields of wheat in Oxfordshire, the price of grain was high, making things extraordinarily tough for people whose diet relied heavily on the bread they baked from this local grain. So the people in this crowd were hungry and angry, and they outnumbered the one farmer driving the wagon. The townspeople of Handborough could easily have made off with a few sacks of grain or maybe the whole cartload, giving them enough to bake dozens of loaves of bread and feel a whole lot better. But that wasn't what happened. The townspeople had no intention of stealing. What they wanted—and were prepared to insist on with force, if necessary—was to buy the grain, but to buy it *at a fair price*.

And so the riot proceeded with a strange sort of chaotic decorum. "Some of the persons assembled said they would give Forty Shillings a Sack for the Flour [considerably below the going rate], and they would have it at that, and would not give more, and if that would not do, they would have it by force," according to one contemporary account of the events. The farmer, apparently seeing the appropriateness of the price adjustment, accepted the lower price, and the grain changed hands at the new going rate. In a similar incident that year, a baker by the name of Thomas Smith was carrying a load of bread on his horse into the village of Hadstock, in Essex, when he was stopped by a crowd of more than several dozen women and children. One of the women, identified only as a labourer's wife, grabbed Smith's horse and asked if there had been a reduction in the price of bread. When he answered no, she angrily replied that he'd better cut his price or he wouldn't be allowed to sell any of his bread in town. At this point, several others in the crowd offered him nine pence for a quarter loaf. But Smith insisted the price was nineteen pence—a price the crowd considered nothing short of highway robbery. Several women grabbed a few loaves from the bread baskets slung over his horse. After reconsidering his situation, Smith agreed to the lower price.

What is striking about these incidents, and all the others like them, is not the boisterousness of the crowd, but almost the opposite. Despite their hunger and neediness, these people seemed very restrained and circumspect in their demands. While they were prepared to use force and threats of force, they were not really thieves. They were basically law-abiding. What angered them was that they felt others were taking unfair advantage of them. Indeed, they had a strong sense of what they felt was right and fair, of what was *morally* justifiable. They were convinced, for instance, that the high price of bread was a result of avaricious human behaviour, which violated their moral standards. Their response was to try to set things right, to pay what was really due.

This sense of morality and fair play is evident in much of what has often simply been dubbed "food rioting." At times, it seems almost absurd to call these people rioters, so mannerly, responsible and fair-minded do their actions appear. In an incident in Portsea, in Hampshire, also in the bad year of 1795, a "mob" approached the town bakers and butchers and demanded to be charged what they considered fair prices for bread and meat. According to a contemporary account of the event, "[T]hose that complied with those demands were paid with exactness." However, the bakers and butchers who did not agree to cut their prices soon found their shops plundered *"without receiving any more money than the mob chose to leave"* (my italics).

The idea of angry rioters calming themselves after a frenzy of plundering so they can carefully count out and leave the exact amount that they consider fair is curious and almost touching. And this sort of insistence on a fair set of rules wasn't restricted to setting a fair price. Equally odious to the "mob" was any kind of cheating, whereby unfair advantage was taken by those who control access to the food supply. Millers and bakers were constantly accused of adding cheap ingredients to the bread—including everything from "Acorns, Beans, Bones, Whiting, Chopt Straw and even dried Horse Dung" to "sacks of old ground bones"—in order to squeeze an extra bit of profit out of their sales. Similarly, millers and bakers were often accused of using faulty measures or weights, or of presenting a loaf of bread as weighing more than it really did. In one bizarre case, a London magistrate happened upon a crowd angrily taking apart the shop of a baker who was accused of selling underweight bread. But once again the action of the crowd—not to mention that of the magistrate—might seem unusual to us. With the arrival of the magistrate, the mob promptly stopped its hooliganism and focused its energies on drawing his attention to the underweight bread, eagerly presenting the scrawny loaves for his inspection. The magistrate carefully weighed and examined the offending loaves and, concluding the crowd had a point, proceeded to distribute the loaves to the rioters.

The magistrate's action makes more sense once we learn that the price of bread was carefully regulated by law. Bread—and ale, for that matter—were considered far too important to be left to the vagaries of the marketplace. Hence the people were demanding that the law—which they considered fair—be enforced. And the magistrate, despite the strong-arm methods employed by the crowd, found merit in their position. Indeed, much of the rioting consisted of hungry people insisting on nothing more than the enforcement of laws designed to protect them from the full force of the marketplace.

This insistence on protection from the caprices of the market is also evident in the enormous hostility towards exports of local food supplies in times of shortage. In such times, dealers tended to buy up local supply and ship it to London, where they could get higher prices. When this happened in Cornwall in 1773, there was a large-scale riot by more than seven hundred local tinners. The crowd was so angry that after they offered the just price and were turned down, they didn't bother with any further politeness. They simply broke down the cellar doors and took the corn, skipping the usual courtesy payment. Even more contemptible than dealers who exported grain to London were those who exported it right out of the country, most commonly to France. In one case in 1740, a merchant in North Yorkshire, who was caught exporting grain during a shortage, was dunked in the river by an angry crowd. To avoid such misfortunes, merchants tried moving grain headed for export during the night. In the shortages of 1795 and 1800, crowds set up night roadblocks, forced the wagons to stop and unload their grain in the dark, and refused to let it leave the local parish when people there were hungry.

Another economic player who came in for strict censure by the community was the middleman—that is, anyone who made profits by inserting himself between the producer and the consumer. In the moral world of the common people, the producer and the consumer were both performing a vital function in society, and each needed the other. What they strongly felt they didn't need was someone coming between them, fiddling with the supply or taking advantage of the demand, and thereby jacking up the price and siphoning off part of the profit for himself. In other words, they strongly felt they didn't need what would today be considered normal business practice.

To prevent these sorts of abuses, strict rules governed the operation of markets and placed restrictions on middlemen. Under the rules, farmers were required to bring all their grain themselves to the local market as soon as it was ready. They were not permitted to sell it to a middleman before it was harvested, nor were they allowed to delay in bringing it to market themselves in the hope that prices would rise. Once at the market, there were more rules. Sales weren't permitted before the ringing of the first morning bell at 8:00 a.m. At the sound of the bell, the poor—the word used to describe the common people—could buy their grain or flour, in the portions they wanted, with authorities carefully supervising the weighing and measuring of their purchases. Once the poor had been taken care of, a second bell rung at about noon and dealers were allowed into the arena. The rules were only slightly more lax at this point. Neither seller nor dealer was allowed to deal in samples, perhaps to prevent a seller from showing an attractive sample and then, once the sale was completed, hauling out a cartload of defective grain. The dealer was also prevented from buying up a quantity of grain or flour, holding it for a few months and then reselling it in the same market or in a nearby market.

What's interesting about these rules isn't even the amount of detail. Our markets today are also full of detailed regulations—although of a different kind. What is striking about these rules from the sixteenth and seventeenth centuries is that they aimed to prevent people from exploiting a situation, from using leverage to advance their own interests, from profiting at the expense of others. In other words, they sought to prevent a very basic part of what the market economy is all about—the maximization of profit by gaining advantage, which implicitly means advantage over others. In a market economy, sellers seek to get the highest price "which the market will bear"—that is, what they are able to collect. If buyers are particularly anxious to get a product, sellers can likely get a higher price for it. They can take advantage, in other words, of the neediness or eagerness of the buyer. The fact that this might put a squeeze on the finances of the buyer is not an issue in a market transaction. Similarly, buyers don't concern themselves with whether sellers are able to make an adequate profit from a sale. Neither buyers nor sellers have any particular concern about the details of each others' lives.

It is precisely this dehumanized aspect of the market system that offended and alienated the protestors of earlier centuries, who hadn't yet adapted to the market mentality. Not being sufficiently schooled in market principles, they seemed unable to grasp—or unwilling to accept—the notion that there was no such thing as a "fair price," that instead the price was whatever the buyer could get away with charging. To the protestors, it seemed intuitively obvious that the price should have a *moral* basis—that is, it should be linked to issues like the amount of work and effort performed by the seller, not the level of desperation of the buyer. Similarly, it seemed *morally* obvious to them that the common people should be able to buy grain at the cheapest price, in the portions they required, since their resources were limited, and that dealers shouldn't be allowed to deny people access to grain so that they could hold it until it was more valuable (and thereby maximize their profit).

This popular insistence that the economy operate according to some moral laws was deeply at odds with the new market-based system. In essence, the market system was all about liberating the economy from moral rules. This represented a dramatic break with traditional approaches to economic issues. What distinguished the earlier approaches was their refusal to separate economics from morality, or a sense of "fairness"—precisely the same insistence we find in the food rioters of the seventeenth and eighteenth centuries. This moral approach is similar to the approach taken by no less an intellectual superstar than Aristotle—who, by the way, would have fit in well with the crowd taking apart the bakers' shops or throwing the sacks of grain off the horse in the eighteenth-century English countryside. In his writings in the fourth century B.C., Aristotle drew a clear moral line between economic activities aimed at providing for the needs of oneself and one's family, which he considered just, and those aimed at acquiring more than one needed, which he considered an unworthy activity.

This moral approach to economics became even stronger and clearer in the medieval period. Medieval thinkers had quite a lot to say about the economy, and what they said was very much in line with the teachings of Aristotle. The most important of these medieval thinkers was St. Thomas Aquinas, a nobleman born in Naples in about 1225, who became the most respected scholar and theologian of his day. Although he didn't live beyond his forties, he managed to produce the massive *Summa Theologiae,* which became the leading philosophical tract and moral guidebook of the Middle Ages. Aquinas was heavily influenced by the writings of Aristotle, whom he referred to with great deference. Like Aristotle, he took a strong moral position on the economy, developing this approach into a comprehensive line of thought.

It's worth noting that Aquinas had no interest in the operation of the economy for its own sake. His interest arose purely in connection with his moral concerns. The *Summa Theologiae* is an intellectually complex inquiry into the question of how humans should behave. First and foremost, they should serve God, Aquinas argued, elaborating at great length. He then turned to the perhaps trickier question of how humans should relate to each other. It is in this section that we encounter questions about the economy. But it won't come as a big surprise that the questions here don't deal with things like how to increase one's earning power or how to corner the market in grain. Rather, all the economic questions arise as moral issues. Aquinas— and the medieval world in general—argued that one should behave in a way that served the common good. By this, the medievalists meant that a person's behaviour must promote social cohesion and harmony, and thereby benefit the community as a whole.

One begins to see the extent of medieval restrictions when one considers that economic activity was supposed to be guided by one basic principle: "Whatsoever ye would that men should do unto you, do ye also unto them." This left little room for market notions like "Whatever the market will bear" or "Buyer beware." The idea that one strives to maximize one's advantage and gain the upper hand in any transaction, an idea central to the market system, would have been unacceptable to medievalists. Aquinas theorizes that the practice of buying and selling must have been introduced into the world for the common advantage of mankind, and therefore for the *equal* advantage of both parties. An equal result could not be achieved, he argued, if an article was sold for more or less than it was worth.

Certainly, the idea that the price of a transaction should be determined by the neediness or strength of feeling of either party was rejected as morally wrong. For instance, if a seller would suffer greatly by parting with something he was selling, Aquinas said that both sides should agree to a price above the object's real value—so as to compensate for the seller's pain! If it was the buyer who would suffer from having to do without, the seller shouldn't take advantage of this by jacking up the price. The buyer might perhaps offer to pay more, to reflect how much he or she cared about the object, but this would be a voluntary additional payment. The historian W. J. Ashley notes that medieval theory held that prices "should not vary with momentary supply and demand, with individual caprice, or skill in the chaffering of the market. It is the moral duty of buyer and seller to try to arrive, as nearly as possible, at [the] just price."

This may leave the impression that medieval price negotiations consisted of each side trying to figure out the extent of each other's pain, and therefore how best to compensate the poor soul. In fact, a group of influential medieval theologians known as the Schoolmen were aware of and allowed for the fact that humans frequently didn't live up to all that was expected of them. The Schoolmen showed themselves to be quite capable of moral flexibility on occasion to allow for a little human frailty. For instance, it was considered a moral duty for a seller not to deceive a buyer about a product—not to boast of the great eyesight of a one-eyed horse, for example. But on the other hand, if it was obvious that one of the horse's eyes didn't work—perhaps it was hanging out of its socket or the horse was wearing an eye patch—then it was fine for the seller not to draw additional attention to the matter. Similarly, a grain dealer wasn't obliged to point out to potential purchasers that other grain dealers were in the neighbourhood and might be willing to sell at a lower price. In analyzing the moral issues involved in the grain-dealer case, Aquinas showed himself capable of as much wiggling as any lawyer. He noted that it would certainly be a sign of moral virtue for the grain dealer to disclose the presence of competitors in the neighbourhood, but if the grain dealer chose to say nothing, he wasn't to be condemned for immorality. After all, grain would drop in price only after the arrival of the other dealers, so if the grain dealer sold his grain before the others arrived, he would technically not be selling at the wrong price.

For that matter, a seller could even get away with selling the one-eyed horse if he had reason to believe the buyer didn't need a two-eyed horse. In other words, it's permissible to sell a defective article under some circumstances, because the product might be adequate for the purposes of someone else. In 1378, a London tanner was accused by the craft association of cordwainers (shoemakers) of selling "false" hides. In a proceeding before the mayor, the tanner conceded that the hides were not of good enough quality to be sold to cordwainers, but he argued they were good enough to be used by other craftspeople. The tanner was clearly well versed in the intricacies of medieval economic thinking, and might have got away with his crime, except that the jury was stacked with a crowd that knew a totally worthless hide when they saw one. With every relevant craft represented on the jury—two saddlers, one pouchmaker, one girdler, two leather bottlemakers, two curriers, two tanners and two cordwainers—it became impossible for the tanner to make the case that his hides could be of use to anyone.

Given these common human frailties, the medieval world considered it appropriate, indeed morally necessary, for the proper authorities of state, town or guild to step in and regulate much of the economy. Certainly, as we've seen, it was standard practice for the authorities to establish a "just price" for some basic goods. The affordability of bread, ale and some other necessities was simply considered too important for the well-being of the community to be left to negotiation. The possibility of an individual gaining leverage over the consumer market—that is, over the people in the community—was simply too great, and this would almost certainly have a negative effect on the well-being and harmony of the community.

So how was this "just price" to be determined without reference to supply and demand? The Schoolmen had other principles in mind. They were strong proponents of the work ethic, and saw an intrinsic merit in human toil and effort. Thus the just price to a large extent

reflected the amount of work effort that was deployed in the prepa-
ration of the product. There was also an implicit recognition of skill,
education or importance of function, and different jobs or crafts or
professions were assigned different levels of reward. Medieval society
was of course highly stratified, and its notion of "justice" involved
giving everyone "that which is his due." And what was due to a cobbler
was deemed to be very different from what was due to a magistrate.
What was due to a cobbler and to an unskilled worker also differed.
There was a standard of comfort—if it's not stretching the concept of
"comfort" too much to apply it to the lifestyle of a thirteenth-century
craftsman—that was accepted by public opinion as appropriate for
the cobbler, and the just price for his products were set at a level that
allowed him to maintain this standard.

Of course, this could be seen as nothing more than an elaborate
justification for tremendous inequality. For that matter, it could be
noted that the medieval criticism of material acquisitiveness was
highly selective. Certainly, there was no prohibition against well-born
members of society—including those within the top ranks of the
Church—living very indulgent material lives. Indeed, one is sometimes tempted to conclude that the medieval lectures against excessive materialistic urges were mostly designed to discourage the lower
orders from having any yearnings for the bounty they saw on their
masters' tables. Undoubtedly, the desire to keep the lower orders in
their place, satisfied with their limited material possessions, played an
important role in the medieval discouragement of greed and acquisitiveness.

But it also seems to go beyond this. Consider the medieval
approach to usury. Despite the clear ban on usury, there were a
number of powerful banking houses that operated in the Middle Ages
openly charging interest on loans. But the customers of these banking
houses were always well-to-do merchants or nobles, even kings—in
other words, people who weren't helpless against an avaricious
moneylender. The point of the ban on usury was to protect the
vulnerable, and it wasn't considered necessary to extend this shield to
those who were able to fend for themselves. So while merchants and

princes borrowed at whatever rate they could negotiate—and often faced quite punishing rates, despite their considerable bargaining power—the poor man in the village was considered too vulnerable to be left in this sort of situation, and was therefore shielded by an elaborate set of laws from the potential tyranny of the moneylender. As a result, he was often able to get the money he needed for free, just as he was expected to help out others like himself when they were in need. The ban on usury, ultimately, was about putting the well-being of the community ahead of an individual's right to accumulate personal wealth. And the lifting of the ban in the fifteenth century was not only "the dawn of modern banking," but the start of the era of elevating greed above all else.

IN THE CONTEXT OF medieval thinking, the moral ideas of the food rioters start to make more sense. Now we can see that the crowd taking apart the baker's shop in Portsea in 1795 was acting on the basis of a moral code that was not unlike the moral code that prevailed centuries earlier, in the Middle Ages. In fact, there was a striking similarity. In both cases, there is a rejection of the market notion that one could and should attempt to gain advantage over others in an economic transaction. Both the medieval theorists and the food rioters—and, let's not forget, Aristotle—believed that personal greed and the pursuit of material gain should be tempered and controlled in the interest of preserving the well-being of the whole community.

Now this raises an interesting question. Where does this idea come from, and how is it passed on from one era to the next? How does it survive after the sixteenth century, when it clearly runs counter to the market principles that increasingly are adopted and encoded in the prevailing laws and cultural attitudes (including attitudes towards religion, which come to co-exist more comfortably with individualism and eventually with market principles)? In the face of this massive change in social, economic and religious thinking, how do the distinctly anti-market, "common good" ideas stay alive in the hearts and minds of the rioters of the sixteenth, seventeenth and eighteenth centuries? It's clearly unlikely that the food rioters in Portsea had been reading Aristotle, or that they were well versed in the thinking of Aquinas and other medieval Schoolmen.

E. P. Thompson addresses this last question, and comes up with an interesting theory. He attributes the persistence of these ideas to a kind of "popular memory," kept alive and passed from generation to generation partly through oral recounting and story-telling. He notes that the defiant actions of the rioters seemed to follow closely the set of rules established in Elizabethan times to deal with emergency food shortages.

These rules, set out in something called the Book of Orders, were a detailed set of measures aimed at protecting the community from the "greedie desier" of those involved in the growing and selling of grain, who "bee not content wth anie moderate gayne, but seeke and devise waies to kepe up the prices to the manifest oppression of the poorer sort." The Book of Orders empowered magistrates and local juries to go right into farmers' barns and granaries to determine the size of the grain stocks and make sure no grain was being held back so it could be sold later at a higher price. Despite the changing times, or perhaps because of them, the moral rules for governing the economy set out in the Book of Orders remained a powerful notion for many people—sufficiently powerful that the Book of Orders, which isn't exactly a page-turner, was republished in 1662 and again in 1758. The 1758 edition included a preface that highlighted the contemporary relevance of the themes in the book to the "wicked combination to make scarcity."

Thompson's case about the "popular memory" is intriguing. But my guess is that this only partly explains the strong moral sensibilities and sense of injustice felt by the protestors. What is going on seems to be even more basic than the memory of an earlier moral code. Rather, I suspect, there is something deep in the human psyche, something perhaps innate, which is surfacing here. It comes back to the idea that we are, first and foremost, social animals. It seems to follow that as social animals, we would have a natural inclination towards figuring out ways to live in communities with minimal friction. And it seems almost intuitively obvious—unless one has been taught otherwise—that an economic system based on personal greed, acquisitiveness and gaining advantage over others is not ultimately conducive to social harmony and community well-being. The kind of moral order envisioned by Aristotle, Thomas Aquinas and the food rioters of later centuries might have been based on a kind of "natural" urge in human beings to build a functional, workable social order—a social order where humans feel their needs are met and they are adequately secure.

This is not to deny that there are also "natural" human urges to be greedy and acquisitive, as well as aggressive and even hostile (and certainly members of a community are often aggressive and hostile towards others outside the community). But the human propensity for greed and aggressiveness is not in doubt; we live in a society that seems to have concluded that greedy, acquisitive, aggressive, even hostile urges are pretty well the only ones that are natural. What is in question—or rather, what is often overlooked in our age—is the "naturalness" of the social aspects of human behaviour, including the tendency to resist the market, with its encouragement of self-serving and anti-social behaviour.

What could be more natural, for instance, than for eighteenth-century English villagers to feel angry and offer resistance as they see grain from nearby fields carted off to France when members of their own community are hungry? To respond as the market theorists teach us to—that is, to let the grain dealer pass by peacefully, confident that we will all be better off in the long run as a result of his foreign sales—is an unnatural response that must be learned. It may or may not turn out to be a sensible response, but it certainly isn't the response that comes naturally. The natural response appears to be spontaneous rage—a rage that the grain dealer's profit is given precedence over the well-being of the community. It's possible that this rage reflects a moral sensibility that is deeply ingrained in our beings.

❧

WHEN WE THINK TODAY of medieval society, on the rare occasions that we do, we tend to focus on its primitive aspects—its barbarism, its lack of human rights, its curious obsession with the construction of churches. All these things were undoubtedly true about it, and in the subsequent centuries, we've largely rejected this world. We've shaken off the obsession with constructing churches, and have struggled to move away from the barbarism and the lack of human rights—although sadly the results on these important fronts have been more mixed. But it's worth noting that there's another aspect of pre-market society that we tend to ignore: the notion of community, and the idea that there is a "common good" that should take precedence over private gain.

The response to this statement might well be that the concept of the common good was mostly rhetoric, that the reverence for community was never what it was cracked up to be, that the teachings of Christian moralists like Aquinas and the Schoolmen concealed massive hypocrisy. There is, of course, considerable truth to these charges, as noted above. While the Church preached Christian love and non-exploitation of one's neighbour in trade and commercial matters, it was itself a massive profit-making institution, riddled with corruption at all levels and the largest property owner of the day. And while the Church publicly denounced greed and materialism, those occupying its senior ranks lived in such splendour and opulence that it was clear they considered the anti-materialist message to be important primarily to others. Similarly, the feudal lords had no trouble endorsing a system that, in addition to providing peasants with a bit of free pasture on less desirable tracts of land, also provided the lords with free peasant labour—labour that was ruthlessly exploited for the benefit of the lord (the one in the manor, not in the heavens). So the desire to assign the medieval world to the trash bin of history is in some ways understandable. Make no mistake: the medieval world was exploitative, brutal, hierarchical, authoritarian, superstitious and hypocritical.

If that sounds like the end of the matter, I would still insist that it shouldn't be. There was much about medieval, pre-market society—

in many ways, a world of very small-scale stakeholders—that worked rather well. And there appears to have been an enormous sense of loss on the part of many when it was taken away. The historian Christopher Hill has brought together a powerful collection of popular seventeenth- and eighteenth-century ballads and poems about the loss of a sense of community—a literature that at times sounds like a painful cry from the heart for the lost world of "merrie England."

It should also be said that even when the medieval world fell dramatically short of the ideals it espoused, there was something inspiring about what it was aiming to achieve. R. H. Tawney points with admiration to the "insistence of medieval thinkers that society is a spiritual organism, not an economic machine, and that economic activity, which is one subordinate element within a vast and complex unity, requires to be controlled and repressed by reference to the moral ends for which it supplies the means."

Undoubtedly, human nature has a greedy and acquisitive side. But is that reason enough to abandon all attempts to create human societies based on other, more socially harmonious traits *which are also part of the human personality?* This is a particularly important question if we add the notion that, if anything, the social instinct, with its implicit desire for social harmony, may be the most basic and constant aspect of our human makeup. If this is correct, giving prominence and free rein instead to the anti-social instincts of greed and acquisitiveness seems to be setting the bar for ourselves needlessly low. In retrospect, the medieval attempt to bring under control, rather than to constantly excite, the appetites of greed and acquisitiveness—to make greed the servant, not the master, of civilization—seems reasonable, even laudable. Despite the huge gulf, then, between theory and practice in the medieval world, Tawney insists that the greatness of what was being attempted "still glows through it all with a certain tarnished splendour."

# CHAPTER SIX

# The Master, the Servant, the Horse and the Grass

FOR A FAIRLY SMALL and ineffectual group, the Luddites have managed to generate a lot of press over the years. Their appearance on the world stage was brief. Between the years 1811 and 1816, this band of unemployed English mechanics carried out physical attacks on the new machinery that had thrown them out of work—in much the same way that in the preceding centuries, small peasant farmers and craftsmen had taken up hoes and cudgels to tear down hedges barring their cows from traditional pastureland. In the end, the impact of the Luddites was virtually nil. But their memory has been kept alive, largely because it serves to illustrate the hopelessness— and foolishness, because they are always held up to ridicule—of anyone resisting new technology and a changing world.

What is arguably most interesting about the Luddites, however, is not widely known. And that is the ferocity of the reaction against them on the part of those trying to put the new economy in place. While destroying machinery was obviously a crime against property, the British Parliament wanted to send a clear message that this sort of interference in the new economy would be treated more harshly than any normal sort of property damage. Thus it passed a bill making such attacks on machinery punishable *by death,* thereby creating a new legal concept—an eye for an eye, a tooth for a tooth and a life for a sewing machine. Despite an impassioned plea against it by Lord Byron, the bill was passed into law by the House of Lords with only three dissenters.

The enthusiasm for the anti-Luddite bill shows that members of the elite understood well the potential appeal of Ludditism—and therefore felt the need to terrify thoroughly anyone toying with the idea of joining the cause. So while the merchants and aristocrats who sat in Parliament championed the new economic system with plenty of references to the freedom and liberty it bestowed, they apparently felt no qualms about ordering death for those who stubbornly insisted on clinging to the old ways. Above all, the anti-Luddite bill reveals that the elite understood that ensuring the new economic ways was not something that could be left to chance; it required the full force and power of the law.

What is striking about the transformation to a market economy is how much state power is required to establish and maintain the new system, first through the creation of the necessary laws and then through the enforcement of those laws by the courts and the police. This may seem surprising. Certainly it is at odds with the breezy view expressed by many pro-market advocates, who equate the market with freedom or, as Adam Smith put it, with "simple and natural liberty." Under this rosy scenario, the market system appears to come into being simply by the removal of restrictive laws—such as those that regulated medieval commerce—and the giving of free rein to natural human impulses to barter, trade and gain advantage over others. In other words, this pro-market view suggests that simply by stripping away the interfering hand of society, the market will naturally come into being. But the complex nexus of legal rules required to create and maintain a laissez-faire economy suggests otherwise. As Karl Polanyi notes, "There was nothing natural about laissez-faire. Free markets could never have come into being merely by allowing things to take their course."

In order to achieve the kind of dramatic change that the market economy required, it was necessary to fundamentally alter some of the most basic aspects of human life and social organization. For instance, it was necessary to transform the relationship of humans to the very land they lived on. Land had to become a marketable commodity, able to be bought, sold, subdivided, parcelled together or treated in whatever other way was necessary to make it desirable to purchasers. But while the creation of a real estate market seems pretty straightforward and understandable to us, it involved nothing less than a revolutionary change in people's attitudes in the Middle Ages. Land, and the lakes and forests on it, had been an integral part of their lives, providing sustenance for their needs and a place for their lives to unfold—a place that was as familiar to them as their own hands and feet, a place that had been there for their parents and grandparents and as far back as anyone could remember. Suddenly, it was to be something that could be freely traded, like a sack of potatoes or a bag of hair ribbons. "What we call land is an element of nature inextricably interwoven with man's institutions," notes Polanyi. "To isolate it and form a market for it was perhaps the weirdest of all undertakings of our ancestors."

Only slightly less weird was the creation of a labour market—that is, a pool of workers who could be induced to enter into contractual arrangements to provide their labour in exchange for a payment or wage determined by market forces. While the concept of a labour market also seems logical to us today, let's not forget that no such concept had previously existed. In pre-market times, the common people had of course always worked, and worked hard. But as Polanyi notes, their labour had been only part of what defined them. Just as important were ties of kinship, clan, neighbourhood, craft and creed. Their labour was just one of the ways they participated in the life of the community.

All this had to change. A functioning labour market required the adoption of a whole new approach to *people*. It required their redefinition as beings whose purpose was really nothing more than to provide labour. All that was needed from them was their ability to work, to enter into contracts to provide their labour. The efficient operation of the market therefore required that they be dealt with purely on this level, without reference to their other human characteristics.

Thus the market demanded some extraordinary changes, since, as Polanyi notes, "labour" is just another word for people, and "land" just another word for nature or the environment. What was being demanded was the fundamental transformation of people and nature into commodities that could be adapted to the needs of the market. The most basic elements of human life and society were to be subordinated to an ideological concept, a mere theory of how things should be organized. The central reality of this new system, then, was that humans and nature would be forced to adapt to the needs of the economy, rather than the other way around. This was—and is—a truly bizarre concept, however you look at it.

The transformation required was not only bizarre, but also enormous. What was involved was a radical overhaul of some of the most basic institutions and traditions in society. As we saw in the previous chapter, a labour market was established by creating a pool of desperate peasants—stripped of their traditional common rights and facing persecution by the state for their resulting poverty—who were now "willing" to work for wages. Similarly, a real estate market was created by removing the litany of traditional legal claims on pieces of land—common-land rights, entails, endowments, rights of redemption and tithes. But the free market wouldn't just spring into being as soon as the old set of rules and restrictions were removed. What was needed was an entirely new set of rules and restrictions enabling the creation of a market system.

Most significantly, what was needed was a set of restrictions transforming property into something exclusive to its owner. As we also saw in the previous chapter, property had in pre-market times been treated very differently; its ownership had been conditional, to some extent, on the competing rights of other individuals and the community as a whole. The new system required a different approach to property—one that strengthened the claims of the owner and excluded the claims of all others. The political theorist C. B. Macpherson noted that in earlier times, there had essentially been two kinds of property rights: the right to exclude others and the right not be to excluded by others. But with the rise of the market economy, only the first right survived. As Macpherson points out, "The very idea of property was narrowed to cover only the right to exclude others."

Supporters of this narrow sense of property as exclusively private have argued that it can be justified on the basis of "natural laws"—laws that a number of theorists, most notably the philosopher John Locke, were apparently able to identify. Locke, writing in the 1680s, was clearly uninterested in the concept of common property. In building a case for the legitimacy of private property—the cornerstone of the capitalist economy—Locke dealt briefly with the idea that land and resources were given by God to "mankind in common." But he wasn't much interested in this shared situation, and he suggested that in this undeveloped state, property wasn't held by all, but rather by none. This left open the possibility that an individual could come along and assert a private claim. Locke then went on to construct a justification for that private claim. He argued that if an individual applies his own labour to the property, he adds something of value to it and, in so doing, develops a legitimate claim to its exclusive ownership. "It hath by this labour something annexed to it that excludes the common right."

This quickness to exclude the common right seems a little questionable, especially when Locke goes on to give what many might consider a fairly feeble justification: "Thus, the grass my horse has bit, the turfs my servant has cut and the ore I have dug in any place where I have a right to them in common with others, become my property." The idea that the labour he has expended in digging ore gives him an exclusive claim to it seems plausible, or at least a reasonable point to argue. But how did the horse and the servant get into the picture? It is far from clear why the bite of his horse or the work of his servant should render something exclusively his. Wouldn't the servant also have a claim, in fact a considerably stronger claim, if labour is the issue here? And how is his horse's eating some grass an example of his labour? On the contrary, it's neither labour, nor his. Perhaps Locke was simply careless in choosing his examples, but it does weaken the persuasiveness of what is already a fairly tenuous debating position. Certainly he never explained how, in a propertyless state of nature, some men had already managed to get command over servants and horses. Were these just possessions delivered directly from God, or by what authority did he gain control of them?

In fact, the real weakness of Locke's case, it seems, is the failure to acknowledge the possibility of any conflicting claims. What if his horse chooses to bite grass that someone else is hoping to eat, weave into a skirt or use to patch a thatched roof? Are we simply talking about a first-come, first-served arrangement, a variation of "might is right"? Locke seems to want to make a more ennobling case for private ownership by invoking the transformative power of labour. But in doing so, he simply brushes aside the notion that anyone other than the person acquiring the property (through his or his servant's or his horse's "labour") could have a claim to it. Now this would not seem surprising if Locke was writing today, when the concept of "common rights" is not a familiar one. But Locke was writing at a time of intense discussion and debate over the elimination of common rights, a time when farmers throughout the land were risking imprisonment—and even sometimes torture and death—to defend these common rights. It's certainly legitimate for Locke to make a case against common rights. But to simply ignore them, to imply that an individual acquires property that is otherwise just sitting there attracting no interest or attention, seems a little disingenuous under the circumstances.

Of course, it's much easier to make a plausible case for private property if, like Locke, one starts with the assumption that the property being claimed originally belonged to no one. Once we acknowledge that others were using it, and indeed relying on it for sustenance, the case for wrenching it out of their hands becomes much more problematic, if not impossible. The political theorist Anatole Anton argues that the "right of exclusion" involved in private property is a right that "defies moral justification." He goes on to insist that, at the very least, the onus should be on those seeking the exclusion to justify it. "Taking something from a group and giving it to a single person . . . cries out to the democratic sensibility for reasons. . . . Private property, from a democratic point of view, amounts to the surrender of democratic control of social resources to private individuals. Surrender might be the right thing to do, but surely some good reasons ought to be given for so doing."

Locke comes up with really just one reason: the fact that the would-be owner transforms the property by providing his or her labour. It's interesting to note that much of the saleability of Locke's argument—to a fairly broad audience over the years—lies in the importance he attaches to human labour. Locke is not suggesting allocating property on the basis of privilege—because, let's say, someone has a better-looking face, is taller or has red hair or is related to someone who's better-looking, taller or red-haired. Instead, Locke wants property ownership to be rooted in human toil and effort—something that can be universally admired and applauded. In this sense, Locke's argument is actually quite similar to that advanced by the Digger leader, Gerard Winstanley, who, as we saw, wrote several decades earlier, at the time of the English Civil War. But Winstanley used the "human labour" argument to justify quite a different result—a world of small stakeholders, each digging and planting their own little plots by the sweat of their own brows. Winstanley's vision at least seems consistent with the idea that labour bestows property rights. By contrast, the notion that labour bestows property rights does *not* seem to fit with the capitalist world—which Locke appears to be endorsing—where the largest property owners often seem to do the least labour.

Of course, we know that Locke went on to include in his imaginary scenario the example of the labour provided by the servant and the horse. This broadens the options significantly, and may help explain why Locke became a hero to modern-day capitalists while Winstanley is hard to locate in many a library. Certainly, if we are able to make a property claim on the basis of labour *done by others on our behalf or in our employ,* we are into more flexible arrangements, and the justification for private property ownership becomes much more wide open. It now becomes possible for Locke's argument to be moulded into a shape that will allow it to be used to defend the property rights of even the largest transnational corporation today. But on the other hand, the addition of the servant and the horse also makes Locke's theory less convincing. After all, there we were, in the midst of an explanation about the evolution of private property, when an already privately owned horse sauntered onto the set. Whoa, Nellie! If Winstanley had built his case this carelessly, it's unlikely he would even have made it into obscure history books.

But if Locke is starting to look like someone who could be found working today in the PR department of Nike or Coke, that's not quite fair to him. Locke went on to add the caveat that someone could claim property as his own only provided there was "enough and as good" left over that would be available to others. Well, this seems to change everything! Certainly it limits the scope of Locke's defence of private property, making it conditional on everyone's having a chance to transform some equivalent piece of property into his or her own. But what if there isn't enough to go around—with land and non-renewable resources the obvious examples? Certainly, agribusiness and the oil industry would have trouble citing Locke in their defence. But this explains why pro-market theorists, despite invoking Locke as the quintessential authority on the legitimacy of private property, often tend to brush over this caveat. It also raises the question of whether Locke might have been something of a closet Digger.

Locke's caveat also helps identify something interesting about private property—that, as the early-twentieth-century U.S. legal scholar Robert Hale noted, it is a form of special privilege conferred by the state. Hale points to the example of land distributed by governments to homesteaders in North America during the nineteenth century. Here the conditions of Locke's caveat were met. There was plenty of fertile land available for all, so in granting a parcel to one pioneer family, a government was not depriving other families (except, of course, Native American families, from whom the land was seized). But once the fertile land was gone, land became scarce and therefore more valuable. The early homesteading family got to hold on to its increasingly valuable parcel of land, thereby joining a privileged minority. What had started out as a gift equally available to anyone willing to provide labour had become a gift of special privilege from the state, available only to the select group that had got there first. Over time, this select group could, and did, reap enormous benefits—for reasons that had nothing to do with the fruits of their labour and everything to do with the fortuitous increase in real-estate values.

Economic liberals will quickly counter that, in today's world at least, the right to acquire property is a general right, available equally to all. While it's true that there's a general right to acquire property, specific property is unattainable. All land is already owned, and unless one is willing to meet the conditions set by the owner, one cannot gain access to it.

Of course, land is a special case, since it is limited in supply and therefore prone to scarcity. Perhaps Locke's theory works better with other forms of private property. But Hale goes on to make the provocative argument that *all* forms of private property ultimately represent a special privilege, conferred by the state. You cannot remove a delightful lawn ornament from a neighbour's yard and then protest to the police and the courts that you were simply exercising your "right to acquire property." The right to acquire property is conditional on a buyer having sufficient money to pay the market price demanded by the existing owner. Someone lacking those resources will find the full force of state power arrayed against her, preventing her from gaining access to the property she desires. In this sense, then, private property is a special privilege, backed up by state power and conferred exclusively on those lucky enough to have sufficient resources to pay for it.

Thus under our legal system, a man has a perfect right to eat. But there's a hitch. "While there is no law against eating in the abstract," writes Hale, "there is a law which forbids him to eat any of the food which actually exists in the community—and that is the law of property." So unless he can afford the price demanded for the food, he will have to go without it. Another option would be for him to grow his own food. Again, our legal system has no law saying he can't do this, so he seems free to do so. But again, there is a hitch. Hale comments, "[I]n every settled country there is a law which forbids him to cultivate any particular piece of ground unless he happens to be an owner. This again is the law of property."

Hale colourfully highlights the privileged nature of private property rights: "One owner, as the result of the entire network of restrictions inherent in property rights, gets the benefit of finding that liberty to use a particular ragged suit of clothes will not be interfered with by the acts of non-owners. Another owner gets the liberty of wandering over a large estate and using a large number of automobiles without interference from others. . . . The benefits conferred by these rights are not equal in any important sense." The most that could be said is that the rights of both these individuals will be equally enforced—although even this is uncertain. The estate owner will likely find that the police respond more quickly when he calls to report his mansion has been robbed than they do when the homeless man calls to report his ragged suit is missing.

Private property exists only because governments have set up elaborate laws that endow owners with certain privileged rights, and at the same time, strictly and forcefully curtail the rights of non-owners. As Jeremy Bentham pointed out, "[T]ake away the laws, all property ceases." Without the benefit of property laws—and police and courts to enforce them—no one could enjoy any piece of private property, since there would be nothing to prevent others from seizing it. For that matter, if the police and the courts simply refused to act to ensure property rights, owners would be forced to rely exclusively on "natural rights"—a favourite concept with philosophers, but not something that has much power to deter thieves.

Without the muscle of the state, the concept of "natural rights" is essentially meaningless, since it is unenforceable. Consider the case of inherited wealth. Critics of taxes on inherited wealth often argue that the right to transfer property to an heir is a "natural" right. But without elaborate state laws ensuring the transfer of wealth from one generation to the next, this right has no practical meaning. When a wealthy woman dies, for instance, her son cannot simply show up at his mother's bank the next day and, invoking his natural rights, demand that her account be handed over. What happens to the mother's property is determined exclusively by the detailed laws establishing the legal process for inheritance. There must be a will, drawn up according to strict legal guidelines and signed by the mother when she met a legal definition of mental capacity. There are further legal restrictions, requiring provision for her spouse, for example, as well as restrictions on her ability to dictate the future use of the property being distributed. If she dies without a will, the distribution of the inheritance isn't left to her family and friends to work out as they choose over a game of cards or a jousting match, but is instead determined by another set of laws.

Ultimately, then, the market economy exists because a legal system has been put in place to enforce it. As we saw, this required a fundamental redesign of society and its laws—a process that involved a great deal of coercion by the state. For all the tossing about of words and expressions like "free," "natural" and "laissez-faire," the market economy exists purely because a set of man-made laws enforce it. The propertied classes deliberately—and with the use of force—created a legal system that protected their own property interests and stripped away the pre-existing common property rights of most of the population. So it would seem bizarre to see these new private property laws as any more "natural" than the common property laws of earlier times. Natural *to whom?* To paraphrase slightly: They call it natural, when themselves feel comfortable.

Even after its creation, the "free" market needed the full force of state legal power to be maintained. Polanyi observed, "Administrators had to be constantly on the watch to ensure the free working of the system." Despite incessant proselytizing from authorities about the merits of the market, the new system proved a hard sell, and there were almost constant attempts to rein in the full fury of market forces before they wreaked too much havoc on people's lives. As Polanyi ironically notes, "While laissez-faire economy was the product of deliberate state action, subsequent restrictions on laissez-faire started in a spontaneous way. Laissez-faire was planned; planning was not." Indeed, if we are looking for something "natural," we find it not so much in the market, but rather in the massive and constant reaction *against* the market.

IT'S NOT AN EXAGGERATION to say that since the early sixteenth century, virtually every segment of society has at some point struggled to protect itself from some aspect of the market. If we consider that the creation of the market economy involved the transformation of people and nature into the commodities of labour and real estate, it is not hard to imagine that this change caused considerable stress and dislocation, to say the least. Polanyi argues that the attempt to carry out this change "disregarded the fact that leaving the fate of soil and people to the market would be tantamount to annihilating them." Resistance to this potential annihilation was therefore predictable and natural.

If the charge of annihilation sounds strong, let's consider for a moment the potential impact a fully unregulated market can have. And we don't need to dream up scenarios—we can get a sense of what actually happened by looking at measures that were passed into law in the middle of the nineteenth century to curb some of the more serious problems created by the largely unregulated market of early-nineteenth-century England. In 1860, for instance, a revision to the Mines Act made it "penal to employ boys under twelve not attending schools and unable to read and write." An 1862 act made it illegal to operate a coal mine with a single shaft; it was in response to the deaths of many miners who became trapped without an escape route when the one shaft in their mine collapsed. In 1863, the Chimney-Sweeper's Act imposed restrictions on how children could be used in the chimney-sweeping business, after a number of little ones had died horrible deaths as a result of being forced to clean out very narrow slots.

These acts of restrictive legislation were strongly protested at the time by market enthusiasts, such as Herbert Spencer, who considered them a betrayal of free-market principles. Polanyi notes, however, that this sort of intervention in the marketplace, which became extensive after 1860, was often advocated by people who were not in any way hostile to the basic principles of the marketplace, but who recognized the necessity of restraining an economic system capable of causing horrendous human damage. Much of the regulation, for instance, involved areas of public health and safety, such as the inspection of gasworks, water supplies, and irrigation and drainage systems. In addition, there was legislation establishing a public fire brigade for London, which meant the provision of fire protection was no longer a matter of private insurance—a troublesome situation if your neighbour in a row of wooden houses hadn't bothered to insure himself. The impetus for market-restraining legislation sometimes came from business interests themselves; this was especially the case when businesspeople wanted state action to prevent others from establishing monopolies, or wanted state subsidies for themselves when the free play of market forces left them unable to compete.

Polanyi argues that the vast array of "anti-laissez-faire" legislation put in place in the second half of the nineteenth century amounted to a counter-movement. This counter-movement was essentially unplanned and spontaneous—a kind of knee-jerk human reaction to the sometimes brutal reality of the marketplace, an instinctive attempt on the part of individuals and society to protect themselves from the dehumanizing nature of what market forces, left unchecked, often delivered.

I've argued earlier in the book that this reflex of self-protection seems to be fairly basic to the human personality, as basic surely as our instinct to accumulate material goods. Economic liberals might reply that individuals do care about protecting themselves and their families, but they don't care about the protection of the broader community. Of course, in taking steps to rein in the full force of the market, individuals *are,* first and foremost, concerned with protecting themselves and their families. But that self-interest doesn't really end at their own front door. If humans are basically social in nature, as Polanyi contends, it follows that that they would want to live in communities that are viable, functional and even harmonious. It feels bad—not to mention uncomfortable or even dangerous—to be surrounded by social breakdown and distrust, even if we're doing all right ourselves. So we don't even need to be particularly sanguine about human nature to argue that humans have a genuine self-interest in ensuring a place for themselves inside a larger community whose survival and well-being is protected.

Furthermore, it seems that people sometimes even care about things that don't affect them personally. It's hard to imagine that the only people who were concerned about young children being shoved into chimney slots were relatives of children in the chimney-sweeping business. Similarly, in the spring of 2001, the huge out-pouring of public concern that accompanied the starvation death of infant Jordan Heikamp in Toronto didn't come only from people who feared that they or members of their family might also end up starving to death. It came from people who, although confident in their own food supply, were outraged that a helpless member of their community had been denied what he needed to live. Similarly, the worldwide pressure on the multinational drug industry to drop the price of medication for African AIDS victims reflects genuine concern on the part of large numbers of people who do not know the victims personally and will probably never travel to Africa.

The point is that there seems to be a natural human tendency to resist the full force of the market, to shield oneself—and sometimes others too—from its fury. This tendency can be muted or perhaps even extinguished, but only with considerable "education" or training in market theory. Perhaps people could, with sufficient attention to the teachings of the market enthusiast Herbert Spencer, learn to accept that sticking children into chimney slots is a reasonable thing to do, that it will encourage them to develop a strong work ethic and be more efficient and productive later in life. But without the "benefit" of such teaching, the *natural* response of most people is the opposite—to punish any adult who would do such a thing, even if they have never met that child or heard his name.

It certainly seems natural that humans would react against the way the market transforms them into "labour"—a mere commodity that, like any other, is subject to the market's rules of supply and demand. Under a market regime, workers must be willing to uproot themselves and move to wherever there is demand for their labour. If they don't want to move—if they don't, for instance, like the place where work is available, or if they yearn to be back home with family and friends—the market doesn't allow for this. Workers must also be willing to accept whatever pay and working conditions the market offers. To hold out for more by refusing to work under the terms offered—either individually or as a group through a unionized action—is to defy the market.

When workers defy the market, they risk ending up unemployed. And if that happens, it's their own fault, according to market supporters. There is no unemployment, they argue, when workers do as the market demands. In this view, which prevailed throughout much of the Depression, it is up to workers to lower their expectations when the market requires it. There can be no intervention by the state that would allow labour to escape the harsh realities of the marketplace. The efficient operation of the market demands nothing less than full human submission to market dictates—that is, full acceptance by people of their status as commodities.

Given the scope of the market's demands, it's understandable that humans would instinctively seek protection from its dictates. The counter-movement, then, was to a large extent about people organizing themselves into labour unions or forming other sorts of pressure groups to force the market to make concessions to human needs. The resulting legislation left them less vulnerable, and therefore in a position to be more demanding about wages and working conditions. That was the whole point—to remove human labour from the orbit of the market and return it to the realm of human decision making, in order to safeguard its humanness.

So Polanyi adds an interesting twist to the idea that the market is an artificially constructed system based on man-made laws. Not only is it artificial, he suggests, but the market might actually be *at odds* with the natural human instinct for self-protection and security. This would seem to present an interesting challenge to John Locke. Rather than asserting that the market and private property rights are rooted in natural law, as Locke and other market supporters would have us believe, Polanyi makes the case that the market is an institution that is contrary to some of our deepest natural human urges. While it is right in tune with our natural instincts for material gain, the market is antithetical to our equally powerful instincts for self-protection.

Rather than being based on natural law, the laws that create the market seem to be based mostly on the narrow self-interest of the propertied classes, who have everything to gain by excluding the rights of others. This was evident in some of the early legal decisions that helped establish the market system. Judges in eighteenth-century England unabashedly rejected common rights simply on the basis of how much "inconvenience" they caused (although presumably not to the people possessing them). In an important case in 1788, Mr. Justice Heath decided to discard the long-established right of the poor to pick up grain left in the field after harvest. As he noted, the "inconvience arising from this custom being considered a right by the poor would be infinite. . . . It would raise the insolence of the poor." The judge had a point; it undoubtedly raised the "insolence" of the poor—that is, their sense of entitlement and empowerment—to be assured of this "gleaning" right, which had enabled them to feed their families. Better simply to remove this right than to risk insolence—which is exactly what the courts did.

Another judge, Mr. Justice Wilson, lending support to Justice Heath's opinion in the gleaning case, made sweeping conclusions about the property owner's natural rights in another case. "The soil is his, the seed is his, and in natural justice his also are the profits." As E. P. Thompson notes, "It is difficult to think of a purer expression of capitalist rationality, in which both labour and human need have disappeared from view, and the 'natural justice' of profits has become a reason at law." The honesty of the judge's position was at least refreshing. There were no soothing bromides here about how the poor, deprived of the rotting grain left in the field, would develop more character. Stamping out the insolence of the poor was the sole reason for taking away their rights, and the judge stated this simple truth without the layers of dissembling rhetoric we so often have to wade through in political debate today.

Ultimately, these rulings seem to reflect nothing more than naked class bias. They certainly reveal the ability of the judges to identify with the property owner, and their total inability to identify with the guy scrounging around in the field for bits of leftover grain. Similarly, Adam Smith was moved by the imagined plight of a property owner who, lacking adequate legal protections for his property, would be unable to "sleep a single night in security." Meanwhile, the far more serious fate awaiting people who lost their common rights didn't lead Smith to concern himself with their ability to get a good night's sleep. This capacity to sympathize with and focus on the plight of the powerful—while ignoring the far-more-distressing fate faced by the powerless—is familiar still, as we saw with Thomas Friedman's identification with today's economic and political elite.

If we free ourselves of this class bias, we are left with a very different picture. Private property rights lose their special sacrosanct status as a natural right, becoming just another competing political claim with no more inherent validity than, say, common rights. And some of our most widely held political beliefs suddenly seem to be based less on overarching principles of natural law and justice and more on special privilege.

THE VITALITY OF THE anti-market impulse can be seen in the evolution of a strong, interventionist role for government. Starting in the late nineteenth century, Western governments were pushed to respond to popular demands to limit the power and scope of the market, and by the mid-twentieth century, they had begun to create a whole new realm of public life outside the market through the creation of social welfare programs. In this public realm, everyone enjoys certain rights and has access to a certain amount of society's resources—not on the basis of property ownership, but on the basis of citizenship (that is, on the basis of simply being part of the community). The creation of this public realm could be seen in many ways as the re-establishment of long-lost "common rights." As we've seen, these common rights had once given ordinary people access to basic necessities, like grass for cattle, wildlife and fruit for eating, wood for building, peat moss for heating. And in the early post-war years, government began to some extent to take on that function, ensuring people had access to certain basic necessities outside the framework of the market—clean drinking water, public systems for health and education, public parks and libraries, financial support for the needy.

It is perhaps no surprise, then, that the central and urgent thrust of the financial elite in the past couple of decades has been the removal of these recently revived common rights—which have proved no less inconvenient to today's rich than the original version was to the rich two hundred years ago.

༎

A CRUCIAL STRATEGY FOR the rich has been the vilification of government and all attempts at collective action to control the market. The market is held up as representing freedom, and any action to limit its powers is portrayed as an assault on human freedom. One of the singular achievements of the pro-market school has been its ability to link the notions of coercion and compulsion exclusively with government.

While government is undoubtedly capable of coercion—and of the worst sort—it has no monopoly on coercive behaviour. The market imposes a coercion of its own that is less obvious but still real and important. The apparently "voluntary" market exchange, in which workers exchange their labour for wages, takes place within a context of mutual coercion, Robert Hale notes. Each side has the legal right to withhold something the other side wants—the labourer isn't obliged to work; the employer isn't obliged to pay—and each side uses that right to try to obtain the most favourable terms from the other. So while neither side is pulling a knife on the other, they are both using a form of coercion to get their way.

If government intervenes in this struggle—with minimum-wage laws, or anti-scab or back-to-work legislation—it can tilt the balance, enhancing the power of one side to impose its terms on the other. But it would be wrong to view the government's intervention as the *introduction* of coercion into the process. Coercion is already there. Government is simply rejigging the power balance, thereby increasing the leverage of one side to dictate the terms. One can dispute the legitimacy of a specific government intervention, but one could also presumably question the fairness of the original distribution of power. One could argue, for instance, that the employer enjoys considerable financial security already—as a result of property laws—and that this financial security gives him an unfair degree of coercive negotiating power through his ability to hold out longer than a hungry labourer. By imposing minimum-wage laws, the government is perhaps only slightly rebalancing a badly skewed power balance, in which the laws of the state have already conferred an enormous advantage on the employer.

It's not even clear that the government's intervention is an infringement of liberty. It certainly is an infringement of the liberty *of one side*. But at the same time, it expands the liberty of the other side. Hale's point is that all sets of rights impose constraints on the rights of others to do as they wish. When governments establish private property rights, they limit the rights of non-property owners, denying them access to property that now belongs to others.

One of the starkest examples of this, law professor Neil Brooks notes, is the way property laws exclude people from getting access to life-saving drugs. This exclusion happens because governments have created an elaborate set of copyright and patent laws to protect so-called intellectual property so that the creator or inventor of a product can claim exclusive rights to sell that product. This exclusivity may not present too much of a problem when the product is a musical recording or a book or a movie. But as we saw in chapter one, it becomes extremely serious when the product is an item essential to human health. There are millions of African AIDS victims facing the prospect of premature death because they are unable to afford the price that drug companies are demanding for access to their products. If it wasn't for laws enforcing the "intellectual property" rights of these companies, other companies would be permitted to produce generic versions of these drugs for a fraction of the amount.

(Of course, the drug companies argue that without these intellectual property rights—which are extensively protected through trade deals like NAFTA—they would not be able to carry out the costly research necessary to invent new drugs. While it's true that research is costly, the drug industry is highly profitable and very reluctant to divulge information about its internal costing systems. Critics charge that the industry routinely inflates the costs of its research to many times what it actually spends. It certainly downplays the fact that government funding has paid for much of the basic research that has led to important medical breakthroughs, including those that have led to new AIDS medications.)

In any event, the point is that intellectual property rights amount to a massive government intervention in the marketplace—an intervention that greatly increases the rights of the multinational drug industry while drastically curtailing the rights of poor African AIDS victims. And the intervention is a highly arbitrary one that is tilted heavily in the direction of the drug industry. If the patent laws were altered, it would change the way the rights are distributed. If drug patents were made to expire in five years or ten years, for instance, rather than the twenty years usually specified by law these days, this would diminish the rights enjoyed by some of the world's richest corporations and greatly expand the rights enjoyed by some of the sickest, most vulnerable people on earth. There is no particular magic in twenty years. The long patent period mostly reflects the enormous clout enjoyed by the drug industry, which, by investing heavily in government lobbying and political contributions, has managed to construct a market to suit its own interests.

THE CORPORATE WORLD TENDS to be blind to the coercive nature of government interventions when those interventions further their own interests, as in the case of intellectual property rights. They are vigilant, however, in detecting coercion when the government intervention negatively impacts on their interests, as in the case of progressive taxation. The allegedly coercive nature of progressive taxation has been central to the financial elite's attack on the welfare state in recent years. The attack ultimately comes down to the argument that government actions to redistribute resources through taxation and social spending amount to a confiscation of property that belongs to the well-to-do. Of course, the rich have always resisted government efforts to redistribute resources towards the less well-to-do. But in the past, their arguments used to revolve more around the importance of creating a strong work ethic by keeping taxes low. These days, their argument seems to be more about the rights of the rich to enjoy what is (allegedly) rightfully theirs. The concept "It's my money—I earned it, and I'm entitled to keep it" seems to have a powerful resonance in an age that encourages endless self-regard.

It is part of the hubris of our times that we think we, as individuals, are the key actors—that we've basically made it on our own, and that we therefore are individually entitled to enjoy the benefits that our personal efforts have reaped. This sentiment is echoed in the concept of Tax Freedom Day—an annual event promoted by right-wing think-tanks in Canada and the U.S. to encourage the notion that taxes are coercive and burdensome. By calculating the number of days in the year that the average person must work to earn enough to pay his or her taxes, the organizers are suggesting that up until this point in the calendar, people are simply "working for the government."

The concept receives widespread coverage in the media, and is treated almost as some kind of neutral and important assessment by a watchdog agency responsible for monitoring the size of government. In fact, the event tries to confuse the issue of taxation. Utterly left out of Tax Freedom Day is any notion that taxes are what we pay to buy services that we all need and use, and that would be much more expensive or even impossible to purchase privately—fire and police protection, highways, roads, canals, coast guard services, snow removal, water purification, schools, hospitals, libraries, etc. Tax Freedom Day could undoubtedly be moved up to early January if we were prepared to walk out of our dwellings that morning onto a dirt path and take our chances on what might befall us.

Furthermore, the suggestion that one has created one's income all by oneself conveniently ignores the complex web of laws and regulations—affecting property, copyright, inheritance, licensing and certification of trades and professions—that plays a major role in determining income. Without all this, individuals wouldn't be able to "earn" and safely enjoy the income at all. Doctors, lawyers, engineers and architects have high incomes not only because their services are in demand, but also because they receive accreditation from government—accreditation that gives the public confidence in their services and restricts would-be competitors who lack accreditation from offering *their* services. Even incomes that seem to be determined without the involvement of government are usually influenced in some way by legislation affecting a whole range of issues revolving around the right of workers to organize into unions and to go on strike. A tilt in the legislation in favour of labour will likely push up wages; a tilt towards management will tend to shift a larger share of the profits to the employer.

So the individual's moral claim to his or her income should be tempered by the notion that society has already had a hand in directing the income to that person in the first place. If the laws had been different, the income distribution would have been different. The claim to a certain amount of income rests, then, on little more than society's choices. As John Stuart Mill noted, the distribution of wealth in any society is a product of human choice, dependent on the laws and customs of that society and subject to alteration at any time.

The notion that we have earned our individual incomes also tends to ignore the huge and often invisible contribution made by others. Just about every innovation or invention is based on a host of previous innovations and inventions by other individuals or teams of individuals, often stretching back a long way in time. Alexander Graham Bell's invention of the telephone or Bill Gates's computer breakthrough couldn't have happened without the previous scientific and mathematical discoveries on which these inventions are based. For that matter, the technical breakthroughs that led to Henry Ford's assembly-line car can be traced all the way back to the invention of the wheel. Sometimes the collective role of society is even more clear-cut. Pharmaceutical companies are able to reap huge profits by finishing off products after the costly basic research has been carried out by government-funded agencies. For that matter, all enterprises are able to function and prosper only because they can rely on a government-provided infrastructure of transportation and telecommunications, as well as a labour force that is educated in government-subsidized institutions. Tax Freedom Day assumes that we can stop paying taxes and these vital, communally paid-for resources will somehow just fall from the sky.

Of course, most people would use a variation of Gerard Winstanley's Digger argument to justify their income, insisting that it is theirs because they have worked hard to earn it. And hard work and effort undoubtedly do play a part in earning income, although they clearly don't tell the whole story, or even much of a story at all. A hard-working executive may well put in many late nights at the office, but he does not necessarily clock more hours than the factory worker who also works part-time as an office cleaner and cashier—and earns a fraction of the pay. Besides, any claim that the distribution of resources in our society is closely linked to effort and hard work has to deal with the blatantly contradictory fact of inherited wealth. Hale argues that inherited wealth accounts for the greatest part of economic inequality. He notes that all other factors, including unequal abilities and talents—no matter how important in determining income—have an impact on only one generation. But inherited wealth allows inequality to be perpetuated over time—even, with proper investment advice, indefinitely.

The role of inherited wealth is simply huge. In addition to receiving actual property and assets, those born into wealthy families also generally have access to countless advantages that allow them to develop the skills, attitudes and social connections that lead to further financial success. These advantages, while recognized, are generally underemphasized, largely because the rich prefer it that way. While they insist on strong laws safeguarding their rights to inheritance, they prefer not to draw too much attention to the source of their prosperity; they want their good fortune to be perceived as a reflection of their own talents, brains and efforts. Yet any system of distribution that relies as heavily as ours does on inherited wealth can make only the feeblest claim to reward people on the basis of effort and hard work.

In fact, what our system does reward people for—beyond the skill of choosing the right parents—is the ability and willingness to perform functions that those with money want performed. This might seem like a fair way to reward people; those who can perform tasks useful to others—from accounting to haircutting to brain surgery—are able to earn a living by selling their services. But several problems, typical of the marketplace, quickly arise. Services that are desired by the wealthy are hugely rewarded, while services needed by those without money are barely compensated. Corporate lawyers reap handsome rewards arranging mergers, even though they might be no more skilled or talented than legal-aid lawyers fighting tenant evictions. Corporate managers who prove adept at enhancing shareholder value—and even some who don't seem particularly adept—can end up with inexplicably large incomes. How can one come up with any meaningful justification for Nortel's CEO, John Roth, earning more than one thousand nurses did in the year 2000, even as he steered his company towards virtual collapse? Clearly, the market does not reward skills on the basis of social usefulness. Indeed, it's hard to come up with any moral justification for these sorts of discrepancies. To people untrained in market theory, such discrepancies are likely to seem unfair, even perverse.

In the face of the arbitrary nature of the market's system of distributing income, what are we to do? The market advocates insist that we should do nothing, that to redistribute resources through the tax system amounts to a coercive intervention. But they are of course ignoring any previous coercive intervention. As Neil Brooks notes, "Redistributive taxation simply changes the starting positions of the parties, and all starting positions involve coercion." Certainly progressive taxation can have the effect of expanding liberty for many, whose life choices will be enhanced through stronger social programs that give them greater access to health care, education and financial security. So constraints on the liberty of the wealthy can lead to expanded liberty for the rest of society. Brooks illustrates the point with an example of a well-to-do taxpayer who owns an acre of land on which he plans to build a log cabin and create a fish pond. Suppose that because of the income taxes he owes, he is obliged to sell his piece of land. With the revenue, the government then purchases the land and converts it into a public park, complete with public fish pond. For the owner, the whole affair represents a limitation on his freedom to do what he wants. For members of the public, who will now have access to a fish pond that would otherwise have been off limits to them, the result is an expansion of their opportunities and horizons. "[T]here is no reduction of freedoms, only adjustments," comments Brooks. "The freedom of nonowners, who could now make use of the park, would be greatly expanded. The tax did not eliminate the freedom to use the land; it simply redistributed it."

There is no question that a progressive tax system can result in a much more equitable distribution of resources among citizens, and that those in the middle- and lower-income ranges are net beneficiaries, because they gain access to vital services that might otherwise be unavailable to them under a pure market system. Amazingly, all this can be accomplished without in any way seriously endangering the economic well-being of the financial elite. Despite loud complaints from members of the financial elite about high tax levels, it's interesting to note that they still manage to live in the finest houses, eat at the best restaurants, shop at the most expensive stores. If this is coercion, we should all experience it. It's clearly a far different sort of coercion from that faced by Maria Sybila Arredondo, who remains locked in a Peruvian prison.

Progressive taxation also, of course, reduces the perversity of the market's distribution of income. While the market distributes income on the basis of one's ability to service those with money, government programs redistribute it on the basis of nothing more than being part of the community. As a member of the community, an individual is deemed to be entitled to a basic level of economic well-being—a level that at least prevents him from having to, say, sleep on a grate. There is also the notion that this is a right, automatically conferred on everyone through citizenship. Note that without the coercion of taxation, such rights would not exist; the poor would receive from the rich only as a matter of charity, and only when the rich chose to give. Through the coercive mechanism of taxation, the rich are *obliged* to give. And the poor receive as a matter of right—just like their peasant predecessors centuries ago had "rights" that allowed them to graze their cattle on the common land even when the lord was not in a generous mood.

It is quite striking, then, the way progressive taxation reimposes the notion of community onto the market economy. Not only are certain "common rights" restored to the people, but the financial elite is once again obliged to take on social duties and responsibilities. Just as the holding of property was conditional on service to the king in medieval times, the holding of wealth and property under a progressive tax system is conditional on the payment of a tax—a payment that goes towards the upkeep of the whole community. And that payment becomes proportionately larger as the property holdings increase in size—reflecting the owner's greater ability to pay and also the fact that he or she is monopolizing a larger share of the resources available to the community. All this reflects the idea that the ownership of property is not an absolute right enjoyed apart from society, but rather is a conditional right, granted by society and entailing social responsibilities. Ultimately, progressive taxation re-establishes the moral authority of society over the marketplace.

So the claim "It's my money—I earned it" is not only embarrassingly egotistical, but also essentially wrong. It should at the very least be qualified, as in, "I earned it, but only with a great deal of help along the way." Taxation is in many ways simply a recognition that the money was not earned by individual effort alone, that, as Edmund James put it, society and the state were silent partners and therefore have a right to share in the prosperity. Those tempted to slough off the helpful role of the state should, as James suggests, "compare the fortune accumulated by Cornelius Vanderbilt in America with what he might have accumulated had he been adopted when an infant by a family of Hottentots."

# CHAPTER SEVEN

# Tearing Down the Fence

JUST AS THE HEDGE APPEARED almost overnight in the world of the medieval peasant, so it was with the Fence. It suddenly encircled the central core of Quebec City to protect political leaders attending the Summit of the Americas in April 2001 and to keep out what could be considered today's equivalent of the medieval peasant. It turns out that whatever the century, people respond badly when confronted with an enormous obstruction in the path of where they want to go.

Back in the sixteenth and seventeenth centuries, they used hoes, pitchforks, axes or anything else close at hand to rip down the offending Hedge. In Quebec City, they went after the Fence with similar gusto; some also threw hockey pucks, beer bottles and pieces of concrete towards the six-thousand-strong phalanx of police behind it. From a distance, the scenes could hardly look more different—one small in scale and pastoral, the other resembling large-scale urban warfare, complete with gas masks and helicopters whirring overhead. And the political realities were different too. Unlike their medieval ancestors, the people in Quebec City weren't facing starvation as a result of the Fence—although they were acting partly out of concern for those who were. In truth, one can find many differences between the situations. But one can also find an overarching theme linking the two protests across the centuries: people don't like to be excluded from the earth's bounty.

And that is precisely what capitalism does. It cordons off—behind fences or hedges or other visible and invisible barriers—most of the world as private property from which non-owners are excluded. The new capitalism simply does this more vigorously and, through mechanisms like the trade deal that was being negotiated in Quebec City that warm April weekend, with a more all-encompassing set of corporate powers. The gulf that separated the two sides of the Fence in Quebec City was thus huge. Outside the Fence, a popular placard among protestors read: "The Earth Is Not for Sale." Inside, those designing the new trade deals had little patience with these sorts of anti-market sentiments. Had they been inclined to state their feelings on placards, they might well have held up one saying: "Get a Grip. Everything's for Sale."

The two positions are irreconcilable. What it comes down to is a fundamentally different set of values—one puts material acquisitiveness at the forefront of human experience, and views this aspect of human behaviour as the centrepoint and defining activity of human life; the other assigns material acquisitiveness a lower status, fitting it in among a range of human activities and aspirations. To this second group, the increasing domination of the market, and its elevation of corporate profit-making rights, is undermining society's ability to deal with other important aspects of life—like the protection of the environment and the creation of viable and inclusive communities. Those in the first group, on the other hand, are happy to hand over power to the market; indeed, they increasingly look to the market for solutions to what seem like complex human and social problems. A Harvard law professor, for instance, came up with a market-based solution for dealing with racial discrimination. Rather than trying to outlaw it, Derrick Bell proposed creating a market for discriminatory behaviour. Employers wanting to discriminate would be free to do so, but they would have to purchase a license.

The market has also made inroads into other surprising domains, including that of human genes. Once the private preserve of the human body, genes have now been recognized for the hot marketable commodity that they are. This has been made possible by recent scientific breakthroughs that have paved the way for scientists to use microscopic stem cells extracted from human embryos to develop dramatic new cures for deadly diseases.

A private company, Geron Corporation of Menlo Park, California, has managed to obtain exclusive commercial rights over key aspects of stem cell research. Geron negotiated these rights with a research foundation at the University of Wisconsin, which holds the patent for embryonic stem cells, after they were first discovered by a research biologist at the university, Dr. James Thomson. Geron's deal raises the prospect that a private company will end up with a monopoly over treatments and products developed from future stem cell research, and that other companies developing their own stem cell lines might be charged with patent infringements. The result could be delays in making treatments available or higher prices, or both. (If it's any consolation, Geron only holds the exclusive commercial rights for stem cell treatments related to six specific body parts—bone, blood, muscle, nerve, liver and pancreas. Whew! It appears there's lots of room for competition in other key body parts—the brain still seems to be up for grabs, for instance, and nobody has yet cornered the market for the stomach, gall bladder, small intestine, leg, etc.)

Market enthusiasts argue of course that these sorts of monopolies are necessary if companies are to recoup the billions of dollars they spend developing new products. As we've seen, however, claims about research costs are often exaggerated. It's interesting to note, for instance, that Geron contributed only $1 million (U.S.) to Dr. Thomson's research—and only after Dr. Thomson had carried out years of related research funded by the U.S. government. In fact, it was while working on federally funded research that Thomson made a crucial breakthrough—he discovered how to extract stem cells from monkeys. He then wrote an academic paper pointing out that this same technique could be applied to humans. Geron, spotting the commercial possibilities, was quick to offer him money to do so.

As the stem cell issue flared up in August 2001, there was plenty of debate about the "morality" of stem cell research. But nobody seemed very concerned about another aspect of the issue—that such a vital discovery, with huge potential to improve human welfare, was being handed over to the marketplace, where the public will have little control over it. Even though public funds were spent on the research leading up to Thomson's important discovery, the U.S.

government will do nothing to ensure that the resulting medications are available to the public at affordable prices. In fact, the government can be counted on to do the opposite. It will enforce patent laws that will allow Geron to keep the price of its medications high and prevent competitors from producing the same products at lower prices.

We have become so steeped in the market mentality that all this simply passes for normal. In fact, this is nothing more than the logical extension of our current way of thinking, with its celebration of the market as the ultimate achievement and the path to human betterment. In an insightful essay, Harvey Cox, a professor of divinity at Harvard University, argued that the focus on religion in earlier centuries has given way to a new focus on the market. Where once we sought salvation through God, we now seek "salvation through the advent of free markets."

It's worth mentioning that as pervasive as the new religion of the market seems, there are probably a lot more sceptics or even atheists out there than is evident from the size of the protests on the streets of Quebec City and Seattle. A poll reported in the *National Post* just prior to the Quebec summit found that while most Canadians generally supported "free trade," almost half had concerns that the trade deals didn't go far enough in protecting the environment and other social rights. A poll conducted for *BusinessWeek* similarly found that 80 per cent of Americans believed that the environment should be a top priority in trade deals; 74 percent also wanted to make labour rights a priority, and a solid majority disapproved of signing trade deals that offered no protection for environmental and labour concerns. What this suggests is that a lot of Canadians and Americans don't fully understand that the new trade deals compromise environmental and labour rights. This is no surprise, since government and business leaders keep implying that the deals are exclusively about trade. But when asked about their priorities, citizens in both countries are unequivocal: unbridled profit-making, at the expense of everything else, is unacceptable. Whether members of the general public realize it or not, their position, as reflected in these polls at least, is closer to that of the demonstrators than to that of the elected political leaders.

The pro-market advocates like to portray the contemporary conversion to the religion of the market as the triumph of reason, and they portray their opponents on the other side of the Fence as soft-thinking sentimentalists who resist the market's indisputable rationality. But in fact, there's no reason to assume that logic and rationality are on the side of the market. Yes, the economics industry has generated some impressive mathematical equations about how markets operate; it can even figure out how to construct a market for racial slurs. But what if some of the assumptions fed into those equations are flawed? Mainstream economics has built an elaborate mathematical model for dealing with a subject that is rooted, ultimately, in human behaviour—which is not exactly known for its mathematical precision.

As noted, even classical economists like Adam Smith assumed humans had a range of motives and thus were capable of behaviour that included generosity, public-spiritedness and sympathy for others. The "neoclassical" economics, which replaced the classical school, concentrated on the purely self-interested, materialistic motive. By isolating this one motive—and if not eliminating all others, then reducing them to near insignificance—economics was able to approach questions more scientifically, or at least in a way that appeared to be more scientific. If human motivation was simple and straightforward, as in the *Homo Economicus* model, it was possible to predict more reliably behaviour and results, and therefore to calculate costs and benefits. If the economy was considered to be made up of individuals rationally pursuing nothing but their own material self-interest, then it could be analyzed and quantified with a degree of precision through the use of mathematical equations.

All this created a wonderful boom for economics, which soared ahead of the other social sciences as the apparently most scientific of the disciplines. Of course, there is nothing scientific about assuming that human behaviour can be reduced to a certain motivation if this isn't in fact the case. What if the economists' assumptions about human motivation are wrong, or simply a distortion of the whole range of human wants and needs? Then all the math in the world won't help us get to where we want to go. It will help us produce sophisticated solutions, but perhaps not to the problems we want solved. What if we don't want a market in racial slurs, but instead want clean drinking water, a decent place to live and streets where we can walk outside the gate?

Even in the one field where economics should have some definitive solutions—the satisfaction of material wants—its answers seem far from unassailable. Its models show us how to maximize wealth, and where its rules have been applied, great wealth has been generated. That much is indisputable—and is borne out by the evidence of the rich enclaves tucked into the most desirable sections of the world's major cities. But the creation of a small class of millionaires and billionaires hardly solves the problem of satisfying the material wants *of all*—if that's the goal. Once we get beyond a relatively small elite, the evidence of the market's ability to satisfy material wants is less clear. Things actually seem to be getting worse for a huge part of humanity.

Economists urge us not to be confused by this apparent contradiction. They tell us that we are on the right track, that we will all be better off; we just need more free trade, lower taxes, deregulation, privatization, etc. They are urging us to believe in their system. Cox, the divinity professor, notes the extent to which faith is required, both in traditional religion and in the new religion of the market-place. In traditional religion, faith was needed to deal with the vexing question of why an all-powerful and benevolent God would allow so many bad things to happen in the world. A similar faith is required in economics, he suggests, "to explain the dislocation, pain and disorientation that are the result of transitions from economic heterodoxy to free markets." Certainly it is doubtful that economists who urge confidence that the market will bring material improvement for all would be willing to make their salaries contingent upon that outcome being achieved.

And once we get beyond the strong suit of economics—the satisfaction of material wants—the profession sure has some explaining to do. By convincing us to elevate greed and material acquisitiveness to a place of honour in our society, it has left at the sidelines just about every other possible human concern. Let's just take one quick example: the survival of the planet as we know it. Washington has long tried to argue that the scientific evidence on global warming is inconclusive. But with the release of the massive United Nations–supervised review of the subject in the spring of 2001, it was no longer really possible to make that case (if it ever was). The review, which involved fifteen hundred scientists worldwide, including virtually every important climatologist on earth, made clear that the world is facing a problem of cataclysmic proportions: reductions of crop yields in regions where food is already scarce; decreased water supplies in arid zones; and at the same time, elsewhere on the planet, massive flooding and destruction from rising sea levels and El Niño–style storms. The impact will be felt most acutely by the poorest parts of the world, but it will eventually be felt everywhere; it will change the physical stability of the earth.

Yet this seemingly vital subject has been given a subordinate status, below the task of generating a higher level of GDP. President George Bush clarified this ranking of priorities in April 2001, when he withdrew U.S. support for the Kyoto accords on global warming and proceeded to develop an energy policy based on increasing access for Americans to the very fuels that cause global warming. Bush explained that he wasn't willing to take the steps outlined in the Kyoto accords—steps that both the scientific world and the international political community had agreed, with a stunning degree of unanimity, were necessary for the future viability of the earth—because he wasn't willing to jeopardize the rate of growth of the American economy.

In what sense is this a rational position?

Perhaps it seems that the sudden melting of the polar ice caps and raging tropical storms have left climatologists, as a group, inclined to be alarmist. Let's hear, then, from paleontologists—scientists who take a longer and broader view, analyzing the overall life of the planet as it evolves over many, many centuries. In a brilliant article in *Harper's*, David Quammen explored the prospects for the environment from the perspective of paleontologists. Among other things, paleontologists make the point that the earth's species—including animal, insect and plant life—are disappearing at a greatly accelerated rate. Between 1600 and 1900, roughly seventy-five species went extinct. Between 1900 and 1979, another seventy-five disappeared from the face of the earth. But since then, with the rapid cutting down of tropical rain forests and other acts indifferent to the world's ecology, things have truly gone haywire. An estimated twenty-five thousand plant species are now considered in jeopardy, along with perhaps hundreds of thousands of different kinds of insects. This has led to speculation that we are headed towards the kind of major species meltdown that has happened only a handful of times in geological history, starting with the first mass species extinction 439 million years ago and ending with the "recent" one that wiped out the dinosaurs.

The disappearance forever of hundreds of thousands of plants and insects that largely inhabit a tropical rain forest may not sound very important. But as Quammen notes, there are certain consequences to leaving the earth's landscape "threadbare, leached of diversity." First, we risk losing valuable pharmaceutical and genetic resources. Second, as the weaker species die off, the more rugged, aggressive, prolific ones—like rats, ragweed, cockroaches and other weed-like species—become more ensconced. As a result, many basic functions of the earth's ecosystems—like the cleaning and recirculating of air and water, the renewal of soil, the decomposing of wastes, the pollinating of crops and the regulating of climate, drought and floods—cease to operate properly. Quammen is not trying to make the case that humans are facing extinction. On the contrary, humans are among the weed-like species—rugged, aggressive, prolific. But he does show that leading paleontologists believe that not very far into the future— say, five or six generations from now—the earth will be a much crummier place to live, a kind of "planet of weeds," with humans "sort of picking through the rubble."

Given that science seems to be telling us we're headed for a species meltdown not seen since the demise of the dinosaur, it might be "rational" to give this matter some attention, to elevate it on our list of priorities to a spot even above that of ensuring higher GDP growth rates. Indeed, responding in any other way seems downright irrational. And yet, mainstream opinion-makers, like those who oversee the *New York Times,* don't seem to find anything out of whack with our sense of priorities. In a low-key editorial analyzing Bush's environmental stance, the paper noted that he was reversing some of the small steps taken by the Clinton administration in the direction of environmental protection, and it went on to point out that the new administration's retreat from the Kyoto commitments "has international ramifications." There was no suggestion of other possible ramifications. Only a system that relies heavily on faith could treat as secondary or inconsequential the sweeping ramifications for life as we know it on this planet.

WHEN ALL OTHER ARGUMENTS fail, the pro-market forces generally resort to the defence of modernity. Today's extreme form of capitalism is simply the reality of the modern world, they insist. Or as the *Globe and Mail*'s Marcus Gee puts it: "At the heart of the anti-globalization movement is a fierce hostility to the very idea of modern life." In one quick swoop, the elevation of greed and acquisitiveness to the central organizing principles of society has become indistinguishable from life in the twenty-first century. Anyone who questions the current ordering of priorities must be yearning to be back in Hammurabi's time.

Had Marcus Gee ever stumbled across Karl Polanyi, he would have no doubt taken him for a fierce hater of modern life. Polanyi spent much of his adult life studying ancient and traditional societies. Nothing was too obscure for him, from the Babylonians, the ancient Greeks and the Egyptians to the Troibidor Indian bands and the medieval world. The point of all this study wasn't nostalgia for the old days or an attempt to apply yesterday's systems to today's world. Rather, Polanyi was in search of the universal. He wanted to discover what mankind's true "economic" nature was, in what way humans naturally dealt with the problem of feeding themselves and satisfying their material needs. And to see this, he felt it was necessary to strip away the lens of the market economy—to see, as it were, the hard-wiring in humans, before capitalism came along and shaped their views and their behaviour.

Probably the most striking thing that Polanyi found in his wide-ranging quest was that human economic behaviour was traditionally interwoven into the overall social fabric—that is, the production of food and material goods was an integral part of the social system. There was no separate thing called "the economy." In fact, until the eighteenth century, there was really no word that meant "the economy." As Polanyi explained it, "Neither under tribal, nor feudal, nor mercantile conditions was there . . . a separate economic system in society." How people functioned and how society produced and distributed material goods among its members were all part of the overall social process, and were largely set by tradition. Each person had his or her place in society and contributed in some way to the material production of the community.

All this changed dramatically, of course, with the rise of the market economy. Where meeting one's material needs had once simply been part of one's routine and overall life—along with religion, family duties and participating in public functions, etc.—in the market economy, the realm of satisfying material wants became separated out, enlarged and elevated in importance. This newly carved realm, called "the economy," was now considered the most important aspect of life, in that it dictated the organization of life and society. People, now reclassified as "labour," were expected, for instance, to answer to the dictates of the market, to work for a wage determined by the market and to move to wherever the market could best make use of their services. Their natural surroundings, now called "resources" or "real estate," were bought and sold, mined and processed or simply left to become a receptacle for the waste generated by the market. People and their surroundings—the very essence of society—had thus become subordinated to the dictates of the market, able to be deployed as the market demanded.

This isn't to say there weren't markets in the past. There were. In fact, markets—or the barter or exchange of goods for a price—were one of the three patterns of economic behaviour that Polanyi identified as recurring throughout history. (The other two, briefly, were redistribution and reciprocity. Redistribution, a concept we're familiar with today, refers to the divvying up of resources among people other than those who produced them. A progressive tax system, for instance, takes money from the rich and redistributes some of it to the poor. Reciprocity, a concept less familiar today but hugely important in early societies, is the mutual exchange of goods or favours without charge between people connected to each other, usually through kinship or clan. Although reciprocity is theoretically at odds with the market system's arm's-length approach to determining the value of everything, it in fact lives on today in an unofficial and often unacknowledged form. Market efficiency may demand, for instance, that job candidates be selected purely on merit. But it is not unusual for other considerations to count as well, such as connections, family ties or the "old boys' network." This kind of reciprocity isn't something that would surprise a tribal king from the ancient world.)

Market exchanges can be found in many historical contexts, stretching back to the fifth century B.C., Polanyi noted. In these earlier contexts, however, market transactions were quite different, with goods generally exchanged at fixed prices. The purpose of the transaction was to attain goods that one didn't produce oneself by selling goods one did produce—for the cobbler to sell shoes in order to buy bread, for example. Beyond this, there wasn't usually an element of personal gain involved; the purpose of the exchange was not to make a lot of money, but rather to get what one needed but didn't produce oneself. With the rise of the market economy, however, markets came to revolve around the concept of maximizing personal gain, or profit-making. The point was not just to get what one needed, but to get all that one wanted—a pit of material desires that was apparently bottomless. So while markets had long existed, the *market economy* that emerged in the West in the past several hundred years was radically different. In the market economy, markets changed in nature and importance. No longer just a part of the social order, they became a focus of their own, and were given dominance over all other considerations and aspects of life.

It is this dominance of the market over all other considerations—the environment, human social needs, the rights of labour—that is the focus of the protests that have become known as the anti-globalization movement. It's doubtful that many of the protestors and the vast numbers of others who share their concerns if not their activism have much knowledge of the different sorts of societies that have existed in history, of how they arranged their economies, and how dramatic the transformation from this traditional world to a market economy was. Still, even without this historical perspective, the protestors are essentially echoing Polanyi's point—that the elevation of greed and private profit-making to a position of dominance over all other human needs and environmental concerns is not some immutable fact of life. It's just the system we have in place now. And it can change.

HAD THEY BEEN ALIVE, Karl and Ilona Polanyi would no doubt have taken great interest in the anti-globalization movement. The values espoused by the protestors in the streets of Quebec and Seattle are the same values that shaped Red Vienna before that euphoric experiment in economic and social democracy was wiped out by Fascist storm troopers. Although democracy finally returned to Europe, Red Vienna was never replicated. The Soviet Union implemented some socialist principles, but without democracy. And Western nations, over the next few decades, experimented with the welfare state, toning down the extremes of capitalism and forcing it to respond to a broader set of public needs. Still, this was a far cry from the truly egalitarian spirit of Red Vienna, where the working population—not the financial elite—actually called the shots.

The experience of Red Vienna never left Karl or Ilona. The city remained a centrepiece of their lives, the place where they had come of age, finding each other against a backdrop of political drama and hope. For both of them, Red Vienna had been a kind of exciting and eye-opening episode that helped them define who they were, and clarified and fortified their deeply held political ideals.

After Karl published *The Great Transformation* in 1944, he gained some degree of international recognition, and went on to teach economic history and anthropology at Columbia University in New York. His seminars were immensely popular, and he attracted a broad range of students across a number of disciplines, as well as a coterie of inspired younger academics. Those young disciples, who included Abraham Rotstein, Harry Pearson, Walter Neale and George Dalton, were keen on advancing the research themes Polanyi had started, and they went on to pursue those themes with him and in their own work, after Polanyi's death in 1964. In the spring of 2001, a new edition of *The Great Transformation* was released, with a preface by Joseph Stiglitz.

For Ilona, life after Vienna was never the same. She was never again able to capture the sense of purpose and adventure that had inspired her early life, first as a fearless and foolhardy young radical in Hungary, and later as a strategic activist, daring to defy Facsist rule in defence of her beloved Red Vienna. It was downhill after that. Because of her past associations with the Communist Party, she was banned from entering the U.S. in the McCarthy years. So she and Karl bought a house in Pickering, Ontario, just outside Toronto, and Karl commuted to Columbia. But that meant he was away much of the time, and Ilona increasingly retreated to cultivating a lovely garden of wildflowers at their Pickering home. She lived fourteen years after his death.

She never lost interest in left-wing political causes and returned often to Vienna and Budapest, where she was generally treated as something of a revolutionary hero. However, her life in Canada was not particularly happy. Although she developed a close friendship with Ursula Franklin, the University of Toronto physics professor and leading political activist, Ilona never really felt connected to the suburban enclave where she lived.

If Karl and Ilona had been alive in the spring of 2001, one can imagine that they would have made their way to Quebec City. And Karl would undoubtedly have watched the protestors with great interest, seeing in their actions the signs of a rising counter-movement, an attempt to re-establish the dominance of society over the economy. Ilona, on the other hand, would probably have been right up there at the front of the protest, tearing down the Fence.

❧

IT'S HARD TO REMEMBER life before Relationship Banking. But I think it went roughly like this: you went to the bank, put money in or took money out, occasionally bought traveller's cheques or money orders, and very occasionally applied for a mortgage or a car loan. With Relationship Banking, however, you now have a Personal Banker who, as the relationship develops, will tailor things to **your individual situation,** a letter from the bank informs me, with these key words in boldface type. To think that, only a few years ago, I went to the bank and simply did my banking, and now when I go there, I have an individual situation. It's enough to give me a swelled head. Life doesn't revolve around me, but they're working on it.

More and more, we are presented with what Ellen Ullman has called the "utlimate baby-world of narcissism"—a consumer world where everything is supposedly catered to you as an individual, a world where you can apparently have whatever you want. If this sort of thing isn't enough to make you feel empowered, Dinesh D'Souza points out that we now have "unprecedented power" and the "ability to will our future." He has in mind the technological advances of robotics and biotechnology, which will allow humans to alter the genetic makeup of future generations, but you could probably also include Relationship Banking in that. It's all part of the new empowerment. It's about you, or rather, it's about **you.**

Certainly there does appear to be a vast consumer world out there, where you can feel powerful, indulged and important. And the computer now allows us to plug into this world without even having to deal with the rest of society. A TV advertisement for Intel starts with a surrealistic image of a broken-down, dysfunctional city of the future, where buildings are mostly in ruins, lineups are endless and people treat each other with suspicion and contempt. Then it cuts to an idyllic scene of a lovely Victorian house surrounded by green grass and a picket fence. Magically, the door to the house opens for us, beckoning us into a cheerful room with a large computer screen full of icons that give us access to anything, anywhere in the world. The window in the room is open, with the curtain gently billowing in the breeze, like the drawing on the front of a grade-school textbook I remember called *Wide-Open Windows*. Except there it meant "Let's go outside and explore!" Here the message is the opposite: "let's stay inside, where it's comfortable and safe." With the computer, you can get anything you want from that outside world, without actually having to go there.

Or can you? If what you want is silk pyjamas, a cocktail dress or an exquisite watch, the possibilities are endless. But there's no icon to click on if you want a clean environment, to save an endangered species, streets that are safe to walk on, a public education system so your children can go a decent school, a public transit system that will take you where you want to go. These sorts of things require some kind of collective action, and increasingly collective action seems to be out of reach. In fact, the flip side of all this focus on personal empowerment is a focus on *disempowering* us collectively. All our public systems—public health care, public education, public pensions, public transit—are underfunded and under attack. Although we are richer in terms of GDP than we've ever been before, we are told we can't afford the level of spending on public programs that we managed to afford in the past. Besides, we're told, there's no point in having public programs with ambitious social goals because government will only screw them up. All our confidence in our ability to act collectively is being undermined, with the subtext message *Whatever it is, the private sector can do it better.*

Never mind that there's no evidence to prove this. Never mind, for instance, that the private U.S. health-care system is 40 percent more expensive *per capita* than the Canadian public system, even though the Canadian system provides full medical coverage for all Canadians and the American system leaves some forty-three million without any coverage at all. This isn't because Canadians are smarter than Americans—it's because we have a public system and they don't. The simple truth is that by pooling resources through our national tax system, Canada has been able to build a public health-care system that takes care of all its citizens—an impressive achievement, when you think about it. One of the reasons we've been able to do this is that a public system is less expensive than a private system—not because the services are inferior, but because the enormous overhead costs of private insurance are eliminated and also because health problems tend to be diagnosed at an earlier stage, before they become more serious and more costly. When you leave health care to the market, it ends up being dished out like every other consumer good: to those who have the means to pay. So some end up with great care, and some end up with no care.

The attempt to discredit public health care—the crowning jewel of the social programs created in the early post-war era—shows the determination on the part of pro-market forces to undermine our confidence in our ability to act collectively. All this is part of an attempt to reshape society, and indeed, to reshape us—to make us more focused on being consumers, and less focused on being citizens. As consumers, we are being offered a world of dizzying possibilities; as citizens, we are being offered a world of shrinking possibilities. If we would all just be like *Homo Economicus,* we could adjust perfectly to the change. After all, the consumer world is a world designed for *Homo Economicus.* It is a world where nothing exists but material possessions—a perfect fit for a person who has nothing but material desires. And it all fits perfectly with the business plans of the corporations that want to sell us those material possessions and not be bothered by our collective impulse to do things like tax them or regulate them or restrict them from dumping their waste wherever they find convenient.

Of course, there are a few problems. Like *Homo Economicus,* this consumer dream world is awfully one-dimensional; it provides for endless personal material indulgence, but it doesn't really deal with a whole range of other human needs and aspirations. Specifically, it doesn't allow us to satisfy some very important needs that require collective solutions, like ensuring that all members of society have access to certain basic things—both for their sake and for overall social cohesiveness—and ensuring that the environment, which we all must ultimately share, will be protected. Without collective solutions for these needs, the world will almost certainly end up an uglier place, a crummier place to live. Thomas Homer-Dixon paints a vivid image of a world of deteriorating environmental and social conditions, where the privileged few drive in an air-conditioned stretch limo through potholed streets lined with homeless beggars. David Quammen imagines that things could break down further, with those inside the limo "drinking bottled water and breathing bottled air and eating reasonably healthy food that has become incredibly precious, while the potholes on the road outside grow ever deeper. Eventually the limo will look more like a lunar rover." And, it could be added, there will be no curtains billowing gently in the breeze on the lunar rover. Sealed portholes, with the faces of a desperate humanity pressed up against the bulletproof glass, will be the closest thing to wide-open windows.

INSTEAD OF A WORLD DESIGNED for *Homo Economicus,* then, here's another idea: a society designed to treat material greed as only one of many aspects of human motivation. Rather than stressing it, massaging it and assuring ourselves that we are capable of nothing else, we could rearrange things so that material acquisitiveness would be obliged to take a number, as it were, and wait in line with all the other human needs and motivations requiring some kind of attention. We could even strive to make greed the servant, not the master, of civilization, and to make markets subject to the dictates of society.

In rejecting the *Homo Economicus* model, the radical economists Samuel Bowles and Herbert Gintis have argued that while selfishness is an important motive, it is by no means the only one. Their work shows, for instance, that there are also important human impulses towards sharing and reciprocity. Gintis notes that people are generally willing to pay their taxes if they believe others are doing so too. Once that perception of fairness and a shared burden is gone—if it becomes known that some businesses or individuals are not paying and getting away with it, for example—then people will resist paying taxes and even seek to cheat as well. Similarly, while pure market theory says that employers cut wages in a recession because workers have little bargaining power, the reality is that employers, particularly in small companies, rarely do this. A sense of fairness, a sense of loyalty or friendship, a desire for harmonious relations may explain their reluctance.

In fact, motivations often overlap. Hugh Stretton and Lionel Orchard note that it is frequently difficult to separate out exactly what motive lies behind specific human behaviour. To illustrate this, they describe the behaviour of a typical individual, Ellie, a thirty-five-year-old wife and mother who works for IBM demonstrating its computer products and training buyers in how to use them. Through a long description of Ellie's daily life and interests, Stretton and Orchard show the complex interweaving of her personal motivation towards material gain and a host of other motivations. She works to make money and seeks promotion, and she claims all tax deductions she's entitled to. But other aspects of her behaviour seem to fit less with the *Homo Economicus* model. She joined a conservation group, originally to defend a historic site in her neighbourhood, but she stayed on to work on other campaigns for saving old buildings—perhaps because she is committed to the principle of conservation, or perhaps because she enjoys the self-image of being concerned about conservation, or perhaps because she likes the camaraderie of the movement. Or perhaps all three.

Similarly, Ellie worked hard during a six-month assignment at the museum, teaching staff there how to operate a new IBM computer program that visitors will be able to access. Her hard work at the museum could clearly be explained by her desire to please her boss, thereby positioning herself for promotion and higher pay, all of which is in line with a *Homo Economicus* model of behaviour. But Ellie also seemed to enjoy the assignment. The museum staff had little knowledge of computers, and they were really impressed by her and grateful for her instruction, which made Ellie feel good about herself. After a while, other branches of the museum started bringing other computer problems to her, making her feel even more important and respected—a feeling she particularly relished as a woman working in the traditionally male-dominated world of computers. Furthermore, she was pleased by the fact that the computer program would help inform and educate visitors to the museum. Perhaps the feeling of helping others like this simply brought her pleasure, or perhaps she just felt better about herself because she knew that even though she worked for a big corporation, she was helping people. Or perhaps both.

The point is that motivation is complex and multifaceted. Motives are at times purely geared to material self-interest, at other times connected to a desire to advance ourselves socially or project an image of ourselves socially, and other times perhaps even based on some kind of principle or moral idea that appeals to us. Or there could be a mixture or combination of any one or more of these. Some motivations could reinforce others; at other times, motivations could be in conflict.

But if we all have many motivations, doesn't it follow that society could benefit by encouraging some of our more socially harmonious motivations, particularly when they can be made to overlap with our self-interest? Let's go back to the case of health care. We are all motivated by self-interest to provide for our health-care needs. A public health-care system has the potential to serve that self-interest as well as the overall public good. By pooling resources through the tax system and providing a high level of care for all, we are able to take care of our individual needs at the same time as we take care of the broader needs of the community. And don't be too quick to dismiss the satisfaction people get from contributing to the broader community. In fact, it is this feeling that underlies the traditional sense of national pride that has long been associated with public health care in

Canada. So public health care is an effective bit of public policy, one that satisfies both private and public ends, and is made possible by the fact that all the motivational ducks are pointed in the same direction.

By contrast, a private health-care system is based only on self-interest and gives no encouragement to the broader needs of the community. In fact, as the U.S. system shows, individuals are soon pitted against each other. In the privatized U.S. system, there is a public program called Medicaid that provides care for the poor. But this creates a real divisiveness in American society. Consider the situation: there are some forty-three million Americans—mostly belonging to the ranks of the lower middle class and the near poor—who don't qualify for this public program. These people, and their family members, often go without necessary medical treatment because they can't afford it, and yet they must pay taxes that enable other members of society to get free medical care. Here, the motivation of self-interest clashes sharply with the motivation to contribute positively to the community—indeed, so sharply that any motivation to help the poor has been largely extinguished.

Given the understandable resentment of the forty-three million uninsured Americans, who have limited resources themselves, there is always political pressure to cut back on funding for Medicaid. As a result, the program provides limited and generally low-level care; it fails to cover many poor people, and it reimburses doctors for their services at such low rates that few will accept Medicaid patients. With the motivational ducks lined up in opposition to each other like this, the results are disastrous for society: inadequate care for the poor, inadequate or sometimes no care for the lower middle class and, overall, an incredibly expensive system to operate. The only real beneficiaries of the U.S. system are the thousands of companies that sell health insurance and provide medical services in the massive and lucrative private health-care industry.

One of the key strategies of the pro-market forces in recent years has been to convince us that collective solutions such as medicare can't properly serve our individual interests, thereby destroying our confidence in these collective solutions. Of course, this is the whole point of public-choice theory, which as we saw in chapter one argues that humans are by nature only self-interested and are therefore incapable of coming up with collective solutions that serve a larger public good. Thus the strong right-wing voice of the *National Post* has continually emphasized the problems of medicare, suggesting that there is a crisis that can best be dealt with through privatization. Similarly, the *Post* has conducted a relentless campaign against our tax system—particularly its few remaining progressive features—in an attempt to convince Canadians that our overall tax and social-transfer system fails to serve their individual interests. To this end, the *Post* has attempted to destroy the connection in people's minds between paying taxes and receiving benefits and things of value. Instead, we are simply told our taxes are too high, particularly in comparison with the U.S., without any acknowledgement of any additional benefits we receive—which, of course, include full health-care coverage and more public support for education. The *Post* seems to be trying to destroy the inclination of ordinary citizens, identified by Bowles and Gintis, to pay their taxes voluntarily, as part of a general socially cooperative attitude and a belief in the viability of collective solutions. Instead, the *Post* seems willing—in fact, keen—to sacrifice the popular motivation towards social cohesiveness and replace it with a individualistic "tax rage."

That a pro-market force like the *Post* would want to do this is perhaps not surprising; the goal of its publisher, the corporate mogul Conrad Black, is unabashedly to lower taxes and reduce the size of government. Similarly, it is hardly surprising that the American health-care industry has relentlessly attacked and undermined any move to try to create a public health-care system in the U.S. But beyond the narrow interests of the corporate world, it would make a lot of sense for the rest of society to structure things so that our private self-interest is lined up, wherever possible, with the broader public interest. While this may seem like simple common sense, it is almost exactly the opposite of what the religion of the market teaches us.

ADAM SMITH'S FAMOUS PASSAGE explaining the wondrous qualities
of human self-interest has become the definitive expression of market
theory, doing for market dogma what the Sermon on the Mount did
for Christianity. Smith's claim that it "is not from the benevolence of
the butcher, the brewer or the baker, that we expect our dinner, but
from their regard to their own self-interest" makes the case that the
broader public will best be served not by a focus on defending the
public good, but by releasing the forces of individual greed and self-
interest. As we've seen, Smith was actually more nuanced in his views
than many of his followers are today. Still, we have from him a powerful endorsement for the idea that if we want to improve the lot of
human beings, we are best to let individual greed do the work for us.
It is not hard to see why this idea has caught on among those keen to
indulge their individual greed.

It has also become a quick way for pro-market types to dismiss
opponents, branding their efforts—because of either misinformation
or selfishness—as actually contrary to the interests of the world's
poor. In this spirit, Thomas Friedman dismissed the protestors in
Quebec City as members of the "Coalition to Keep Poor People
Poor." It's an ingenious argument, and it makes for a canny debating
point. Anything that advances the cause of private profit-making can
be defended because, well, it's ultimately going to help poor people
in Afghanistan and Guatemala. Criticism can then instantly be
deflected by accusing critics of wanting to keep Afghanis and
Guatemalans poor.

Given the strength and pervasiveness of this Adam Smith position
in our culture, it is striking, as I've argued earlier in this book, that so
little evidence exists to back it up. It is an argument made constantly
and confidently, even triumphantly, by pro-market forces—even as,
under their watch, the conditions of the world's poor have deteriorated drastically in recent years. The Coalition to Keep Poor People
Poor might as well disband; its apparent goal is being accomplished in

spades by pro-market forces. If the prospect of the world's poor improving their lot is one that supposedly upsets anti-capitalist protestors, they can confidently put away their gas masks and get back to the shopping mall—global capitalism can be trusted to keep the poor in check without any help.

Of course, lack of evidence has never been a problem for religions. That's where faith comes in handy. It would certainly be hard for Christianity to make the case that God, at any given moment, is acting fairly, and that justice and good are being properly rewarded in the world. But God, we're told, works in mysterious ways, and things will look very different after death. Indeed, it is in the afterlife that everything is supposed to be tallied up and worked out fairly; this is where the evil ones among us finally get their comeuppance in the fires of hell. And although it's often frustrating that the evil ones don't get a little pre-taste of unpleasantness right now just so we can be sure, it all comes down to faith. We have to believe that justice will be done in the end.

And so it is with the market. Even if progress for the world's poor seems slow, we must have faith that by releasing the full force of individual greed, all will turn out well in the end. For many pro-market types, sitting in the comfort of their lavish homes, this faith seems easy to come by, and they have no trouble being patient and channelling their efforts into making sure that individual greed is fully released. For others, that faith may be harder to come by, particularly given the fact that the market lacks the escape hatch of an afterlife. This is a major stumbling block. Unlike Christianity, the market is supposed to make good on its promises in this world—a much more exacting demand.

But if the market lacks the advantages of an afterlife, it does have the next best thing—the long run. If things don't seem to be working out so well now, pro-market types will argue that it takes time, that the poor will do better *in the long run*. It's not as airtight an argument as "things will be better in the afterlife," but it's not bad, particularly since there's never any time limit on the long run. So market theologians can at least stall for time. But there's also the problem of the visibility of the preliminary evidence. In Christianity, the results promised for the afterlife have the advantage of being entirely located in another world, beyond human inspection. Market theology, on the other hand, promises results in this world, where everything is on full display—and so far, things aren't looking good. Given the extent and intractability of world poverty, the market case appears even flimsier than the Christian one. Certainly, believing in the beneficent powers of the market requires a faith that is profound indeed.

WHEN PUSHED INTO A CORNER, pro-market forces have a final position to retreat to: even if individual greed does not eventually enrich the world, it is all we are capable of anyway. It all comes down, then, to our friend *Homo Economicus,* the one-dimensional creature who supposedly defines us all, and whose self-centred nature apparently prevents us from working out collective solutions that would further the public good. When all is said and done, it is *Homo Economicus,* and the limited view of human potential that he represents, which is the ace up the sleeve of the pro-market types.

Of course, it's interesting to note that as much as the pro-market types cling to *Homo Economicus* and sneer at any other model of human behaviour as naive and gullible, they aren't entirely convinced themselves. Their position is that humans are greedy and self-interested and no more, but just in case that's not true, they insist on putting in place sweeping laws to enforce the rights of individual greed and strike down collective measures aimed at defending the public good. The basic thrust of the new trade deals is to empower corporations to knock down collective attempts at defending the interests of society—which is odd if one dismisses the notion that humans are collectively motivated to protect the interests of society. I suspect that, deep down, the pro-market types don't actually believe this *Homo Economicus* stuff any more than we do. That's why they're so determined to get these trade deals in place, to make sure that we don't achieve the potential for collective action that they fully understand we are capable of.

Karl Polanyi considered the concept of *Homo Economicus* an insult to humans. "To reduce human behaviour to acquisition and profit-making is a travesty—a libel on human beings," says Abraham Rotstein, the Polanyi scholar. It may well be that the *Homo Economicus* character is such an extreme representation of human nature that it is more laughable than libellous. In the 2001 movie *Lucky Numbers,* starring John Travolta and Lisa Kudrow, Kudrow plays a woman involved in a scheme to rig the lottery, and her character is pure *Homo Economicus*. Greedy and selfish to a fault, she never thinks of anything but her own self-interest, and her character is so extreme it is comical.

Rather than end on such a low note, I will offer up what could be considered a sort of antidote to *Homo Economicus* and his ilk, which I first encountered years ago and which has stayed with me ever since. In a wonderful essay, "The Bird and the Machine," Loren Eisley describes how he was reading in his morning paper about the brilliant advances of science and how machines can now replicate virtually everything humans can do. Eisley, a professor of the history of science at the University of Pennsylvania, wasn't questioning the advances of science, but as he read the article in the paper, he was suddenly struck by the memory of an encounter with a pair of birds years earlier.

He had been on a research expedition in a remote desert when he came upon a pair of sparrow hawks and was instructed to entrap them so they could be brought back to the city, where they would be put in a zoo. In his attempt to capture the birds, one put up such fierce resistance that its mate managed to get away. Eisley finally caught the first bird and kept it in a small cage overnight. The next morning he noticed that the young hawk seemed to have lost its will to live, and now lay mostly limp and spiritless. Checking to make sure no one was watching, Eisley opened the cage door and let the bird go. Straining to watch the hawk soar into the air, he was astonished to see the bird's mate circling high in the sky overhead, "where she must have been soaring restlessly above us for untold hours." As he watched the birds hurtling towards each other "from far up, ringing from peak to peak of the summits over us, came a cry of such unutterable and ecstatic joy that it sounds down across the years."

Eisley's point was that while machines may be able to do amazing things, "the machine does not bleed, ache, hang for hours in the empty sky in a torment of hope to learn the fate of another machine, nor does it cry out with joy nor dance in the air with the fierce passion of a bird."

It could be added that *Homo Economicus* probably also wouldn't bleed, ache or hang for hours in a torment of hope to learn the fate of another *Homo Economicus*. After all, what would be in it for him? While we may not all possess the fierce passion of a bird, it seems clear that there's a lot more to us than *Homo Economicus* lets on. If so, there's hope for us yet.

# Epilogue

IN THE LATE 1970S, the economics department at McGill University was a fairly interesting place to be for progressive-minded students like Marguerite Mendell. University economics departments had already begun rejecting Keynesian solutions and veering towards more pure-market economics, but McGill's department still included some impressive left-leaning economists. There was long-time social democrat Jack Weldon, up-and-coming international financial expert Tom Naylor and Third World development specialist Kari Levitt, who had just made a big splash with her best-selling book, *Silent Surrender,* about foreign ownership of the Canadian economy. So for Marguerite Mendell, who was working on her PhD in economics at the time, McGill was a stimulating and eclectic environment, and she eagerly took up studying Marx under Weldon and development economics under Levitt. But what really changed the course of Mendell's intellectual development—and her life—was a chance discovery of the work of Karl Polanyi.

Polanyi's work wasn't assigned on any of her courses or reading lists, and she had come upon a reference to it almost by chance, in some extra reading she was doing on economic anthropology. Mendell looked up some of Polanyi's books in the library and was immediately overwhelmed by the power of his ideas and observations, and their relevance to broader political and economic issues. She was surprised, however, to discover that Jack Weldon, despite his knowledge of economic history and left-wing political movements, was unaware of Polanyi. She was even more surprised to discover that Kari Levitt, whom she had come to know quite well through their common interest in Third World issues, was Karl Polanyi's daughter.

Mendell ended up doing her thesis on Polanyi, and over the course of the next decade, she and Kari Levitt became immersed in exploring the intellectual world of Polanyi's ideas. With the death of Ilona in 1978, Kari had inherited an enormous collection of papers—drafts of Polanyi's books, articles, diaries and lecture notes, as well as his voluminous correspondence in several different languages. Kari offered the papers to several Canadian universities, including McGill, but got little response. In the end, she and Mendell painstakingly sorted through the massive material themselves, spending most of two years in a basement reading through and cataloguing the documents. Later, a grant from the Rockefeller Foundation helped them create an extensive computerized archive of Polanyi's work. They also set up the Karl Polanyi Institute of Political Economy, headed by Mendell, at Concordia University in Montreal. The institute holds biennial international conferences and seeks to foster research and thought in areas explored by Polanyi.

It's somehow appropriate that the Karl Polanyi Institute is located here in Canada, even though Polanyi was a Central European whose intellectual interests were enormously wide-ranging over time and space. Much of the Polanyi family still lives in Canada, including Kari Polanyi-Levitt and Karl Polanyi's nephew John Polanyi, winner of the Nobel Prize for Chemistry in 1986, who lives in Toronto with his family. There is also perhaps a subtler but more profound way in which Karl Polanyi is connected to Canada. Abraham Rotstein, who was deeply influenced by his studies under Polanyi and his close friendship with Karl and Ilona, went on to become an important figure in Canadian intellectual life. Both as a prominent professor of economics at the University of Toronto and formerly as editor of the left-leaning, nationalistic *Canadian Forum* magazine, Rotstein has had an impact on a large number of Canadians, both inside and outside the academic world, and has helped bring Polanyi's *The Great Transformation* to a wider audience in recent years. Rotstein's vigorous support for a Polanyian perspective has helped reinforce a strain of anti-market thinking that has been a recurrent theme in Canadian culture.

It would be a mistake to put too much emphasis on this anti-market strain. At times, Canada's culture seems almost indistinguishable from the corporate culture of Disneyland and McDonald's emanating from south of the border. And certainly Conrad Black's *National Post* has done its best in the past few years to extinguish any notion that Canadians should want a separate identity or should in any way resist the market culture of America. The *Post*'s constant message has been that things are better in the U.S., and that any Canadian with any sort of ability would want to leave immediately for those greener American pastures. *Frank* magazine captured the spirit of the *Post*'s relentless "brain drain" campaign with the satirical headline: "Brane drane excelorating: If you kin reed this sentins, Unkle Sam wonts you."

Still, it does seem there's some small strain of independent, anti-market thinking here, which is partly why Black and the neoconservative editors he's hired to run the *Post* find Canada so irritating. Canadians seem deeply attached to egalitarian, collectivist solutions such as medicare—an attachment that Black himself has ridiculed. This attachment springs largely from the Canadian affinity for equality—something that the market is notoriously poor at delivering. Canadians bristle at the notion of the kind of rampant inequality visible in the market culture south of the border, where the emergency departments of private hospitals routinely turn away patients because they lack medical insurance.

A bit of anti-market rebelliousness also seemed to be behind the widespread hostility of Canadians to the proposed merger of four of the country's biggest banks in 1998. When the federal government responded to this popular sentiment by rejecting the merger requests, there was much negative commentary in the business press, particularly the *Post*. Among those lamenting the anti-bank sentiments of Canadians was B.C. economist David Bond, who ended his column in the *Post* simply with the words: "How sad. How Canadian." He meant it as an insult: that this reckless defiance of the dictates of the marketplace had a distinctly Canadian stamp to it.

But I felt a small surge of national pride when I read that. The thought that there's something deep in the Canadian psyche that leads us to occasionally defy the dictates of the market seems almost inspiring. I suspect that the vision of Karl Polanyi has played a role in keeping that defiance alive.

# Notes

**CHAPTER ONE:** *Nudists and Capitalists*

p. 1    *Like any crime* . . . The trial of William le Bole is described in W. J. Ashley, *An Introduction to English Economic History and Theory* (London: Longmans, Green & Co., 1906), Part 1, *The Middle Ages*, p. 189.

p. 2    *Usurers seemed to fare particularly badly* . . . Ibid., pp. 148–53. See also Jacques Le Goff, "The Usurer and Purgatory," in *The Dawn of Modern Banking* (New Haven, Conn.: Yale University Press, 1979), and John W. Baldwin, *Master, Princes and Merchants: The Social View of Peter the Chanter and his Circle* (Princeton, N.J.: Princeton University Press, 1970), vol. 1.

p. 3    *If there was one thing the executives* . . . The legal aspects of the Metalclad case are set out in the *ICSID Review—Foreign Investment Law Journal* (forthcoming issue). The ICSID (International Centre for Settlement of Investment Disputes) operates under the auspices of the World Bank. Its Web site is www.worldbank.org/icsid. For a more popular account, see Anthony DePalma, "NAFTA's Powerful Little Secret," *New York Times*, March 11, 2001.

p. 7    *The late economic historian* . . . Karl Polanyi's major work is *The Great Transformation* (Boston: Beacon Press, 1957). *The Great Transformation* was first published in 1944.

p. 8    *In her tiny jail cell in Lima* . . . Details of the Arredondo case can be found on the Web site of the United Nations Human Rights Committee, www.unhchr.ch. Follow-up information on the case is drawn from personal correspondence between the author and Paul Oertly, spokesman for the UN committee.

p. 13    *But while the case for* Homo Economicus . . . The social nature of humans is an important theme running through Polanyi's work. In addition to *The Great Transformation*, see "Aristotle Discovers the Economy" and "The Economy As Instituted Process," in Polanyi, Conrad M. Arensberg and Harry Pearson, eds., *Trade and Market in the Early Empires* (New York: The Free Press, 1957), and "Jean-Jacques Rousseau: Or Is a Free Society Possible?" text of a lecture given by Karl Polanyi at Bennington College,

Vermont, April 27, 1943. See also Marguerite Mendell and Daniel Salee, "Introduction," in Marguerite Mendell and Daniel Salee, eds., *The Legacy of Karl Polanyi* (New York: St. Martin's Press, 1991), and Gregory Baum, *Karl Polanyi on Ethics and Economics* (Montreal and Kingston: McGill-Queen's University Press, 1996).

p. 14   *"[M]an does not aim at safeguarding . . ."* Karl Polanyi, "Our Obsolete Market Mentality," in George Dalton, ed., *Primitive, Archaic and Modern Economies: Essays of Karl Polanyi* (Garden City, N.Y.: Anchor Books, 1968), p. 65.

p. 15   *"In Iroquois society . . ."* Author interview with Abraham Rotstein.

p. 15   *Robert Heilbroner makes a similar point . . .* Robert L. Heilbroner, *The Worldly Philosophers* (New York: Simon and Schuster, 1992), pp. 24–27.

p. 16   *"Rank and status . . ."* Polanyi, "Obsolete Market Mentality," p. 67.

p. 18   *Even Adam Smith . . .* For Smith's views on the importance of human virtue, see Adam Smith, *The Theory of Moral Sentiments* (New York: Augustus M. Kelley Publishers, 1966), p. 213.

p. 20   *Such people, who would be considered smart businesspeople . . .* Quoted in E. P. Thompson, *Customs in Common,* (New York: The New Press, 1991), pp. 253–54.

p. 20   *But in our celebration . . .* Polanyi, *Great Transformation,* p. 156.

p. 23   *Polanyi questions the wisdom . . .* Polanyi, "Obsolete Market Mentality," pp. 71–72.

p. 25   *So merciless is the tyranny . . .* R. H. Tawney, *Religion and the Rise of Capitalism* (Toronto: Penguin Books, 1990), p. 73, (italics added).

p. 26   *"By having their minds constantly employed . . ."* Quoted in Heilbroner, *The Nature and Logic of Capitalism* (New York: W. W. Norton and Company, 1985), p. 114.

p. 27   *We will return to this subject . . .* See *World Development Report 2000–2001: Attacking Poverty* (New York: Oxford University Press, published for the World Bank, 2001), p. vi.

p. 27   *The latest numbers from the World Bank . . .* Branko Milanovic (World Bank Development Research Group), "True World Income Distribution, 1988 and 1993: First Calculation Based on Household Surveys Alone" (Unpublished paper, November 2000). Additional information from author interview with Branko Milanovic, May 25, 2001.

p. 28   *But this claim, as Heilbroner notes . . .* Heilbroner, *Nature and Logic of Capitalism,* p. 113.

p. 28   *"[T]he economic problem has been solved. . . .* Dinesh D'Souza, *The Virtue of Prosperity* (New York: The Free Press, 2000), p. 231.

p. 28   *A recent Wall Street Journal . . .* William McGurn, "Globalization Gospel Reaches the Eternal City," *National Post,* Dec. 23, 2000 (reprinted from the *Wall Street Journal*).

p. 29 *"Short-term inequality remains a problem . . ."* D'Souza, *Virtue of Prosperity,* p. 108.

p. 29 *"We are living in an astonishing . . ."* Ibid., p. 229.

p. 29 *As Heilbroner notes* . . . Heilbroner, *Nature and Logic of Capitalism,* p. 46.

p. 30 *Even Adam Smith acknowledged* . . . Quoted in ibid., p. 46.

p. 30 *Comments John Gray* . . . John Gray, *False Dawn: The Delusions of Global Capitalism* (London: Granta Books, 1998), p. 8.

p. 30 *The principle that everyone in society* . . . Polanyi, *Great Transformation,* p. 163.

p. 31 *This explains why the drug industry* . . . Médecins Sans Frontières, "Campaign for Access to Essential Medicines" (MSF Briefing for the European Parliament). See also James Orbinski and Avi Denburg, "Focus on the Neglected Diseases," *Globe and Mail,* July 11, 2001, and Linda McQuaig, "Big Parma Fails the Poor and Sick," *National Post,* July 3, 2001.

p. 32 *Gro Harlem Brundtland* . . . G. Brundtland, "Towards a Strategic Agenda for the WHO Secretariat: Statement by the Director-General to the Executive Board at Its 105th Session," Jan. 24, 2000, p. 7.

p. 34 *These academics, who became known as public-choice theorists* . . . For an excellent discussion of public-choice theory, see Hugh Stretton and Lionel Orchard, *Public Goods, Public Enterprise, Public Choice: Theoretical Foundations of the Contemporary Attack on Government* (New York: St. Martin's Press, 1994).

p. 35 *The extreme nature of some public-choice theories* . . . Ibid., p. 44.

p. 36 *The absurdity of public-choice theory* . . . Quoted in ibid., p. 51. See also, Amartya K. Sen, "Rational Fools: A Critique of the Behavioural Foundations of Economic Theory," in *Philosophy and Public Affairs,* 6, no. 4 (Summer 1977).

p. 36 *"Public-choice theory is . . ."* Lars Udehn, *The Limits of Public Choice* (London: Routledge, 1996).

p. 38 *Stretton and Orchard note.* . . . Stretton and Orchard, *Public Goods,* p. 20.

**CHAPTER TWO**: *Remaking the World*

p. 41 *Yes, we are back to the subject of the new trade deals* . . . For a description and analysis of the Methanex case, see William T. Waren, *Paying to Regulate: A Guide to Methanex vs. United States and NAFTA Investor Rights* (working paper for the Harrison Institute for Public Law, Georgetown University Law Center, Washington, D.C., March 26, 2001). See also Linda McQuaig, "NAFTA: Viagra for Corporations," in *National Post,* April 9, 2001.

p. 44 *The Canadian government did take initial steps* . . . Scott Sinclair, "Canadian Government Retreats on NAFTA Investor-State Concerns," in *Briefing*

*Paper Series: Trade and Investment,* vol. 2, no. 3 (Canadian Centre for Policy Alternatives: June 11, 2001). See also Linda McQuaig, "Chrétien Sings a Familiar Tune," in *National Post,* June 18, 2001.

p. 45   *And Sergio Marchi . . .* Quoted in Sinclair, "Investor-State Concerns," p. 1.

p. 45   *The concerns raised by Pettigrew . . .* Pierre S. Pettigrew, "Chapter 11 debate," *National Post,* March 23, 2001.

p. 46   *Indeed, the U.S. released a copy of a letter . . .* The letter, to the U.S. trade representative Robert Zoellick, is included as an appendix in Sinclair, "Investor-State Concerns." It was also published in *World Trade Online,* the electronic service of *Inside U.S. Trade.*

p. 46   *He cheerfully told the House of Commons . . . Hansard Parliamentary Debates,* April 24, 2001.

p. 48   *In 1948, fifty-four countries met in Havana . . .* The background story of the Havana conference, the changing approach to international trade in the post-war decades and the origin and negotiation of the Canada-U.S. Free Trade Agreement is adapted from my book *The Quick and the Dead: Brian Mulroney, Big Business and the Seduction of Canada* (Toronto: Viking, 1991).

p. 56   *When the NAFTA tribunal's decision favouring Metalclad . . .* The appeal of the NAFTA tribunal's ruling in the Metalclad case was heard by Mr. Justice Tysoe of the Supreme Court of British Columbia in the spring of 2001. Judge Tysoe released his decision on May 2, 2001.

p. 57   *As Pettigrew himself put it . . .* Pettigrew, "Chapter 11 debate."

p. 57   *This explains why Ottawa backed off . . .* For details on the MMT case, see Steven Shryman, *A Citizen's Guide to the World Trade Organization* (Ottawa: The Canadian Centre for Policy Alternatives, 1999), pp. 132–34.

p. 58   *Defenders of NAFTA see no problem with this . . .* Barry Appleton, "NAFTA Protects the Public," *National Post,* April 16, 2001.

p. 58   *In the case of California's MTBE ban . . .* William T. Waren, *Paying to Regulate.*

p. 58   *If corporations have had little luck . . .* Information on the operation of NAFTA tribunals comes from the author's interview with Antonio R. Parra, deputy secretary-general of ICSID, May 17, 2001. See also DePalma, "NAFTA's Powerful Little Secret."

p. 60   *The Auto Pact itself was grandfathered . . .* Scott Sinclair, *GATS: Sequel to Seattle: How the World Trade Organization's New "Services" Negotiations Threaten Democracy* (Ottawa: The Canadian Centre for Policy Alternatives, 2000), pp. 42–43.

p. 61   *Ottawa trade lawyer . . .* Author interview with Howard Mann.

p. 62   *Faster than a speeding horse . . .* Information on the UPS NAFTA claim is from *United Parcel Service of America, Inc. vs. Government of Canada,* "Notice of Intent to Submit a Claim to Arbitration under Section B of Chapter

11 of the North American Free Trade Agreement," filed by Appleton and Associates, Washington, D.C., Jan. 19, 2000. See also Sinclair, *GATS*, and Donald Mazankowski, "UPS Delivers a Threat to Canadian Business via NAFTA," *Globe and Mail*, Feb. 8, 2001.

p. 66   *Trade critic Maude Barlow* ... Maude Barlow, "The Free Trade Area of the Americas and the Threat to Social Programs, Environmental Sustainability and Social Justice in Canada and the Americas," on the Web site of the Council of Canadians, www.canadians.org. Also on that Web site, Murray Dobbin, "NAFTA's Big Brother: The Free Trade Area of the Americas and the Threat of NAFTA-Style 'Investor-State' Rules."

p. 67   *Given the tightness of the security system* ... Information on the World Bank and the IMF is drawn from *World Development Report 2000–2001, World Development Indicators 2000* (Washington: World Bank, 2000), and *News and Notices for IMF and World Bank Watchers* vol. 2, no. 4 (spring 2001), and vol. 2, no. 2, (spring 2000), prepared by the Globalization Challenge Initiative, Washington, D.C., and also available on-line at www.challengeglobalization.org. See also *The All-Too-Visible Hand: A Five-Country Look at the Long and Destructive Reach of the IMF.* (Washington: Friends of the Earth and the Development Gap, 1999).

p. 68   *It's interesting to note that* ... Mark Weisbrot, "Globalism for Dummies," *Harper's*, May 2000, p. 15.

p. 69   *"We're not going to apologize ..."* Author interview with Milan Brahmbhatt, Dec. 14, 2000.

p. 73   *Journalist Greg Palast* ... Greg Palast, "An Internal IMF Study Reveals the Price Rescued Nations Pay: Dearer Essentials, Worse Poverty and Shorter Lives," *Observer*, Oct. 8, 2000. See also *Structural Adjustment Program (SAP) Information Alert on the April 2000 IMF Loan to Ecuador* (Washington: Globalization Challenge Initiative, 2000).

p. 74   *In a breath-taking piece of logic* ... "The Push for Water Privatization and Full Cost Recovery," in *News and Notices* 2, no. 4 (Spring 2001), pp. 22–29.

p. 74   *A report prepared for the government* ... Cited in ibid.

p. 75   *An analysis of IMF loan policies* ... Sara Grusky, "IMF Forces Water Privatization on Poor Countries" (release from Globalization Challenge Initiative, Feb. 2001).

p. 75   *As a result, well-off farmers in Tanzania* ... Ross Hammond, "The Impact of IMF Structural Adjustment Policies on Tanzanian Agriculture," in *The All-Too-Visible Hand*, p. 58.

p. 76   *Enthusiasts for the new global economy* ... Peter Foster, "Here's an Idea! Hurl a Cobblestone," *National Post*, Sept. 27, 2000.

p. 76   *But nobody's asking why Ugandans* ... Report and Recommendation of the President of the International Development Association to the Executive Directors on a Proposed Credit of SDR 116.2 Million to

Republic of Uganda for a Poverty Reduction Support Credit, Report No. P7442-UG, March 23, 2001 (document of the World Bank, marked for official use only).

p. 76 *Why, for instance, was it necessary for the Ugandan finance minister* . . . Letter from Hon. Gerald M. Ssendaula, Minister of Finance, Uganda, to James D. Wolfensohn, President of the World Bank and the International Development Association, March 9, 2001, attached to ibid. The IMF and World Bank program is called the Poverty Reduction Strategy Papers (PRSP), but Uganda qualified under its existing Poverty Eradication Action Plan (PEAP).

p. 77 *As the Washington-based Center for Economic and Policy Research* . . . Figures for declining growth in the developing world are from Mark Weisbrot, Dean Baker, Robert Naiman and Gila Neta, *Growth May Be Good for the Poor—But Are IMF and World Bank Policies Good for Growth?* (Washington: Center for Economic and Policy Research, 2000). The 20 per cent decline in Mexican wages is cited in David Crane, "The Downsides to New Trade Deal," *Toronto Star*, April 22, 2001.

p. 79 *Even the World Bank acknowledges* . . . *World Development Report* 2000–2001, p. 64.

p. 79 *Instead, bank officials tend to attribute the lack of success.* . . . Ibid., p. 65.

p. 79 *In fact, an earlier draft of the report* . . . Charlotte Denny, "World Bank Dilutes Report: Agencies Claim Poverty Document Was Censored," *Guardian*, Sept. 13, 2000.

p. 80 *That is the conclusion of another bank economist* . . . Mark Drajem, "IMF, World Bank Reforms Leave Poor Behind, Bank Economist Finds," Bloomberg News Service, Nov. 7, 2000.

p. 80 *The evidence suggests not only a failure* . . . Milanovic, "True World Income Distribution," and author interview. For more on Milanovic's study, see also "Global Shares," in *Left Business Observer*, no. 93 (Feb. 10, 2000.)

p. 81 *It's not often one finds oneself in the back of a limo.* . . . Author interview with Joseph Stiglitz, Jan. 8, 2001. Information about Stiglitz and his views are drawn from this interview, as well as from a number of other sources, including Stiglitz, "What I Learned at the World Economic Crisis," *New Republic*, April 17, 2000; Stiglitz, "The Role of Government in the Economies of Developing Countries," in Edmond Malinwand, ed., *Development Strategy and Management of the Market Economy*, vol. 1 (Oxford: Clarendon Press, 1997); and Louis Uchitelle, "World Bank Economist Felt He Had to Silence Criticism or Quit," *New York Times*, Dec. 2, 1999. See also Lucy Komissar, "The Progressive Interview: Joseph Stiglitz," *The Progressive*, (June 2000), pp. 34–38, and Owen Ullmann, "Mad Dog," *The International Economy*, (March/April 1999), pp. 25–27.

p. 91 *"I know Joe well* . . . *"* Author interview with Paul Martin, July 17, 2001.

CHAPTER THREE: *Loot Bags and the Triumph of the Market*

p. 95    *This proliferation of new baubles . . .* Robert H. Frank, *Luxury Fever: Why Money Fails to Satisfy in an Era of Excess* (New York: The Free Press, 1999).

p. 98    *For instance, one index developed by the Ottawa-based . . .* Lars Osberg and Andrew Sharpe, "Trends in Economic Well-Being in the 1990s," in *The Review of Economic Performance and Social Progress* (Ottawa and Montreal: Centre for the Study of Living Standards/Institute for Research on Public Policy, 2001).

p. 101    *There is strong evidence to support this conclusion . . .* John F. Helliwell, "How's Life? Combining Individual and National Variables to Explain Subjective Well-Being" (unpublished paper, April 2001).

p. 101    *Richard Easterlin . . .* Richard A. Easterlin, "Will Raising the Incomes of All Increase the Happiness of All?" *Journal of Economic Behaviour and Organization* 27 (1995), pp. 35–47.

p. 102    *Along these lines . . .* Heilbroner, *Nature and Logic of Capitalism*, p. 52.

p. 102    *There's an interesting study . . .* Frank, *Luxury Fever*, pp. 128–129.

p. 103    *Or as Karl Marx put it . . .* Quoted in ibid., p. 122.

p. 105    *But as Robert E. Lane has shown . . .* Cited in Stretton and Orchard, *Public Goods*, p. 133.

p. 106    *The Vancouver anti-poverty activist . . .* Jean Swanson, *Poor-Bashing: The Politics of Exclusion* (Toronto: Between the Lines, 2001).

p. 107    *Now, these men were engaging . . .* Journalist Tom Walkom described how phrases like "risk-taking" have been taken over by the business world in recent years. Thomas Walkom, "Torytalk," *This Magazine* 18, no. 6 (Feb. 1985).

p. 109    *"Social systems have to be built . . ."* Lester C. Thurow, *Building WEALTH: The New Rules for Individuals, Companies and Nations in a Knowledge-Based Economy* (New York: HarperCollins, 1999).

p. 110    *Hence, the demand for this kind of material . . .* Thomas Frank, "It's Globalicious!" *Harper's*, Oct. 1999.

p. 115    *Enter Thomas Friedman . . .* Thomas Friedman, *The Lexus and the Olive Tree: Understanding Globalization* (New York: Anchor Books, 1999).

p. 119    *More people may be investing than ever before . . .* A study by MIT economist James Porterba and Dartmouth College economist Andrew Samwick shows that the top quarter of U.S. households own 82 per cent of all stock. The Porterba-Samwick study is cited in Aaron Bernstein, "Sharing Prosperity," *Business Week*, Sept. 1, 1997. See also Adam Harmes, *Unseen Power: How Mutual Funds Threaten the Political and Economic Wealth of Nations* (Toronto: Stoddart Publishing, 2001). Harmes argues that "mutual funds and pension funds are serving to concentrate power within the financial markets in a way that is reducing the diversity of the investor base. . . . [D]ecisions relating to investing are becoming increasingly concentrated as more individuals delegate control over their savings to the professional fund managers" (p. 31).

## CHAPTER FOUR: *Love and Revolution in Red Vienna*

p. 124 *The arrival of the young woman* . . . The story of the lives of Karl Polanyi and Ilona Duczynska is drawn from a number of sources, including several long interviews with their daughter, Kari Polanyi-Levitt. Other important sources include Lee Congdon, *Exile and Social Thought: Hungarian Intellectuals in Germany and Austria* 1919–1933 (Princeton, N.J.: Princeton University Press, 1991); Kenneth McRobbie and Kari Polanyi-Levitt, eds., *Karl Polanyi in Vienna* (Montreal: Black Rose Books, 2000); Kari Polanyi-Levitt, ed., *The Life and Work of Karl Polanyi* (Montreal: Black Rose Books, 1990); and Judit Szapor, "The Possibilities and Impossibilities of This Century: Three Generations of Women of the Polanyi Family" (unpublished paper, 2000). The historical and political background of Central Europe in the early part of the twentieth century is drawn mostly from G.E.R. Gedye, *Fallen Bastions: The Central European Tragedy* (London: Victor Gollancz Ltd., 1939); Adolf Sturmthal, *The Tragedy of European Labour* 1918–1939 (London: Victor Gollancz Ltd., 1944); Laszlo Kontler, *Millennium in Central Europe: A History of Hungary* (Budapest: Atlantisz Publishing House, 1999); and Carl E. Schorske, *Fin-de-Siècle Vienna: Politics and Culture* (New York: Vintage Books, 1981).

p. 146 *Von Mises and his young research assistant, von Hayek* . . . See John Casssidy, "The Price Prophet: The Long-Forgotten Economist Whose Controversial Theories Help Explain Today's Market Mania," *New Yorker*, Feb. 27, 2000.

p. 146 *The issue struck Polanyi as profound* . . . For the debate between Von Mises and Polanyi, see Peter Rosner, "Karl Polanyi on Socialist Accounting," in Polanyi-Levitt, ed., *Life and Work of Karl Polanyi*, and Marguerite Mendell, "Karl Polanyi and Feasible Socialism," in ibid.

p. 155 *In the end, the rank and file* . . . Ilona Duczynska later wrote her own account of the Schutzbund resistance. Ilona Duczynska, *Workers in Arms: The Austrian Schutzbund and the Civil War of* 1934 (New York: Monthly Review Press, 1978).

p. 156 *The plan was to broadcast a message* . . . The story of the illegal radio broadcasts is told in Barbara Striker, "This Is the Voice of Radio Schutzbund," in McRobbie and Polanyi-Levitt, eds., *Karl Polanyi in Vienna*.

p. 158 *To Polanyi, the education of* . . . Marguerite Mendell, "Karl Polanyi on Socialism and Education," paper presented to the Third International Karl Polanyi Conference (Milan, Nov. 1990).

p. 160 *In the powerful words of the eighteenth-century poet Oliver Goldsmith . . .* Quoted in Christopher Hill, *Liberty Against the Law: Some Seventeenth-Century Controversies* (London: Penguin, 1996), p. 43.

## CHAPTER FIVE: *Behind the Hedge*

p. 161 *It may be hard for us to imagine . . .* My account of the impact of the enclosure movement on the peasants and their resistance to it is drawn from a number of sources, particularly Hill, *Liberty Against the Law;* R. H. Tawney, *The Agrarian Problem in the Sixteenth Century* (New York: Longmans, Green and Co., 1912); Thompson, *Customs in Common;* Brian Manning, *The English People and the English Revolution 1640–1649* (London: Heinemann, 1975); and Roger B. Manning, *Village Revolts: Social Protest and Popular Disturbances in England, 1509–1640* (Oxford: Clarendon Press, 1988).

p. 163 *As a result, notes the historian R. H. Tawney . . .* Tawney, *Agrarian Problem,* p. 35.

p. 163 *The loss of this access . . .* John Clare, quoted in Hill, *Liberty Against the Law,* p. 28.

p. 164 *An important legal principle . . .* Manning, *Village Revolts,* p. 27.

p. 164 *As Tawney notes: "In practice, the whole body . . ."* Tawney, *Agrarian Problem,* p. 245. Tawney describes the co-operative approach of managing the land as amounting to a form of "practical communism."

p. 164 *The co-operative way a village operated . . .* Ibid., pp. 251–52.

p. 166 *The medieval historian Bede Jarrett . . .* Bede Jarrett, *Social Theories of the Middle Ages 1200–1500* (London: Ernest Benn Limited, 1926), p. 132.

p. 166 *The thirteenth-century philosopher . . .* Ibid., p. 133.

p. 169 *Not far away, an enclosure dispute in Welcombe . . .* E. K. Chambers, *William Shakespeare: A Study of Facts and Problems* (Oxford: Clarendon Press, 1930), vol. 2, pp. 144–52.

p. 171 *"We hardly have poor enough to do . . . "* Quoted in Hill, *Liberty Against the Law,* p. 64.

p. 171 *Or as Lord Goderich succinctly put it . . .* Quoted in Thompson, *Customs in Common,* p. 167.

p. 174 *Tawney makes the point that, at the time, nothing seemed . . .* Tawney, *Agrarian Problem,* p. 178.

p. 175 *The Diggers and the Levellers . . .* David W. Petegorsky, *Left-Wing Democracy in the English Civil War: A Study of the Social Philosophy of Gerard Winstanley* (London: Victor Gollancz, 1940). See also Hill, *Liberty Against the Law,* pp. 48–49.

p. 177 *As the historian Brian Manning has noted . . .* Manning, *The English People,* p. 119.

p. 177 *"What aroused alarm . . .* Tawney, *Agrarian Problem,* p. 179.

p. 177 *Karl Polanyi argues that if the propertied classes . . .* Polanyi, *Great Transformation,* p. 76.

p. 178 *At first glance, the "food riot". . .* Thompson, "The Moral Economy of the English Crowd in the Eighteenth Century," in Thompson's *Customs in Common.*

p. 184 *This moral approach to economics . . .* For the medieval approach to economics, see Tawney, *Religion and the Rise of Capitalism;* Jarrett, *Social Theories of the Middle Ages;* and Ashley, *English Economic History and Theory.*

p. 193 *R. H. Tawney points with admiration . . .* Tawney, *Religion and the Rise of Capitalism,* p. 73.

p. 193 *Despite the huge gulf then . . .* Ibid., p. 72.

**CHAPTER SIX:** *The Master, the Servant, the Horse and the Grass*

p. 194 *For a fairly small and ineffectual group . . .* For an interesting account of the hostility towards Luddites, see Neil Postman, *Building a Bridge to the Eighteenth Century* (New York: Alfred A. Knopf, 2000), pp. 36–37.

p. 195 *As Polanyi notes, "There was nothing . . ."* Polanyi, *Great Transformation,* p. 139.

p. 196 *"What we call land . . .* Ibid., p. 178.

p. 197 *The political theorist C. B. Macpherson . . .* Cited in Anatole Anton, Milton Fisk and Nancy Holmstrom, *Not for Sale: In Defence of Public Goods* (Colorado: Westview Press, 2000), p. 3. See also C. B. Macpherson, "Capitalism and the Changing Concept of Property" in Eugene Kamenka and R. S. Neale, eds., *Feudalism, Capitalism and Beyond* (London: Edward Arnold, 1975).

p. 198 *Supporters of this narrow sense of property . . .* For an interesting discussion of Locke's approach to property, see Thompson, *Customs in Common,* pp. 160–61, and Heilbroner, *Nature and Logic of Capitalism,* pp. 112–13.

p. 199 *The political theorist Anatole Anton . . .* Anton, et al, *Not for Sale,* p. 14.

p. 201 *Locke's caveat also helps identify . . .* For an excellent discussion of the theories of Robert Hale, see Barbara H. Fried, *The Progressive Assault on Laissez-Faire: Robert Hale and the First Law and Economics Movement* (Cambridge, Mass.: Harvard University Press, 1998).

p. 203 *As Jeremy Bentham pointed out . . .* Quoted in ibid., p. 77.

p. 204 *Polanyi observed, "Administrators . . ."* Polanyi, *Great Transformation,* p. 140.

p. 204 *As Polanyi ironically notes . . .* Ibid., p. 141.

p. 205 *In 1860, for instance . . .* Ibid., pp. 146–47.

p. 205 *These acts of restrictive legislation . . .* Ibid., p. 145.

p. 209 *Judges in eighteenth-century England . . .* Thompson, *Customs in Common,* pp. 140–141.

p. 209 *Another judge, Mr. Justice Wilson* ... Ibid.

p. 209 *Similarly, Adam Smith* ... Quoted in ibid., p. 162.

p. 211 *The apparently "voluntary" market exchange* ... Fried, *Progressive Assault,* pp. 49–50.

p. 215 *As John Stuart Mill noted* ... Cited in ibid., p. 78.

p. 217 *As Neil Brooks notes* ... Neil Brooks, "The Rhetoric of Tax Politics: The Attack on Citizenship," in Richard Krever, ed., *Tax Conversations: A Guide to the Key Issues in the Tax Reform Debate* (New York: Kluwer Academic Publishers, 1998), pp. 132–33.

p. 219 *Taxation is in many ways simply a recognition* ... Quoted in Fried, *Progressive Assault,* p. 75.

## CHAPTER SEVEN: *Tearing Down the Fence*

p. 221 *The market has also made inroads* ... Sheryl Gay Stolberg, "Patent Laws May Determine Shape of Stem Cell Research," *New York Times,* August 17, 2001.

p. 223 *In an insightful essay* ... Harvey Cox, "The Market as God," *Atlantic Monthly,* March 1999, pp. 18–23.

p. 223 *A poll conducted for* Business Week ... "Globalization: What Americans Are Worried About," *Business Week,* April 24, 2000, p. 44.

p. 226 *But with the release of the massive UN-supervised* ... Bill McKibben, "Some Like It Hot," *New York Review of Books,* July 5, 2001.

p. 226 *In a brilliant article in* Harper's ... David Quammen, "Planet of Weeds: Tallying the Losses of Earth's Animals and Plants," *Harper's,* Oct. 1998.

p. 228 *In a low-key editorial* ... "Watching Mr. Bush on Earth Day," *New York Times,* April 22, 2001.

p. 228 *Or as the* Globe and Mail's ... Marcus Gee, "What Globalization Did for Deth," *Globe and Mail,* April 19, 2001.

p. 229 *There was no separate thing called the "economy"* ... Polanyi, *Great Transformation,* p. 71.

p. 233 *More and more, we are presented with* ... Ellen Ullman, "The Museum of Me," *Harper's,* May 2000.

p. 236 *Thomas Homer-Dixon paints a vivid* ... Quoted in Quammen, "Planet of Weeds," p. 64.

p. 236 *In rejecting the* Homo Economicus *model* ... Samuel Bowles and Herbert Gintis, *Democracy and Capitalism: Property, Community and the Contradictions of Modern Social Thought* (New York: Basic, 1986).

p. 237 *In fact, motivations often overlap* ... Stretton and Orchard, *Public Goods,* pp. 1–7.

p. 241  *Adam Smith's famous passage* . . . Adam Smith, *The Wealth of Nations* (New York: Random House), Book 1, Chapter 2.

p. 241  *In this spirit, Thomas Friedman dismissed* . . . Friedman, "Protesting for Whom?" *New York Times,* April 24, 2001.

p. 244  *Rather than end* . . . Loren Eisley, "The Bird and the Machine," in Malcolm Ross and John Stevens (eds.) *In Search of Ourselves* (Toronto: J. M. Dent and Sons, 1967), pp. 229–39.

# Acknowledgements

THE IDEA FOR THIS BOOK came from Christopher Lind, who developed a strong interest in the work of Karl Polanyi while studying economics under Abraham Rotstein at the University of Toronto. When Christopher approached me three years ago with the suggestion that I write a book popularizing Polanyi's ideas, I was immediately interested.

I am indebted to many people who helped me with this project. I would like to thank Abraham Rotstein for generously offering his time and extensive knowledge, and for the many very pleasant lunches we had discussing Polanyi's ideas. Marguerite Mendell provided invaluable feedback on the manuscript, sending it back again and again in an effort to get things right. Her passion for the subject is infectious, and her ability to spot a weakness in an argument is impressive. As with my other books, Andrew Sharpe generously offered his time and provided some very useful analysis and feedback. I'm also grateful for the help of Ursula Franklin, Judit Szapor, Gord Evans, Kenneth McRobbie, Mel Watkins, Adam Harmes, Steven Zikopoulos, David Perry, Jim Stanford, Roy Adams, Timothy Canova and Randall Dodd.

My wonderful friend Tom Walkom has always been interested in the broad themes addressed in this book, and in many ways, he sparked my interest in them back when we were both teenagers. It's always been fascinating discussing these sorts of things with Tom; his ideas have greatly influenced my thinking. I'd also like to thank Neil Brooks for his insightful comments, and for being such a source of inspiration over the years. Speaking of inspiration, Noam Chomsky provided great thoughts on some of the themes in this book over a very enjoyable dinner last year.

Many thanks are also due to Penguin's highly professional team, who were a pleasure to work with: Cynthia Good, Diane Turbide, Craig Pyette, Martin Gould and Sandra Tooze, as well as freelance copy editor Janice Weaver and proofreader Maryan Gibson. Also much valued are the considerable talents of my agent, Bruce Westwood, and my researcher, Sarah Ives. David Kilgour, my long-time editor, performed his usual crucial function; I appreciate his abilities as an editor more with each book.

On a personal note, I'd like to thank my parents, Audrey and Jack McQuaig, for always encouraging me. I'd also like to quickly mention some important friends: Barbara Nichol and David Cole (who have re-established the Oakville situation in Toronto), Jane Spanton, Linda Diebel, Ken Finkleman, Linda Manzer, Gene Allen, Leslie Elver, Ross Elver, Charlotte Montgomery, Clayton Ruby, Harriet Sachs, Rick Salutin, Peter Duffin and Bhagya Patel. And last—but first in my heart—is my remarkable, loving and delightful daughter, Amy.

# Index

Also by Linda McQuaig

*The Cult of Impotence: Selling the Myth of Powerlessness in the Global Economy*

*Shooting the Hippo: Death by Deficit and Other Canadian Myths*

*The Wealthy Banker's Wife*

*The Quick and the Dead: Brian Mulroney, Big Business
and the Seduction of Canada Behind Closed Doors*

# Other titles by
# LINDA McQUAIG

## THE CULT OF IMPOTENCE
### *Selling the Myth of Powerlessness in the Global Economy*

In this provocative book, Linda McQuaig delves into the economic issues of government cutbacks, jobs and social programs across Canada and disputes the notion that dire financial straits have forced the Chrétien government to slash as much as it has.

"Linda McQuaig's magnificent new book, *The Cult of Impotence*, is the slap upside the head we all sorely need." —*London Free Press*

**ISBN 0140262210**

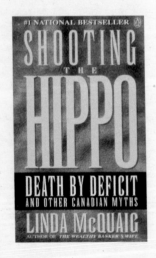

## SHOOTING THE HIPPO
### *Death by Deficit*

"Part thriller, part financial expose... McQuaig has written an accessible and essential introduction to Canada's economy for all Canadians... I intend to send a copy to my federal MP, and hope that the book gives him the kind of nightmares it gave me." —*The Gazette* (Montreal)

"McQuaig has laid out sufficient material to throw serious doubt on the economic policies that dominate our society." —John Ralston Saul, *The Globe and Mail*

**ISBN 0140174753**

PENGUIN
CANADA